WILLIAM LAWES

STUDIES IN THE HISTORY OF MUSIC

EDITED BY EGON WELLESZ
C.B.E., F.B.A., Hon. D. Mus. Oxon.
Fellow of Lincoln College

Uniform with this Volume

MUSIC IN MEDIEVAL BRITAIN
by Frank Ll. Harrison

THE FUGUE IN BEETHOVEN'S PIANO MUSIC
by John V. Cockshoot

Facsimile of the portrait said to be William Lawes
which hangs in the Faculty of Music School
in Oxford.

WILLIAM LAWES

by
MURRAY LEFKOWITZ

Routledge and Kegan Paul

LONDON

*First published 1960
by Routledge & Kegan Paul Limited
Broadway House, Carter Lane, E.C.4*

*Printed in Great Britain
by Butler & Tanner Limited
Frome and London*

TO MY WIFE

CONTENTS

CONTENTS

PREFACE

T HE full extent and importance of William Lawes' work has not hitherto been known, not even to the few enthusiastic scholars who have made limited investigations. The reasons for the neglect of so rich a heritage of music are fourfold. First, Lawes' complete works have, until now, never been catalogued and only one or two of his important pieces have ever been published. Second, the sweeping generalities which have condemned the decadence of so much of the courtly arts of Jacobean and Caroline times have, by association, helped to keep Lawes' music in obscurity. Third, because of the composer's early death at the siege of Chester in 1645, his memory has been greatly overshadowed by the contemporary popularity of his older brother, Henry Lawes, and the latter's close association with the foremost poets of the age, this despite the limited production and inferior quality of the older musician's work. And finally, William Lawes had the misfortune of being part of an unpopular era, an era which saw the royal household grow away from the masses of the English people to become oversophisticated in the extreme, an era which culminated in a bloody civil war, the execution of the King and the stringent edicts of a confused Commonwealth. Indeed, the age of the Carolines is only just now beginning to excite more popular interest. It is fitting, therefore, that the music of William Lawes be 'awakened from its centuries-long slumber', that it be examined and sifted so that the finest of the composer's compositions may occupy their rightful niche in the performer's repertory.

The task of locating, cataloguing, transcribing and evaluating Lawes' works has not been an easy one. I have to thank the United States Fulbright Commission for the original grant which enabled me to conduct my research at the University of Oxford from 1951 to 1953. I also wish to thank Dr. Raymond Kendall and Dr. Pauline Alderman of the University of Southern

California for additional aid which has facilitated the completion of this book. To Professor J. A. Westrup, Heather Professor of Music at Oxford, under whom I worked, I extend my gratitude for valuable criticism. I further wish to thank Mr. C. B. Oldman of the British Museum, Dr. Hunt of the Bodleian Library, Mr. Hiscock of the Christ Church Library, Dr. Carlton Sprague Smith of the New York Public Library, the staff of the William Andrews Clark Memorial Library in Los Angeles and the librarians of the Royal College of Music in London, St. Michael's College in Tenbury, and the various other libraries in which I worked or with whom I have had correspondence. I am grateful also to the Lord Chamberlain and to the Sub-Dean of Her Majestie's Chapel Royal at St. James's Palace for allowing me to examine manuscripts and certain signatures in the Cheque Book of the Chapel Royal, and to Dr. David Wodlinger of the Institute of International Education in New York.

My thanks also to the three members of the English Consort of Viols, Mr. Marco Pallis, Mr. Richard Nicholson and Mrs. Elizabeth Goble, who instructed me in the art of playing the viol and allowed me to participate in their consorts, as well as to Mr. Thurston Dart, Mr. William B. Coates, Mr. John Hough, Mr. Denis Stevens and Miss Margaret C. Crum, all of whom have been helpful in offering information which has been of value to this book.

MURRAY LEFKOWITZ

LOS ANGELES, CALIFORNIA
June 1958

As this book goes to press I have located what appears to be the autograph volume of William Lawes' music for lyra viol. This manuscript is now in the Houghton Library at Harvard (MS. Mus. 70), and by its description it is probably the lyra viol autograph mentioned in the *Catalogue of the William H. Cummings Library* which was sold at auction in 1917 (see p. 30). I intend to publish an article concerning this manuscript in the very near future.

M. L.

LOS ANGELES
September 1959

I

A BIOGRAPHICAL INTRODUCTION

T HE facts relating to the life of William Lawes, the man, are meagre indeed. They are confined to some knowledge of his family background, the dates and circumstances of his birth and death, a fleeting hint as to his early education, his presence in London from at least the year 1633, an anecdote or two—and that is all. Lawes, the King's musician, however, presents a more rewarding avenue of approach, from the numerous glowing tributes paid to him by his contemporaries, by his activities in the 'private musick' of Charles I, and from the accounts of a few musical chroniclers; but above all, it is through his music that we may know him.

William Lawes was baptized in the Close at Salisbury Cathedral in the county of Wiltshire on May 1, 1602.[1] His

[1] The date of Lawes' birth has been the subject of notable error. Various encyclopaedias, dictionaries, books and articles have confused William Lawes, the subject of this study, with a second William Lawes, *alias* Coldbeck, who from the year 1591 was successively a singer in the Cathedral choirs of Winchester, Salisbury, Chichester and the Chapel Royal. It is due to this confusion of personalities that the present William Lawes is referred to in many sources as the elder half-brother of Henry Lawes, and that his birth date is given in the early 1580's. Moreover, no evidence has been uncovered to even suggest that Lawes, *alias* Coldbeck, was any relation to William and Henry Lawes. This mistaken identity was first discussed and proven in detail by Henry Hatcher in his account of the Lawes brothers in *Old and New Sarum*, Vol. VI of *The History of Modern Wiltshire*, edited by Sir Richard Colt Hoare (London: 1843), pp. 623–7. William Lawes' baptismal date was also recorded by Hatcher, whose account was based on the entries in the Salisbury Cathedral Register and in the Penruddocke Register, pp. 67, 69,

father, Thomas Lawes senior, was a bass choir singer who came, at an unknown date, from Dynder in Somerset to the small parish of Dinton, Wilts., where, on February 3, 1594, he married Lucris Shepharde, daughter of Jennie Shepharde, a widow. In Dinton, William's famous older brother, Henry Lawes, was baptized on January 5, 1596. But at some time before William was born the family had moved into the Close at Salisbury, some eight miles distant, where Thomas Lawes received an appointment as a Lay Vicar in 1602. The Lawes home in the Close seems to have been one of the more important stone dwellings, since it boasted a private postern door which opened into the Cathedral. This would suggest that Thomas Lawes senior was a man of at least moderate means and of some status within the Close. The family was certainly in adequate circumstances, for they were able to keep a servant, one John Luxon.[1] Thomas and Lucris Lawes had, in all, five children. Besides Henry and William, there was one sister, Elizabeth, who was baptized on October 20, 1605, and two more brothers, John, whose birth date has apparently not been recorded, and Thomas junior, christened on June 3, 1608.[2] The latter remained all of his life at Salisbury and followed his father's

73 and 75. Dora Robertson, *Sarum Close* (London: Jonathan Cape Ltd., 1938), pp. 167–71, apparently used Hatcher's account in reporting the error. Willa McClung Evans, *Henry Lawes* (Oxford University Press, 1941), pp. xiv–xvi, also deals with the subject. The present author is able to add perhaps the final note to this case of mistaken identities, inasmuch as a comparison of William Lawes' autograph signatures in the several autograph volumes of his music in the Bodleian Library at Oxford and in the British Museum, with the signature of William Lawes, *alias* Coldbeck, in the Cheque Book of the Chapel Royal at St. James's Palace, proves beyond any doubt that there were two William Lawes'. The signature of the older man is definitely in the old sixteenth-century script, whereas the signature of our William Lawes is in the new seventeenth-century style of writing. These signatures may be compared if the reader will see the signature of Lawes, *alias* Coldbeck, on the frontispiece of Edward F. Rimbault, *The Old Cheque-Book . . . of The Chapel Royall* (London: 1872), and that of William Lawes in the Bodleian MSS. Mus. Sch. B.2 or B.3.

[1] Hatcher, op. cit., p. 310, cited by Evans, op. cit., p. 15, n. 43. For a more detailed account of the Lawes family and life at Sarum Close in the early seventeenth century, see the latter work and also that of Roberston, op. cit.

[2] Hatcher, op. cit., p. 624, cited from the Salisbury Cathedral Register, where the baptismal dates of all the Lawes children, except John, are recorded.

profession. John rose to greater eminence and became a 'sing-ing-man' at Westminster Cathedral.

Of William's childhood and early education, apart from music, little if anything is known for certain. It is probable that he attended the free Grammar School within the confines of the Close, which was then run by a schoolmaster of somewhat dubious merits, Master John Sharpe, who was supposed to instruct the children of the Close in the fundamentals of read-ing, writing, grammar, Latin, Greek and the Catechism. Of William's earliest musical education, it is again not possible to be sure. Reared as he was in a home of fine musicians, it is likely that his first musical instruction came from his father. It is possible also that William, as a boy, should have been one of the choristers of the Cathedral, since the Lawes family was known for its fine voices. Indeed, much of the history of early English music might be told in the works of professional musical families like the Lawes'.[1] If young William was a chorister at Sarum, his lot could not have been a happy one, for the singing-boys at the time were under the supervision of an unscrupulous master, John Bartlett, whose treatment of the boys was such that it finally developed into a full-fledged public scandal.[2] The boys, who resided in the Choristers' House in the Close, were neglected by Bartlett, who neither taught them the music lessons he was supposed to, nor provided for the food, clothing and other necessities which was their due. Nor did he oversee the discipline of the group, so that the choristers became dis-orderly in their behaviour and aroused the wrath of the Cathedral Chapter.

Who William's friends were during these early years is again a matter of conjecture. His brother, Henry, was six years his senior and is known to have had devoted childhood friends at Salisbury, fellow choristers such as Edward Lowe and Francis Sambrooke. The former later became organist of Christ Church in Oxford and copied some of William's manuscripts. Sam-brooke, a capable amateur musician, became an attorney. The latter also contributed commendatory verse to the Lawes

---

[1] One has but to mention such musical families as the Bassanos, the Lupos, the Ferraboscos, the Laniers, Dowlands, Simpsons, Gibbons' and Purcells to understand the validity of this statement.

[2] Robertson, op. cit., pp. 172–4.

brothers' publication of *Choice Psalmes* in 1648 and is responsible, together with Lowe, for the copying and preservation of much pre-Commonwealth music. William Lawes, it seems, liked to associate with boys older than himself, at least if the example of his later years is any indication. Undoubtedly, this was the result of his close association with his brother and the latter's friends as well as with other musicians who were older than himself.

Salisbury and its surroundings were a stimulating area for a young lad of talent and musical ambition in the early seventeenth century. Sarum itself had a long and noble tradition of music, great organists, composers, and excellent choirs of boys and men. The previous generation alone had benefited from the work of John Farrant the elder, one of a long line of English church organists and composers. When the elder Farrant left Salisbury it was finally his son, John Farrant the younger, who succeeded to the post of organist at the Cathedral. The young Farrant was Vicar Choral and organist there from about 1598 until his death in 1618. It may have been this musician who introduced Lawes to the organ and its literature. The Cathedral Choir, on the other hand, offered an opportunity for the boy to hear and perhaps participate in some of the finest performances of religious choral music then known, and to become familiar with a large part of the literature as well. The Sarum Choir had a formidable reputation for its excellent training. Thus, the noted English antiquarian, John Aubrey (b. 1626, d. 1697), tells us that 'The Quire of Salisbury hath produced as many able musicians, if not more than any quire in this nation'.[1]

In addition to the musical activity within the Close, much was also going on in those days in the field of secular instrumental and vocal music in the immediate vicinity of New Sarum. At Amesbury and Wulfall—the estates of Edward Seymour, Earl of Hertford—the two great innovators of early Baroque English instrumental and vocal music, John Cooper (*alias* Giovanni Coperario) and Alfonso Ferrabosco, held sway.[2] Nearby also

---

[1] John Aubrey, *The Natural History of Wiltshire*, written between 1656 and 1691, and edited by John Britton (London: J. B. Nichols & Son, 1847), pp. 80–1.

[2] Loc. cit. Aubrey states, 'Jo. Coperario, whose real name I have been told was Cowper, and Alfonso Ferrabosco, lived most in Wiltshire, sc. at

4

was Wilton House, the estate of the Earls of Pembroke, who were generous patrons of musicians and artists. Both Hertford and Pembroke were benefactors of the Cathedral at Salisbury and were ever on the alert for exceptional talent for their magnificent household establishments. It is not surprising, therefore, that Edward Seymour interested himself in a precocious child like William Lawes and indentured him to his own household under the musical tutelage of Giovanni Coperario. Thomas Fuller supplies us with the full account:

'William Lawes son of *Thomas Lawes a Vicar Choral of the* Church of *Salisbury* was bred in the *Close* of that *City*, being from his *Childhood* inclined to *Musick*. *Edward* Earl of *Hertford* obtained him from his *Father*, and bred him of his own cost in that *Faculty*, under his Master *Giovanni Coperario* an *Italian*, and most *Exquisite Musician*. Yet may it be said that the *Schollar* in time did *Equal*, yea Exceed his Master.

'He afterwards was of the *Private Musick* to King *Charles*, and was respected and beloved of all such *Persons*, who cast any looks towards *Vertue* and *Honour*.' [1]

Amesbury and Wulfall, with Edward Earle of Hertford, who was the great patrone of musicians.' The activities of Coperario and Ferrabosco are difficult to follow from about the year 1610 to 1625. Aubrey, ibid., p. 88, also states that 'Alphonso Ferrabosco, the son, was Lord Philip (the first's) [Philip Herbert, 4th Earl of Pembroke] lutenist. He sang rarely well to the theorbo lute. He had a pension in Baynard's Castle [Pembroke's London house].' It seems likely that he should also have been active at Wilton. At the same time Ferrabosco is known to have been instructor in the art of music to Prince Henry, and after the latter's death, to Prince Charles, as well as one of the viols or violins in the King's private music since 1604. In fact, he was one of the musicians who played at the funeral of Queen Elizabeth; see Walter L. Woodfill, *Musicians in English Society from Elizabeth to Charles I* (Oxford University Press, 1953), pp. 300-3; p. 310, n. 87, n. 104. Coperario too seems to have been officially in the King's music. He was one of the musicians of Prince Charles and taught him to play viol da gamba; ibid., pp. 302-3, 309, n. 81. At the same time it is suspected that he taught John Egerton, future Earl of Bridgewater, at his Ashridge estate. It may well be that the King's musicians circulated a good deal more than we have hitherto believed, but in any case, until further research reveals more complete details in respect of both Coperario's and Ferrabosco's activities during the first quarter of the century, their presence or rather the exact dates of their presence in Wiltshire cannot be ascertained with any degree of certainty.

[1] Thomas Fuller, *The History of the Worthies of England* (London: 1662), under the section Wiltshire, p. 157. Fuller lived from 1608 to 1661. His book

There is no reason to suppose that Fuller's account is not authentic, excluding, of course, the statement that Coperario was an Italian. The latter was in fact an Englishman, John Cooper, who, it is rumoured, went to Italy some time before 1604 and affected the Italian *nom de plume* upon his return.[1] Anthony Wood, in his unpublished notes on the lives of English musicians which are in the Bodleian Library at Oxford, copied Fuller's account of William Lawes verbatim into his own notes concerning the composer. It is significant, however, that he crossed out 'an Italian'. He did not change any of Fuller's other statements but added a list of printed publications in which. Lawes' works were to be found, and the following note:

'Will: Lawes of ye private musick to K. Ch. I and an excellent composer for instrumentall musick—but to indulge the ear—he broke sometimes ye rules of mathematicall composition.

'An improver and approver of the Lyra-viol.

'His things before and after ye restoration alwaies culled out.'[2]

Since it was Benjamin Rogers, the organist and composer, a contemporary of William Lawes, who supplied Wood with a good deal of his material and critical comments for the manuscript, we have a tacit acknowledgement that Fuller's information is indeed correct.

At what age Lawes was apprenticed to Coperario we can only guess from Fuller's statement that William was inclined to music from his childhood and that the Earl 'obtained' him from

was published posthumously. It is significant that William Lawes was the only Wiltshire musician whom Fuller considered of sufficient stature to be honoured in his volume.

[1] Besides Aubrey, Roger North (1650–1734), perhaps taking his cue from the latter, says that Coperario 'was plain Cooper but affected an Italian termination', *Musicall Gramarian*, edited by Hilda Andrews (Oxford University Press, 1925), p. 10. It has often been stated that Coperario went to Italy, but as yet no definite proof of this has been forthcoming. See also the remarks of Manfred Bukofzer to this effect in the facsimile edition of Coperario's *Rules How to Compose* (Los Angeles: Ernest E. Gottlieb, 1952), intro. p. [1].

[2] Anthony Wood, unpublished manuscript notes on the lives of the English musicians in the Bodleian Library at Oxford (Wood D. 19 (4), No. 106, folio 83^r).

6

his father. From this the author suggests a date of *c.* 1612, when the boy was ten years old. Fuller makes it quite clear, however, that Lawes left his parents and Sarum Close to join Hertford's household. What is not clear, is exactly where William was entrusted to Coperario's care and tutelage. Was it at Amesbury or Wulfall nearby to Salisbury, or was it at the Hertford's London house in the big city? And was his brother, Henry, also apprenticed to Coperario and was he with William? Neither of these questions can be answered with certainty. Coperario's activities do not seem to have kept him in any one place for any length of time. In fact, it is possible that the student may have been with his master in several places between about 1612 and perhaps 1620, including the Wiltshire estates of the Earls of Hertford and Pembroke and the Royal Court in London, among others. As for Henry, there is positively no evidence that he studied with Coperario or ever left Salisbury before he was about twenty years of age.[1] If he had been with William, it seems likely that Fuller or one of our other sources would have mentioned it. And one cannot by any stretch of the imagination compare Henry Lawes' music with the essentially polyphonic style of Coperario. The former neither worked in Coperario's forms nor did he write for instruments, whereas it will be shown in the succeeding chapters that William Lawes' music shows Coperario's influence to a marked degree, contrapuntally, formally, harmonically, in the instrumentation and otherwise.

As Coperario's pupil it is probable that the young William Lawes had certain duties to perform in accordance with the seventeenth-century code of apprenticeship. It is not too far-fetched to assume, for example, that the boy acted in the capacity of a servant to his tutor, helping him with his musical instruments when the latter had to travel, copying parts from his scores, securing supplies, reading over his music, etc., this in return for his lessons and his teacher's good favour. The course of study which the boy must have followed under Coperario may be understood from the latter's manuscript treatise, entitled *Rules How to Compose*.[2] This includes the traditional contrapuntal rules of intervals and melodic progressions (with

---

[1] See also the remarks of Bukofzer in Coperario, op. cit., intro., p. [2], and those of Evans, op. cit., p. 24, n. 15.

[2] Op. cit., passim.

the significant difference that Coperario counts his intervals from the bass upwards), four-part harmonic progressions regulated by the bass, rules for figuration or 'division', the handling of suspensions and dissonances, especially in cadence, and imitation or 'fuge'. Again, in the following chapters we shall see how well Lawes mastered his lessons. Indeed, it is possible that Coperario may have written the treatise for his young student. The date, *c.* 1610, which has been ascribed to the manuscript, is not too far off to detract from the plausibility of this assumption.

It is likely also that under Coperario's tutorship William Lawes acquired a thorough knowledge of the musical instruments of his day. These were first and foremost the viols *da gamba*, from the small treble viol to the large 'consort bass'. From his compositions we may also assume that he was a competent performer on the violin, since by far the largest proportion of his works feature that instrument. It is also probable that he studied the theorbo-lute, the lyra viol and division viols, the organ, and perhaps other keyboard instruments as well as the chromatic harp. In fact, if Henry Lawes' statements are to be accepted at face value, then 'neither was there any instrument then in use, but he compos'd to it so aptly, as if he had only studied that'.[1]

As Coperario's pupil too, Lawes must have had the opportunity of listening to and taking part in the performance of a great deal of music, and probably with many of the best musicians of the age. Even at this period in his life he may have made the acquaintance of some of his lifelong friends and colleagues, such as Alfonso Ferrabosco II, John Jenkins, and Simon Ives. And with others of Coperario's pupils, including some influential members of the nobility, Lawes may have taken part in 'consort', i.e. chamber-music playing. Indeed, it is not impossible that through this medium he may have been brought into contact with the two Royal Princes, who were also studying music with Coperario, as well as Ferrabosco at the same time. In particular, it may have been during this period that Lawes first met the future Charles I. The then Prince Charles was studying bass viol with Coperario at about the

[1] In his introduction *To The Reader*, of the Lawes brothers' *Choice Psalmes*, (London: 1648), q.v. on pp. 28-9.

same time that Lawes was the former's pupil.[1] It is entirely possible, therefore, that they may have played in 'consort' together. Indeed, the King's immense respect for William's ability possibly began here, leading to the remark by Fuller that Charles I was particularly fond 'of his deare servant Will: Lawes . . . whom he loved when living, and commonly called the Father of Musick'.[2]

It is significant that Lawes' friends, apart from his brother, were in the main instrumental composers. Coperario himself was primarily an instrumental musician. So were Ferrabosco, Jenkins, Ives, Tomkins and the rest. From Coperario and perhaps Ferrabosco, both older men with a great deal of knowledge and experience, William had more than ample opportunity to learn his art well. Ferrabosco was considered one of the foremost exponents of viol-playing in England. Indeed, his fame as a violist had spread over all of Europe and his numerous compositions for viols were popular abroad. While Ferrabosco is not known to have taught the younger man, Lawes later made use of one of Ferrabosco's bass lines in setting one of his best works, paying tribute to the older composer in the title and referring to him simply as 'Alphonso'.[3] In another of his finest compositions William did the same for Coperario, thereby honouring both men. The importance of Coperario and Ferrabosco in the development of early English baroque instrumental style is paramount. They may be said to have taken the first significant steps in transforming the older 'motet style

[1] Woodfill, op. cit., pp. 302–3, 309, n. 81. We know that Charles I liked to take part in 'consort' playing, since, according to John Playford, he was exceedingly fond of playing 'those incomparable Phantasies of Mr. Coperario to the Organ', *Introduction to The Skill of Music* (London: 1697 ed.).

[2] Fuller, loc. cit. Evans' claim, op. cit., p. xvi, that Fuller confused Lawes with the older William Lawes, *alias* Coldbeck, in making the statement that the King called him the 'Father of Musick', has no foundation in fact. There is no evidence that Lawes, *alias* Coldbeck, was ever in the service of Charles when the latter was Prince. Nor is there any music extant by this man or any record of any significance except that he was a 'singing-man' in the Chapel Royal. Moreover, Coldbeck seems to have been an unstable personality, to say the least, frequently changing positions and under the charge of possessing two wives. The fact that Charles I was two years William Lawes' senior also does not alter the case, since the phrase 'Father of Musick' primarily denotes ability and not necessarily age.

[3] For more about this composition see Chapter VI, pp. 140–1.

9

for instruments' into characteristically instrumental writing. This fact was recognized by Roger North in the early eighteenth century. He states:

'Upon the wearing out of this dull style [i.e. the imitation of vocal polyphony] there arose a set of musicians who were deservedly famous for the advances they made in Improving ye musicall style, as Alfonso Ferrabosco, Coperario (who by ye way was plain Cooper but affected an Italian termination) & others as may be found in old musick books.'[1]

Lawes' music is in fact indebted most to these two instrumental pioneers of the transition period between late Renaissance and early Baroque. He is their rightful heir and successor. It is their forms which he uses and expands, their counterpoint and harmonies which he develops, their instrumentation which he employs and their 'Italianisms' and dissonances which he intensifies; the major difference being that, as Fuller observed, 'the *Schollar* in time did *Equal*, yea Exceed his Master'.[2] Unlike his older colleagues William Lawes possessed that vital spark which distinguishes between genius and what Bukofzer called the 'first-class second rater'.[3]

We do not know how long William Lawes studied with Coperario, nor do we know when and where Lawes was employed before his appearance on the Court scene in 1634 as the composer, together with his friend Simon Ives, of the music for James Shirley's monumental masque *The Triumph of Peace*. He may have remained in the service of the Earl of Hertford's family. It seems likely that the Earl, having reared the boy from childhood and having paid for his training under Coperario, would have expected some service in return for his patronage.[4] Indeed, Lawes himself must have become attached to the Earl and his family. But the pages are quite blank during these years. Even an extensive search of his several extant autograph volumes does not help to establish Lawes' exact whereabouts from about 1620 to 1633. Once again we are forced to speculate.

There is, however, one significant point concerning the com-

---

[1] North, op. cit., p. 10. [2] Fuller, loc. cit.
[3] Coperario, op. cit., intro., p. [3].
[4] Edward Seymour, Lawes' original patron, died in 1621. He was succeeded in the earldom by his grandson, William Seymour (1588–1660).

poser's extant vocal music which may offer a clue. As it will be shown in Chapter VIII, Lawes wrote much of his vocal music for the theatre. This entire production falls between the years 1633 and 1642. Not a single song or instrumental composition has been identified with a play or court masque prior to this period. This fact alone would tend to support a theory that William Lawes was otherwise engaged during this time, namely, in the composition of his larger contrapuntal chamber music for viols and violins. If the composer was still in the employ of the Hertford family or some other of the nobility where 'consort' playing was the particular delight of the patron, it would have been only natural for Lawes to produce compositions in that vein. Then too, he may still have been under the influence of Coperario and Ferrabosco at this time.[1] Later, when William joined his brother at the Court, he may have begun his period of vocal and dramatic composition as well as the lighter *concertante* style of dance music, such as the later version of the *Royall Consort.*

It is known that Coperario, like Ferrabosco, remained in the service of the Court until his death. Thus he continued as Prince Charles' musician until the latter succeeded to the throne in 1625, and immediately thereupon was made special 'Composer of Music to the King'.[2] Moreover, a petition dated May 12, 1625, suggests that Coperario actually had a group of his own within the larger musical establishment run by Nicholas Lanier, who was then 'Master of the King's Music'.[3] In this petition a John Woodington affirms that he had been employed 'in Coperario's music' for three years. This may be merely a reference to the fact that Woodington was one of Prince Charles' musicians who were under the supervision of Coperario, but it does indicate that Coperario was in charge of his own group. Moreover, both Henry and William Lawes were rumoured to have been in the service of Charles before he ascended the throne. While this is entirely possible and the

[1] Coperario died in 1626 and Ferrabosco in 1627.

[2] Woodfill, op. cit., pp. 303, 311, n. 114; cited fromt he *Calendar of State Papers Domestic*, 1625–6, p. 569.

[3] Woodfill, op. cit., p. 309, n. 81, cited from the *Historical Manuscripts Commission Reports*, 23, *Cowper MSS.*, 195; also discussed by Bukofzer in Coperario, op. cit., p. [2]. Several such groups actually existed within the King's larger musical establishment; see Woodfill, op. cit., pp. 186–7.

brothers Lawes may indeed have been in some way connected with a group headed by Coperario from about 1620 to 1626, no definite proof to this effect has as yet turned up.[1] If Coperario was in a position of influence, however, it seems natural to assume that one of the first to have benefited by it would have been his most talented student. Lawes may, therefore, have been in the service of the Court long before his actual appointment in 1635.

Evans has pointed to the fact that Henry Lawes seems to have established himself in London from about the year 1615.[2] If young William Lawes spent much of his time under Coperario's instruction at the Hertfords' London house, then it was probably during this period that the two brothers, drawn together in a large and strange metropolis, away from home and parents, developed that close attachment which characterizes their relationship in later years, a relationship which prompted the Royalist poet, Aurelian Townshend, to describe them as 'Brothers in blood, in Science and Affection, Belov'd by those that envie Their Renowne'.[3] Henry Lawes, at the time, was a lad of twenty, probably seeking his fortune in the big city with an eye to establishing himself at Court.[4] William was a boy of thirteen, still engaged in his music lessons and already under the notice of the Court. When we read the many contemporary accounts which describe Henry as a most benevolent and kindly individual, admired, beloved and respected by all who knew him, we can well understand that the young man must have felt a great responsibility for his talented young brother's welfare in London. William, on the other hand, was in a position to introduce his older brother to influential courtiers and musicians. Through William, Henry Lawes may have become acquainted with Coperario, and through the latter he may have been recommended to teach the children of John Egerton, soon

[1] Hatcher, op. cit., p. 627, on undisclosed evidence, states that William, 'Before he was twenty-three years of age, . . . was selected as one of the private musicians to Prince Charles, and when his royal patron ascended the throne, he was continued in the same post, with additional marks of favour.'

[2] Evans, op. cit., p. 22.

[3] In his commendatory verse in the Lawes brothers' *Choice Psalmes* (London: 1648), q.v. on p. 22.

[4] Evans, op. cit., pp. 21–3.

to become Earl of Bridgewater.[1] The relationship between Coperario, the Egertons and Henry Lawes is established by Coperario's treatise, *Rules How to Compose*. This manuscript is known to have been in John Egerton's possession before 1617, the year Egerton received his title.[2] Egerton himself may have studied with Coperario and had the *Rules* copied out for him by a scribe. Henry Lawes taught the Egerton children, though probably not from Coperario's text. Thus, it is likely that in some way all three were known to each other and may have benefited from their association.[3]

Undoubtedly, William and Henry Lawes entertained hopes of rising to the highest position a musician in seventeenth-century England could hope to attain, that of 'musicians in ordinary' in the 'private musick' of the King. The Royal Court in London was the centre of English cultural life, in music as well as in the other arts, literature and sciences. The musical establishment begun by Henry VIII had grown to the proportions of a great academy and the Stuarts made ample use of it to display the power and magnificence of the Crown and to indulge their tastes for fine music. The best musicians from all over the British Isles were drawn to the Court for the prestige, security, artistic stimulation and better pay which the King's Musick and the Chapel Royal offered them. The English monarchs also attracted many foreign musicians who brought with them new ideas, new techniques and new styles in music from abroad. Competition was keen as the English as well as Italian, French and Dutch musicians attempted to captivate the sharp ears of a sophisticated aristocracy, many of whom, including the King himself, were discriminating musical amateurs. Thus, the society which the Lawes brothers hoped to invade was well informed on matters of music and art, and highly exclusive.

But in that age an artist's ambition to penetrate court circles could not be fulfilled on the strength of the applicant's ability

[1] Ibid., p. 25.

[2] Egerton signed his name twice on the title page, once before 1617 as John Egerton, and again after 1617 as J. Bridgewater. See also Evans, op. cit., pp. 24–5, and Bukofzer in Coperario, op. cit., intro., p. [2].

[3] This relationship is suggested by Evans, op. cit., p. 25, and Bukofzer in Coperario, op. cit., intro., p. [3].

alone. There were two necessary adjuncts: to have come from a family of recognized and famous musicians, and to have the recommendation and support of a powerful patron. It has not yet been established whether the William Lawes, *alias* Coldbeck, who had been a Vicar Choral at Salisbury, was any relation to William and Henry Lawes. The first William Lawes succeeded in becoming a Gentleman of the Chapel Royal in 1602 and in at least, as Evans observes, establishing the name of Lawes in the music at Court, if only in the Chapel.[1] In Salisbury too, one of the centres of English musical training, the Lawes family was well known for its musicians. As for powerful influence, what better patrons could William and Henry desire than the Pembrokes, Bridgewaters and Hertfords? William Herbert, third Earl of Pembroke, became Lord Chamberlain of the Royal Household in 1616. A native of Wiltshire, he was regarded as a special benefactor of Salisbury and its music and maintained his own elaborate establishment at Wilton House, a few miles distant. Like Edward Seymour, Earl of Hertford, Pembroke was also a great patron of musicians. Next to Buckingham he was the most influential man in all of England. It is significant that Pembroke, who was also a poet of some ability, had several of his poems set to music by both William and Henry Lawes. William Herbert's brother, Philip, fourth Earl of Pembroke, was a great friend of Charles I who often visited him at Wilton. It was Philip Herbert who, together with Charles I, petitioned the Dean and Chapter of Salisbury in 1632 in order to secure a Vicar Choral's place in the Cathedral for the elder Thomas Lawes.[2] Philip also attained the position of Lord Chamberlain for a brief period after his brother was made Lord Steward in 1625. And it was during Philip's term of office that Henry Lawes was appointed Epistoler of the Chapel Royal in 1626.

Of the private life of the Lawes brothers in London during the late twenties and early thirties, little is known. Apparently they mixed freely in the company of poets, actors and musicians that surrounded the Court. In particular, William, Henry, and John Wilson, another composer destined for the King's 'private musick', seem to have hit it off well. The follow-

---

[1] Evans, op. cit., pp. 33–4.
[2] For these petitions, see Evans, op. cit., pp. 69–71.

ing anecdote from the manuscript of Jests and Stories by Sir Nicholas L'Estrange describes one of their nightly visitations to the local 'pub':

'Willson, and Har: and Will: Lawes were at a Taverne one night; Wilson being in worst case of the three, swore he would Quarrell with the next Man he mett, who was a meere stranger and a sober gentleman; whome he thus accosted; are not you a Catholicke? yes marry am I; Then ya're a Knave says he; the Gentl: having past by a little way, stepps backe to him; and bids him not swallow an Error, for sayes he, I am no Catholicke: why then ya're a scurvy Lying Knave sayes Willson. upon that out flew their swords, but the Lawes parted them presently.'[1]

Harry, Will and 'Jack' are probably the original 'Three Merry Boyes', referred to in William Lawes' popular catch, 'The Wisemen Were But Seven'.[2] Indeed, the numerous catches and rounds of the Lawes brothers and Wilson were undoubtedly dashed off on the spot, in the tavern of an evening, and immediately sung by the three friends. Thus, the text of another of William's catches begins, 'If you will drink Canary at the Paul-head, let's meet old Harry . . .'[3]

The first of the little band to be appointed to the select group of the King's private musicians was Henry Lawes, who in 1631 was sworn in as 'musician in ordinary for the lutes and voices' in the place of Robert Marsh, deceased.[4] During this period there is still no record of William being employed in any capacity at the English Court. And yet William's fame seems to have grown sufficiently for the great parliamentarian, Bulstrode Whitelocke, to choose him for one of the most important commissions that any composer enjoyed during the century, the music for James Shirley's *Triumph of Peace*, which was presented by the four Inns of Court for Charles I and his

[1] British Museum, Harleian manuscript 6395, Story No. 361.

[2] This catch may be seen in Chapter VII, p. 85, Ex. 29.

[3] In Oxford, Bodleian Library, Mus. Sch. B.2, p. 109. Also printed in Hilton's *Catch that Catch Can* (1652) and Playford's *Musical Companion* (1667, 1673 ed.). Also E. F. Rimbault, *Rounds, Canons and Catches of England* (London: 1865).

[4] H. C. de Lafontaine, *King's Musick* (London: Novello and Co. Ltd., 1909), p. 75.

Queen early in 1634.[1] The younger Lawes apparently succeeded well in this task, for from this date his name appears
much more frequently in the accounts of the productions at
Court. As a matter of fact, even in the previous year William
had composed a piece of music for Ben Jonson's *Entertainment
at Welbeck*, where he seems to have been a part of the Royal
entourage of the King, who was then on his way to Scotland
to accept the Scottish Crown.[2] This entertainment was produced
at Welbeck Abbey by the Earl of Newcastle, with whom the
Lawes brothers seem to have had some relations later on. How
William happened to be a member of the King's party, it is
difficult to determine. Henry, who already had his Court
appointment and still held his post as Gentleman of the Chapel
Royal, would naturally have accompanied Charles, since it is a
matter of record that the Gentlemen of the Chapel did attend
the King on his progress to Edinburgh. But William's connection is puzzling, unless he was indeed in some manner unofficially attached to the Chapel or the Sovereign's household.
There is no mention in the Cheque Book of the Chapel Royal
of William Lawes ever having been a member of the Chapel,
and yet, in the Chapel Royal Anthem Book of 1635, there are
two anthems clearly by him.[3] We know too that William composed a good deal of religious music. All of this, in addition to
previous suggestions and facts presented here, indicates that he
was active in the King's Musick, if not yet acknowledged by
a regular appointment.

By this time, 1633, Henry Lawes was well on his way toward
achieving fame as a composer of *continuo* song. He had an
excellent voice and was well liked and respected at Court. The
Royal poets fawned over him and were only too pleased when
the King's musician would set their lyrics to music. William
Lawes too enjoyed this popularity among the Court poets, and
his songs in the declamatory vein are quite similar to those of
his brother. Though less in quantity they are by no means
inferior in quality. William's chief poets were all courtiers of

---

[1] A full account of this masque is given in Chapter IX, pp. 209–21.

[2] Lawes' music for this entertainment is discussed in Chapter VIII,
p. 196.

[3] British Museum, Harleian manuscript 6346. See the discussion in
Chapter X, pp. 256–7.

one type or another: Sir John Suckling, George Sandys and Thomas Carew, all members of the King's privy council; Robert Herrick, Chaplain to Buckingham; William Davenant, dramatist for the King's Men Players and later poet-laureate; James Shirley, a member of Gray's Inn, and many others. In fact, both William and Henry Lawes shared in the services of all these men, although William seems to have preferred the poetry of the above-mentioned writers most of all.

Isolated instances over the next decade strongly suggest that William and Henry worked closely together in their duties at Court. In 1634, after the success of the *Triumph of Peace*, Henry Lawes did the music for Carew's masque, *Cœlum Britannicum*, and shortly afterwards he was busy preparing the music for his friend John Milton's masque of *Comus*, which was to be presented at Ludlow Castle on the Welsh border in honour of the Earl of Bridgewater's inauguration there on Michaelmas Day. It is not known whether William Lawes assisted his brother in this production by writing the instrumental music for the masque. None of William's works has been identified with *Comus*, despite the fact that modern editors have furnished their editions with instrumental pieces by the younger brother.[1] The possibility does exist, however, that William was at Ludlow Castle with his brother and did help with the music. Later in the same year, both Lawes' appear to have taken part in some activity at Harefield House, the estate of the Countess of Derby, grandmother of the Egerton children.[2] At this time, too (December of 1634), William wrote music for the production of William Davenant's play, *Love and Honour*, which was produced at the Blackfriars Theatre by the King's Men Players on December 12. It was after this performance that William Lawes finally received his appointment as one of the King's musicians

---

[1] See, e.g., the edition of the *Masque of Comus* by Sir Frederick Bridge (London: Novello and Co. Ltd., 1908), in which seven of William Lawes' instrumental compositions from the *Royall Consort* and Playford's publications were included.

[2] In an uncatalogued manuscript belonging to the Hastings Library and now at the Huntington Library, the following items are to be found in the records of the expense of the stables: 'Oate Mr. Lawes horse . . .xi^d', 'To Hussie for fetching Mr. Lawes horse & his brothers from Lond . . .ii^s ii^d'. Cited by Evans, op. cit., p. 107.

in ordinary 'for the lutes and voices', on April 30, 1635.[1] He took the place vacated by one John Laurence, deceased. John Wilson, the Lawes brothers' friend, also received his appointment in this year. William's salary was to be forty pounds per annum and in the months that followed he received the customary allowances for livery that were the due of every Court musician.[2]

In the following year, William and Henry collaborated on their first major work together, *The Triumphs of the Prince d'Amour*, a masque written by William Davenant for the Middle Temple of the Inns of Court. The occasion was the celebration of the arrival in England of the King's nephews, Charles and Rupert, the famous Palatine Princes. In August of the same year, 1636, the Lawes brothers participated in Archbishop Laud's preparations for welcoming the King to Oxford, and again William and Henry worked together. Three plays, which required much incidental music, were performed for Charles I during his short stay. William's activities in the dramatic field from this time increased many-fold and are traced in some detail in Chapter VIII. Another work upon which the brothers collaborated was Sir John Suckling's *Aglaura*, which was presented at the Cockpit-in-Court in February of 1638. The record indicates that in the composition of dramatic music, William and Henry had by this time practically become a team. It is not possible to say, however, that Henry Lawes was responsible for the vocal music of these productions and William Lawes, the instrumental pieces. Practically no instrumental music, apart from the latter's short 'simphonies' for the masques, has been identified with the plays for which the brothers wrote. It is true, of course, that William was much the more famous for his instrumental compositions. (Indeed, Henry seems to have written hardly any instrumental music at all.) Yet, once again the record shows that much more of the extant *vocal* music which has thus far been identified with plays and masques upon which the two collaborated, is by William Lawes rather than by his older brother. No doubt

---

[1] Lafontaine, op. cit., p. 91.

[2] Lafontaine, op. cit., pp. 91, 98–9, 101, 105–6, 107. In March 1636, both William and Henry Lawes received ten pounds apiece for the purchase of two lutes; ibid., p. 93.

William wrote the instrumental music for these productions as well, but his activity in the vocal dramatic field deserves far more than just passing mention, as a later chapter will prove. It is likely also that many of William's instrumental pieces, which we have in the form of short dance tunes in some of the publications of John Playford after the middle of the century, were originally composed for these performances. Some of these have been identified.[1]

The year 1639 already brought with it the distant rumblings of civil war. The outbreak of the Bishops' Wars in the North saw King Charles and many of his loyal followers depart for the battlefield. Among those with commissions in the King's army were many members of the Royal household, including some of Lawes' poet friends, Sir John Suckling and Richard Lovelace, whose poems the Lawes brothers had set to music. William's activities during 1639 and 1640 are difficult to trace. He wrote music for only one play, Suckling's *Tragedy of Brennoralt*, and no mention of him, except in the King's household accounts, has otherwise been found. Nor has any of his other music been traced to those years. As a young and loyal cavalier, he may well have joined his poet friends and his King in the army, but no evidence for this assumption has been discovered. We do know that in 1640 Henry Lawes was living at the 'Little Almonry'. Robert Herrick was also a tenant here at the same time.[2] It is likely that William, too, if he wasn't with the King's army, was living here in London, with his brother and the poet whose verses both of them cherished for their songs. This year, 1640, also saw the death of Thomas Lawes the elder, at Salisbury, and it is probable that the brothers journeyed to Sarum for the burial in early November.

In 1641, William Lawes wrote music for three more plays, and that is the last we hear of him until his death at the Siege of Chester in 1645. In 1642 Parliament closed the theatres and by March 1643 Charles I had commanded his entire household to report to the Court at Oxford. There are no records of William Lawes having produced any music during the Court's residence at Oxford, though he may well have done so. However, at

---

[1] For the identification of instrumental pieces in Playford's collections see Chapter IX, pp. 228 ff.

[2] F. W. Moorman, *Robert Herrick* (London: John Lane, 1910), p. 121.

some time during the Oxford reign he received a commission and enlisted in the Royalist forces. Thomas Fuller supplies the account of what followed:

'In these *distracted times* his [William's] Loyalty ingaged him in the War for his *Lord* and *Master* and though he was by *General Gerrard* made a *Commissary* on designe to secure him (such *Officers* being commonly shot-free by their place, as not Exposed to danger,) yet such the *activity* of *his Spirit*, he disclaimed the *Covert* of his *Office*, and betrayed thereunto by his own adventurousness was casually shot at the Siege of *Chester*, the same time when the Lord *Bernard Stuart* lost his life.

'Nor was the *Kings soul* so ingrossed with *grief* for the death of so near a *Kinsman*, and *Noble a Lord*, but that hearing of the death of his *deare servant William Lawes*, he had a particular Mourning for him when *dead*, whom he loved when living, and commonly called the *Father of Musick*.' [1]

Fuller's account of Lawes' death has been interpreted by some to mean that the composer strayed too near the firing line and was accidentally shot. This interpretation, however, does not appear to be entirely the case. To understand the circumstances of Lawes' death it is necessary to review the action which took place at the battle of Chester in 1645. [2]

Charles I was on his way up from Hereford to relieve the beleaguered city of Chester near the northern Welsh border, thinking afterwards to continue north and effect a junction with Montrose's main force in Scotland. The parliament general, Poyntz, who was informed of the King's intentions, drove his forces hard in an attempt to catch Charles at Chester. Upon approaching the city, on September 23, 1645, the King sent Sir Marmaduke Langdale, with a strong force of cavalry, over Holt Bridge toward Rowton Heath which was a few miles south-east of the city. During the ensuing battle Colonel Jones, the Com-

---

[1] Fuller, op. cit., p. 157 (Wiltshire).

[2] The following account of the battle of Chester and the Campaign of Rowton Heath is based on the details in Samuel R. Gardiner, *History of the Great Civil War 1642–9* (London: Longmans, Green, and Co. Ltd., 1889), Vol. II, pp. 323–5; also Edward Clarendon, *The History of the Rebellion and Civil Wars in England* (Oxford, 1703), Vol. II, pp. 549–50. An incomplete account was also given by Bulstrode Whitelocke, *Memorials of the English Affairs . . .* (London: 1682), p. 160.

mander of the parliament forces, fell back in order to join hands with General Poyntz who came to his support. This movement was erroneously seen by the Royalists as a retreat. They immediately started in what they thought was 'pursuit', and so did many of the garrison and townspeople of the city who ran to join them. It was probably at this point in the battle that William Lawes 'disclaimed the *Covert of his Office*', and like the others ran to join in the 'rout'. In the meantime Jones had joined with Poyntz and the whole of the rebel forces turned and charged their onrushing pursuers, who were then virtually cut to pieces by Poyntz's cavalry. It was one of the bloodiest slaughters of the war. When the smoke of the battle was over, two of the many hundreds who fell were the Lord Bernard Stuart and William Lawes. A tablet in the city wall at Chester still marks the spot where King Charles looked down to see the utter annihilation of his forces there, on September 24, 1645.

A second glance at Fuller's statement concerning Lawes' death will show that it is not inconsistent with the facts as outlined in the above account of the battle. To this we may add the statements by Henry Lawes in his dedicatory remarks to King Charles I in the *Choice Psalmes*, in which he affirms that his brother 'fell a willing sacrifice for your Majestie'; and again in his epistle *To The Reader* he says that William 'lyes in the Bed of Honour, and expir'd in the Service and Defence of the King his Master'. John Jenkins, in his elegaic dialogue 'on the sad losse of his much esteemed Friend, Mr. William Lawes, servant to His Majesty', also says:

> *Treble:* What caus'd his fate?
> *Bass:* A fatall breath of honour
> Challeng'd death with death.
> *Treble:* What tempted?
> *Bass:* Vertue.
> *Treble:* Why?
> *Bass:* To have a loyall fame,
> A royall grave.

Lawes' death was a severe blow to his musician and poet friends, but most of all to his older brother. Because none of William's works had been published during his lifetime, Henry decided to print a memoriam of his psalms in three parts as a tribute to William's genius and as a testimonial of his own undying love and admiration for his younger brother. To William's collection he added an equal number of his own similar compositions and invited the chief poets and musicians of the age to add their verses and music in several elegies and commendatory poems. This was the *Choice Psalmes* of 1648. The verses were furnished by four of the brothers' friends: Aurelian Townshend, the Royalist poet; James Harington, author of *Oceana*; John Milton, and their devoted companion of childhood days, Francis Sambrooke. Townshend's poem is interesting in that it points up the fundamental difference in emphasis followed by the brothers in their musical compositions. Presumably it was William Lawes, the instrumentalist, who sounded 'the depth of Musique', and Henry, the song composer, who 'took his flight into the aire':

To the Incomparable Brothers, M^r· *Henry* and M^r· *William Lawes* (Servants to His Majestie) upon the setting of these Psalmes.

The Various Musick, both for Aire and Art,
    These Arch-Musicians, in their sev'rall waies
Compos'd, and Acted, merit higher praise
    Then wonder-wanting knowledge can impart.
Brothers in blood, in Science and Affection
    Belov'd by those that envie their Renowne;
In a False Time true Servants to the Crowne:
    Lawes of themselves, needing no more direction.
The depth of music one of them did sound,
    The t'other took his flight into the aire:
O then thrice happy and industrious paire,
    That both the depth and height of Musique sound.
Which my sweet Friend, the life of Lovers pens,
    In so milde manner hath attain'd to do,
He looks the better, and his hearers too;
    So in exchange all Ladies are his friends.
And when our Meditations are too Meane
    To keep their raptures longer on the wing,
They soar'd up to that Prophet and that King,
    Whose love is God, and Heav'n his glorious Scene:
Setting his Psalmes, whereby both they and we
    May singing rise to immortalitie.

                                                    A. TOWNSHEND

Francis Sambrooke paid equal tribute to his beloved friends in a poem of considerable merit:

> To my worthy Friend (and Countriman,) Mr. *Henry Lawes*, upon his owne, and his Brother Mr. *William Lawes's* incomparable Works.
>
> Where shall I place my wonder, when I see
> Such right in both to't, such equalitie
> Of worth in either, that it cann't be knowne
> Which does the greatest, and the highest owne?
> So when two Tapers mixe their beames, we say,
> Not this more lustre has, or that more ray;
> But each has title to the light, and they
> Make up one, common, undistinguish'd day:
> Or, as when th'*Flamen* divers incense fires,
> The perfume severs not, but in one aspires;
> So that from this Spice, or that piece of Gum,
> We cannot say, such, or such odours come:
> But mounting in a generall unknowne cloud,
> The wonder of the breath's to each allow'd;
> So here, such equall worth from each does flow,
> That to each light, to each we incense owe.
>
> . . . .
>
> FR. SAMBROOKE

While not included in the commendatory verses of the *Choice Psalmes*, other elegaic poems were written upon the death of William Lawes by the more renowned poets of the age, such as Robert Herrick, Robert Heath and John Tatham.

In his introduction to the *Choice Psalmes* Henry Lawes tells us that many such elegies on the death of William Lawes were written by his 'Noble Friends' and inscribed in a 'peculiar Book', but the latter volume is either not extant or has not yet been discovered.

At the end of the *Choice Psalmes* were printed eight musical elegies by William's friends and colleagues, each a noted composer in his own right. The list includes Henry Lawes, John Wilson, John Jenkins, Simon Ives, John Hilton, John Cobb, John Taylor and Captain Edmund Foster. The longest composition is that of John Jenkins, the 'grand old man' of English chamber music. Despite the fact that Jenkins was ten years Lawes' senior, the two appear to have been close friends. The older man's elegy is indeed a testimonial of his affection and high regard for his young colleague, to whom he refers as '*Amice*'. Jenkins' verses are also valuable in that they paint a revealing portrait of William Lawes, a portrait which agrees in every detail with the one said to be Lawes which now hangs in the Faculty of Music School at Oxford and is reproduced as frontispiece of the present volume.[1] The text of Jenkins' elegy begins as follows:

> *Treble:* Why in this shade of night? *Amice say:*
> How is thy light put out?
> Thy cheerfull day turn'd into frownes?
> The sprightly aire that once danc'd
> On thy smiling brow, and oft convers'd
> With thy quick sighted genius?
> Prithee, prithee tell, my deare *Amice*;
> All I feare's not well.

In the Oxford portrait William is shown as a handsome and somewhat debonair cavalier, with broad-brimmed hat, wide embroidered collar, slashed coat and long curly hair. The thin smile on his lips and the quick sparkle in his eyes betray an adventurous and daring spirit. There is the look of the Court favourite about him too, of a confident and gifted young genius who is fawned upon and indulged by his older colleagues and peers. Indeed, there is little evidence, in his outward appearance at least, of the turbulent romanticism and brooding melancholy of his major works. Apparently this side of William Lawes' character was not for the canvas, nor for the Court.

Jenkins entitled his elegy, '*An Elegiack Dialogue on the sad losse of his much esteemed friend, Mr. William Lawes, servant to His Majesty*'. It is by far the longest of the elegies appended to the *Choice Psalmes*, and shows the older man's respect for Lawes as a musician. In his 'dialogue', which closes with a three-part chorus, Jenkins refers to Lawes as 'the soul of mine and all our

---

[1] The portrait was presented to the Music School late in the eighteenth century by Philip Hayes. It is exactly the same size as a similar portrait of Henry Lawes, which is also in the Music School. The chief doubt about the authenticity of William's portrait has always been the fact that he appeared younger than Henry, but with the proof that he was indeed a younger man this doubt has now been removed. The two portraits seem to have been done at the same time and by the same artist, since the style and materials are the same.

harmony', a statement of some significance, since Lawes'
counterpoint was indeed the most daring of the period and may
well have influenced Jenkins in his own compositions.

Simon Ives also appears to have been more than a casual
friend. It will be remembered that he shared the honour with
Lawes of composing the music for the *Triumph of Peace* in 1634.
His elegy is dedicated as, '*An Elegie On The Death of His Deare
Fraternall Friend and Fellow, Mr. William Lawes, servant to His
Majesty*'. The verse is short:

> Lament and Mourne, he's dead and gone
>> That was the most Admired one, renowned Lawes.
> Generall of the Forces all in Europe that were musicall.
>> Have we not cause to weep and mourne,
> When as the children yet unborne may make us sad,
>> To think that neither girle nor boy
> Shall ever live for to enjoy such *Lawes*
>> Such *Lawes* as once we had.

John Hilton, the famous editor and contributor to Playford's
Catch that Catch Can (1652), set the following verses:

> Bound by the neare conjunction of our soules,
>> Thus I condole thee, thus bedew they Herse;
> And whilst my throbbing, throbbing heart, thy Exit towles,
>> Accept this sacrifice of weeping verse.
> What eyes can drily stubborne be when Lawes resteth
>> At such a long continued pause?
> Let teares, like pendents, garnish every note,
>> Wav'd to and fro with gales of mournfull sighes,
> And let the widowed muses joyntly vote,
>> To celebrate with griefe thy obsequies:
> For with thee vanish't all their aerie pride,
>> Muffled in the clay, that erst was stellified.
> Since then i'th Center sleeps true harmony,
>> Let him (that's greedy of that sacred gaine)
> Close to his mother earth his eare apply,
>> There wait to heare some sad melodious straine.
> Within this Womb hath pale impartiall death
>> Too soon confin'd the Quintessence of breath.

Captain Edmund Foster's words contain a single message:

> Brave spirit, art thou fled?
> And shall not we,

> Since thou so soon art dead
> > Shed teares for thee?
> O let our eyes like limbecks be
> > Still dropping teares for thee.

John Cobb, organist of His Majesty's Chapel Royal, paid tribute to Lawes' skill as a composer:

> Deare Will is dead,
> > Will Lawes, whose active braine
> Gave life to many sweet harmonious straines;
> > Whose boundlesse skill made music speak such sense,
> As if't had sprung from an intelligence.
> > In his just proportion'd songs there might you find
> His soule convers'd with heav'n with his mind
> > And in such language Rhetorick never knew
> For his Rhetorick and sweet Musick too
> > Like that which brought from the imperiall skie
> Angels to men, from men made Divels flie.
> > Oh he's dead, he's dead
> To heav'n is he gone? The life of Musick
> > And laus, the life and laus of our Nation.

John Wilson, who was by this time Doctor of Music, dedicated his elegy '*To the Memory of his Friend and Fellow, Mr. William Lawes, servant to His Majestie*':

> O doe not now lament and cry,
> > 'Tis fate concludes we all must die;
> Rather rejoyce that he is there
> > Mending the musique of the Spheares:
> We are dull soules of little worth,
> > And coldly here his praise set forth,
> Who doth that truly sure must be instructed by divinity.
> > Harke, O harke the celestiall Quire doth pause,
> To heare his sweeter lyre:
> > There he is set free from vaine feares,
> Or heav'd sighs or brinish teares.
> > Could'st thou thy fancy send us downe in Musique,
> We would place a crowne, so harmonious on thy faire Herse,
> > Should out-tongue Ovid in his sweetest verse.

The most tender of all of the elegies is that of Henry Lawes. It is entitled, '*A Pastorall Elegie to the memory of my deare Brother, William Lawes*':

Cease you jolly Shepherds, cease your merry layes;
  Pipe no more, pipe no more in meadowes green,
Crown'd with Ivie and with Bayes:
  Let your flockes no more be seen
On the verdant hillocks spread;
  But tune your oaten Reeds with saddest notes,
With saddest notes to mourne:
  For gentle *Willy*, your lov'd *Lawes*,
Your lov'd *Lawes* is dead.
  Weep, weep, weep Shepherd Swaines
For him that was the glory of your plaines:
  He could appease the sullen seas,
And calme the fury of the mind;
  But now (alas) in silent urne
He lyes, hid from us
  And never must returne, never must returne,
And never must returne, and never must returne.

The full extent of Henry's grief may be understood even more from his dedicatory epistle to King Charles I, and from his preface *To The Reader*:

'To His Most Sacred Majestie, CHARLES, by the Grace of God, King of great Brittaine, France and Ireland, Defender of the Faith, &c.

'I could not answer mine owne Conscience (most Gracious Soveraigne) should I dedicate these Compositions to any but Your Majestie; they were born and nourish'd in Your Majesties service, and long since design'd (such as they are) an Offering to Your Royall hand. Many of them were compos'd by my Brother (*William Lawes*), whose life and endeavours were devoted to Your service; whereof, I (who knew his heart) am a surviving witnesse, and therein he persisted to that last minute, when he fell a willing Sacrifice for Your Majestie: I were unworthy such a Brother, should I tender ought that is his, or mine, to any but our Gracious Master (from whose Royall Bounty both of us receiv'd all we injoy'd;) and such an Inscription would not only seem a Theft and Alienation of what is Your Majesties, but (which I most abhorre) would make me taste of these ungratefull dayes. Your Majestie knowes when the Regall Prophet first penn'd these Psalmes, he gave them to the Musitians to be set to tunes; and they humbly brought them to

David the King. Besides, Mr. *Sandys* inscribes his Translation to Your Sacred Majestie; so that this I offer is Your Majesties in all capacities, and doth not so properly come, as rebound back to Your Majestie. I was easily drawn to this presumption, by Your Majesties known particular affection to *David's* Psalmes, both because the Psalter is held by all Divines one of the most excellent parts of holy Scripture; as also in regard much of Your Majesties present condition, is lively described by King *David's* pen. The King of Heaven and Earth restore Your Majestie according to Your own righteous heart, which is the daily earnest prayer of

Your Majesties most humble
most loyally devoted Subject and Servant,
HENRY LAWES.'

To the Reader

'These following Compositions of mine and my Brothers, set at severall times, and upon severall Occasions, (having been often heard, and well approv'd of, chiefly by such as desire to joyne Musick with Devotion) I have been much importuned to send to the Presse, and should not easily have been perswaded to it now, (especially in these dissonant times) but to doe a Right (or at least to shew my Love) to the Memory of my Brother, unfortunately lost in these unnaturall Warres; yet lyes in the Bed of Honour, and expir'd in the Service and Defence of the King his Master. Living, he was generally known, and (for his Parts) much honoured by Persons of best quality and condition. To give a further Character of him I shall forebeare, because of my neer relation, and rather referre that to those Elegies which many of his noble Friends have written in a peculiar Book: But, as to what he hath done in Musick, I shall desire the present and the future Age, that so much of his Works as are here published, may be received, as the least part of what he hath compos'd and but a small Testimony of his greater Compositions, (too voluminous for the Presse) which I the rather now mention, lest being, as they are, disperst into private hands, they may chance be hereafter lost; for, besides his Fancies of the Three, Foure, Five and Six Parts to the Viols and Organ, he hath made above thirty severall sorts of Musick for Voices and Instruments: Neither was there any Instrument then in use, but he compos'd to it so aptly, as if he had only studied that. As for that which is my part in this Composition, I had not thought at all (though much urg'd) to publish; but that, as they had their birth at the same time with his, and are of the same kinde, so they might enter both into the light together, and accompany one another being so neere allied; Mine taking precedence of order only, not of worth. I may be thought too partiall in what I have spoke of a Brother; but here are following many of our Friends and Fellowes, (whose excellency in Musick is very well knowne) who doe better speak for him, while they mourne his Obsequies: yet I (oblig'd before all other) cannot but bewaile his losse, and shall celebrate his memory to my last houre.

HENRY LAWES'

One cannot help but feel that there existed between the brothers Lawes one of the finest and most sincere relationships in the entire history of the English musical scene. Henry Lawes, as seen from his own testimony, respected and guarded the genius of his younger brother. He was concerned that posterity should know of William's voluminous works in every style of composition, and that he should be honoured after his death. There is also that deeply-rooted affection which is so evident in Henry's every phrase, and which remained with him until his dying day, so that in his last will and testament made shortly before his death, his last words were:

'I give and bequeath unto . . . Mr. Frances Sambrook my chest of Violls and chest in which they are consisting of two treble violls, two tenor violls, and one Base Violl with the bookes of ffancyes, Pavins and Almans of ffive and six parts for the violls and six bookes of Consort lessons bound in bleu leather, all which were the compositions of my deare Brother William Lawes.'[1]

Whether the manuscripts which Henry Lawes bequeathed to Sambrooke are among the autograph volumes of William Lawes' works which are now in the Bodleian Library at Oxford and in the British Museum has not yet been established for certain. At least nine autograph volumes are known to be

[1] Henry Lawes' will is filed in Somerset House and dated 1662, the year of his death.

extant. Six of these, originally belonging to the library of the Oxford Music School, are now in the Bodleian Library. They, and their contents, are as follows:

autographs		contents
Mus. Sch. B. 2.	(in score)	Fantasias, Pavans and Aires in five parts; Masques; Catches, Rounds and Canons; miscellaneous Songs; Suites for two Bass Viols and Organ; Violin Sonata in D Major; pieces for Two Lutes.
Mus. Sch. B. 3.	(in score)	Fantasias, In Nomines, Pavans and Aires in Five and Six Parts; selected 'Harpe' Consorts; Forty pieces from the Royall Consort.
Mus. Sch. D. 238–40.	(in parts; three books)	Violin Sonatas; 'Harpe' Consorts; Suites for Two Bass Viols and Organ.
Mus. Sch. D. 229.	(organ book)	The organ part for the Fantasias, Pavans, In Nomines and Aires in Five and Six Parts; the Violin Sonatas; and the Suites for Two Bass Viols and Organ; also the harp part for the 'Harpe' Consorts.

Two more of Lawes' autograph volumes are in the British Museum. They are:

autographs		contents
Add. 31432	(in score)	Solo songs; Dialogues; Three-part Drinking Songs (all with an unfigured thorough-bass).
Add. 17798	(bass part only)	Fantasias, In Nomines, Pavans and Aires in Five and Six Parts.

The ninth autograph volume contains Lawes' music for lyra viols in tablature. It was part of the library of William H. Cummings, which was sold at auction in 1917. The present owner has not yet been traced.

The authenticity of William Lawes' autograph is supplied by an inscription on the reverse side of the first folio of British Museum, Add. 31432, which reads as follows:

'Richard Gibbon, his booke, given to him by
Mr. William Lawes all of his owne pricking
and composing.
'Given to me J. R., by his widow, Mrs. Gibbon.
J.R.'

All nine autograph volumes are bound exactly alike, in brown calf, with the Royal Arms of Charles I stamped in gold on the covers, and on either side of the design an initial, first W. and then L.[1] Almost every piece in the autographs is signed by William Lawes in a beautiful and distinctive hand, which leaves little doubt that these are autograph signatures. The signatures in all volumes correspond exactly. From the inscription by Richard Gibbon in Add. 31432 it is probable that William Lawes himself arranged the contents and had them bound, perhaps during the Court's establishment at Oxford. This may also explain the presence of the autographs in the Music School collection. Indeed, all of the volumes appear to be part of one large set which was meticulously arranged and guarded. However, while Lawes' autographs are gathered into sets representing his various collections, they offer little or no basis for an attempted chronology of his works. The composer's Court masques, for example, are included in reverse order from their actual dates of composition. Likewise, an elegy written on the death of John Tomkins in 1638 is found on page 101 of Bodleian, Mus. Sch. B.2, whereas the music for *Britannia Triumphans*, which was composed in the same year, is on pages 16 to 18.

An examination and identification of the watermarks of the various autographs supports the claim that they were for the most part all of the same set, as well as the suggestion that the set was compiled in Oxford, *c.* 1642–3. Except for the flyleaves, each volume contains paper which is uniform in size, weight and watermark. This paper has printed staffs of five lines, which are also uniform. All of the volumes, except Mus. Sch. B.2 and B.3, have the same watermarks, a peacock in a circle. This corresponds with No. 174 in Edward Heawood's *Watermarks*, (Hildersum: 1950), which is given as 1628 in Venice. The paper used in the two Bodleian autograph scores has the watermark No. 2174 in Heawood, a cluster of grapes with the initials A.R. on either side of the stem, and is listed much earlier, *c.* 1579. The watermarks on the flyleaves of the latter volumes approximate Nos. 479–81 in Heawood, which are the same as that on the paper of Giovanni Coperario's *Rules How to Compose* of

---

[1] Bodleian, Mus. Sch. B.3, has the initials H. L., although the manuscript contains only autographs of William Lawes.

c. 1610. The latter watermark, however, is listed as early seventeenth century to 1624. These watermarks tell us little, since we know that some of the contents of the manuscripts were not entered until 1638 or later. The most significant of the watermarks is that on the flyleaves of the organ book, Bodleian, Mus. Sch. D.229, which approximates Nos. 649–672 in Heawood and indicates that the paper was made between the years 1640 and 1680. This strongly supports the suggestion that Lawes himself had the book bound in the early 1640's, while with the Court in Oxford, and therefore, that he may have copied and arranged his autograph volumes during the same period. We know that the autographs were not copied chronologically and the presence of music written in at least 1638 or later, at the beginning of one of the major volumes, further strengthens this contention.

It is certain that several of Lawes' autograph volumes are either missing or no longer extant. These would include the five remaining part books of the original set of parts to the five- and six-part fantasias, In Nomines, pavans and aires, of which British Museum, Add. 17798 is one; the six books of consort 'lessons' (probably the parts to the *Royall Consort*), mentioned by Henry Lawes in his will; and the lyra viol autograph listed in the catalogue of the Cummings collection. In addition, the present author believes that the following additional autograph volumes have not yet been discovered or are no longer extant:

1 The three-part psalms.
2 The verse anthems.
3 The madrigals in three, four and five parts.
4 The suites for lutes.
5 Additional consort 'lessons' or dances for instruments.
6 Pieces for wind instruments (*perhaps*).
7 Works for the keyboard (*perhaps*).

Evidence for this claim is based on the fact that in some cases several works do exist of the type mentioned above, but not in autograph. It is important to remember here also, the statement by Henry Lawes, that his brother composed, besides his fantasias of three, four, five and six parts for the viols and organ, more than thirty different kinds of music for voices and instruments, and that William composed for every instrument 'then in use' so well, that one might have thought 'he had only studied that'. And, as the older brother also stated, William Lawes' works were 'too voluminous for the Presse'. Additional evidence for the possible existence of other manuscripts may be seen in the case of Lawes' vocal music.

In examining the contents of the vocal autographs and comparing these with the complete list of Lawes' vocal and dramatic works it becomes evident that a number of pieces which are ascribed to the composer in other manuscripts and in Playford's publications, cannot be authenticated by autographs. Many of these songs, however, are attributed to Lawes in so many manuscripts and publications that little if any doubt should be cast upon their authenticity. In fact, some of the composer's most popular tunes fall into this category, including the three-part dance song, 'O My Clarissa', and perhaps the most famous of all seventeenth-century catches, 'The Wisemen Were But Seven'. It is curious indeed that these works should have been left out of the carefully planned autograph volumes. Even more perplexing is the fact that at several points in the autograph, Bodleian, Mus. Sch. B.2, quite a few pages have been torn out close to the binding. All of these mutilations occur immediately following, immediately preceding, or in the midst of vocal music. Moreover, in some cases part of a piece of vocal music, or even a complete song, has not been torn out, but scratched out in pen and ink, so that instrumental music on the same page or on the reverse side of the folio might be preserved. Undoubtedly someone, probably William Lawes himself, deliberately removed much of the vocal and dramatic music from this autograph volume. Fortunately however, all of the pieces and fragments that remain in the scratched-out form are still decipherable. They are identical with versions found in other manuscripts and publications. It is therefore likely that they were removed for the purpose of binding with other vocal and dramatic music of the same type. In addition, these pieces are mainly part-songs in the style of the late Renaissance madrigal. They are among the finest of Lawes' vocal works.[1]

The *Choice Psalmes* proved to be the first of many publications which contained music by William Lawes. The astute music

[1] The vocal autographs and the mutilations occurring in them are further discussed in Chapter VII, p. 178 f.

publisher, John Playford, who styled himself 'Philo-Musicae', seized upon Lawes' music for his early publications. The second part of the very rare *A Musicall Banquet* (1651), entitled *Musica Harmonia*, which contained music for a treble and bass instrument, was practically dedicated to Lawes.[1] The title page reads as follows:

MUSICA HARMONIA:
or
Choice Almans, Corants, and Sarabands, for one Treble & Basse.
By that rare and accomplished Master in Musick
Mr. William Lawes, Deceased:
and by severall other Excellent Masters in Musick now living.

Twelve of the pieces in *Musica Harmonia* are by Lawes, twice the number of the second most represented composer, John Jenkins. Other contributors are Christopher Simpson, author of *The Division-Violist* (1659), Charles Coleman and Richard Cooke. Part I of *A Musicall Banquet*, entitled *Musick and Mirth*, also included three catches by William Lawes.

The next Playford publication which contained music by the composer was John Hilton's *Catch that Catch Can*, printed in 1652. Only about one-third of the pieces in this volume, however, are by Hilton. William Lawes was the second largest contributor with eighteen pieces. Indeed his catches were much the most popular of the day and outlasted those of Hilton by a number of years. In the same year, 1652, Lawes' music was also featured in Playford's *Musick's Recreation On The Lyra Violl*, and also in the same year Playford brought out an unauthorized version of Henry Lawes' *Select Ayres and Dialogues*, in three books, containing songs by Henry and William Lawes, John Wilson, Charles Coleman and William Webbe. Six of the songs were by William. In 1653, Henry Lawes, at Playford's expense, brought out his own collection of *Select Ayres and Dialogues*, also in three books, in which he complained about inaccuracies in the unauthorized version of the year before. This time William Lawes was represented by eight works.

In 1655 Playford published his *Court-Ayres*, in two parts, for a

---

[1] To the best of the author's knowledge, the only extant copy of *A Musicall Banquet* which is complete is that in the Bodleian Library at Oxford.

treble and a bass, for viols or violins. In the preface 'To All Understanders and Lovers of Musick', the publisher explained his plan of publication:

'About three years since I published a Booke called the *Musicall Banquet*, there being in it a small taste of Musick in four severall Tracts. The first was some *Rules for Song and Violl*. The second had in it about 30 Lessons for *Lyra Violl*. The third contained about 27 Lessons of *Two* Parts, *Basse* and *Treble*. And the fourth consisted of about 20 Rounds and Catches.

'That little Booke finding such acceptance among all lovers and Practitioners in Musick (and the Impression now totally sold off) I resolved to inlarge each of these tracts, and to Print them in severall Books, which I have now (through God's permission) accomplished. The first Book I call, *A Brief Introduction To The Skill of Song and Violl*. The second, *Musick's Recreation*, wherein is 117 Lessons for the *Lyra Violl*. The third is intituled *Court-Ayres of Two Parts*; treble and Basse, containing 246 Lessons. The fourth is called *Catch that Catch Can*, or *Catches*, *Rounds* and *Cannons*, for 3 or foure Voyces, containing at least 150, whereby you have a much larger Banquet than you had before.'

The *Court-Ayres* contained fifty-four pieces by William Lawes. But the pieces in this publication are not the original form of Lawes' works. Many are 'watered-down' versions which are mere skeletons of his larger compositions. Some are also from his masques. In later publications, Playford himself admitted that larger works, containing divisions or variations, or large instrumental compositions in many parts, were too expensive for publication. Indeed this probably explains why none of Lawes' really important works were ever printed during the seventeenth century. Later, in the eighteenth century, his work was forgotten, and the style of composition had so changed that there was little hope of anyone taking the time to interest himself in the composer's autographs.

The second edition of the *Court-Ayres* was entitled *Courtly Masquing Ayres* and was published in 1662.[1] Lawes' pieces make up the first section of this work and include new selections

---

[1] A complete copy of the *Courtly Masquing Ayres* may be found in the music library of the Royal College of Music in London.

from his masques. In 1663 Playford brought out his first collection of music for the virginals, which he entitled *Musick's Handmaide*. Once again Lawes was represented, this time with eight compositions. Whether or not these pieces were originally composed for the virginals, or were even arranged for that instrument by William Lawes, it is difficult to say, since some of the pieces exist in other forms as well. In fact, the only other works for an independent keyboard instrument which are attributed to William Lawes are extant in just a few manuscripts. There are, as far as we know, no solo keyboard works in any of his autographs.

After Playford's publication of music for the virginals, three years elapsed before more of Lawes' music appeared in print. In 1666, however, Playford, acceding to popular demand, published a simple edition of music for the cittern, a plucked instrument which was far less difficult to play than the lute, since it had only four pairs or 'courses' of wire strings. The title of this volume was *Musick's Delight On The Cithren*. It was written in tablature and, according to Playford, was 'Restored and Refined to a more Easie and Pleasant Manner of Playing than formerly; And set forth with Lessons Al a Mode, being the Choicest of our late new Ayres, Corants, Sarabands, Tunes, and Jiggs. To which is added several New Songs and Ayres to Sing to the Cithren.' Eleven pieces were attributed to Lawes, eight of which were versions of his songs to be sung to the accompaniment of the cittern. Two of these songs, however, were wrongly attributed.[1] One of the composer's most popular dance suites, entitled the *Golden Grove*, made up the few purely instrumental works. All of the pieces in the cittern book were reduced to a single melodic line with but a few chords at cadence points. They were probably arranged by Playford himself.

In 1667 another edition of *Catch that Catch Can* appeared with the co-title, *The Musical Companion*. This contained additional catches and rounds as well as those printed in the first edition of 1652. It also had a second part made up of songs of two, three and four parts. Twenty-nine of the pieces in this publication were by William Lawes. Two years later Playford put out another large edition of the *Select Ayres and Dialogues*, with the

[1] These songs are 'Silly Heart Forbear', which is really by Nicholas Lanier, and the catch 'A Boate, A Boate', by John Jenkins.

new title *The Treasury of Musick*, in three books as before. Nineteen of the songs in this volume were by Lawes, eight of which were wrongly attributed to other composers or anonymous.[1] In 1673 another edition of *The Musical Companion* appeared in which Lawes' vocal pieces figured as the largest single contribution (twenty-three songs and catches). The commendatory verse of this publication included a poem by Thomas Jordan, 'Gentleman', in which a reference to William Lawes' death in connection with the civil wars was made:

> When pestilential Purity did raise
> Rebellion 'gainst the best of Princes,
> And Pious Confusion had untun'd the Land
> When by the Fury of the Good old cause
> Will Lawes was slain, by such whose Wills were **Laws**.

This play of words on the composer's name was employed often in the commendatory verse of the period, as evidence also the elegies of the *Choice Psalmes*. In fact, to musicians and poets at least, the death of William Lawes had become a symbol of the excesses of the Puritan Rebellion. In a manuscript in the British Museum, Add. 29,290, which contains the organ parts to Lawes' violin sonatas, is a brief notice of the composer's death and the following 'Monumental Inscription', which makes use of the same word play:

> Concord is conquered, in this urn there lies
> The Master of great Musick's mysteries:
> And it is a riddle, like the cause,
> Will Lawes was slain, by those whose wills were **Lawes**.

It is not known whether or not the above inscription was actually used on Lawes' gravestone. Presumably the composer was buried at Chester, but the whereabouts of his burial place there is not known. There is no record either that he left any will or last testament, or that he was ever married.

The last seventeenth-century publication to feature William Lawes' music in any quantity was the *New Ayres and Dialogues*, published by John Banister and Thomas Low in 1678. The editors' selection of sixteen of Lawes' finest songs included, for

---

[1] Further to this see Chapter VII, p. 159.

the second and last time in print, the beautiful 'Amarilis'.[1] This same volume also contained several new songs by a rising young composer named Henry Purcell. That Lawes' music continued in high esteem throughout this period is evident from the writings of Thomas Mace, who accords to William Lawes first place over John Jenkins and Christopher Simpson as one of the three greatest masters of the age:

'*These last Ages* have produc'd very many *Able*, and most *Excellent Masters* in *Musick*; *Three only* (*of which*) '*I will instance in, in This Particular*; because they were so *Voluminous*, and *very Eminent in Their Works*, viz. Mr. *William Lawes*, Mr. *John Jenkins*, and Mr. *Christopher Simpson*.

'*These Three Famous Men*, although *Two of Them* be laid *asleep*, (or as we say, *Dead*;) yet by *Their most singular and Rare Works*, *They Live*; and may so easily be *Distinguished*, *the one from the other*, and as *Exactly known*, *which is which*, as if they were present in person, and should speak Words.'[2]

Lawes' continued popularity during and after the Restoration may also be seen in the *Diary* of Samuel Pepys, who was especially fond of both William and Henry Lawes' music. Pepys and his friends often played and sang the Lawes brothers' psalms during their many evenings of sober discourse and music-making.[3]

After about 1680 the English musical scene changed rapidly. New influences from abroad brought with them new vogues in both vocal and instrumental composition. But for Henry Purcell, who brought the heritage of William Lawes and his fellows to its culmination, the great age of English vocal and instrumental music begun during the reign of King Henry VIII was drawing to its close. As for William Lawes, his work lasted a brief span of about thirty-five years after his death and then receded into the archives of a few great libraries, where it has lain dormant ever since.

[1] This song is printed and discussed in Chapter VII, pp. 161–4. It was first printed by John Playford in the *Treasury of Musick* (1669), where it was wrongly attributed to Henry Lawes.

[2] Thomas Mace, *Musick's Monument* (London: 1676), p. 151.

[3] Samuel Pepys, *The Diary of Samuel Pepys* (New York: The Limited Editions Club, 1942), 10 vols., ed. by Henry B. Wheatley, i, p. 271; iii, p. 247; v, pp. 105, 113, etc.

II

'FOR Yᵉ VIOLLS':
THE FANTASIAS AND AIRES

Iᶠ it is at all possible to penetrate Lawes' 'quick-smiling' exterior and to capture the spirit of his turbulent romanticism it is through the music he wrote for larger consorts of viols. Lawes' 'active braine' gave birth to many 'harmonious strains', as John Cobb put it, but the daring genius of the large viol fantasias is quite another thing. The fantasia was the only existing musical form which allowed ample space for the free reign of the composer's imagination. It was therefore particularly well suited to Lawes' highly introspective style. Here, the composer, alone with himself, soars far above the ordinary techniques of his contemporaries, beyond the understanding of the Royal Court, and into an emotional and intellectual realm fashioned from forces of his own choosing.

The fantasia was the English 'sonata movement' of the late sixteenth and seventeenth centuries. As such it was composed for chamber music groups or 'consorts' of from two to seven viols. The form was an outgrowth of the sixteenth-century vocal motet, and the designation 'fantasia' seems to have been borrowed from a contemporary and similar Italian form.[1]

'Fantasia', however, does not in this case imply an instrumental composition of a free form as we are prone to understand it, governed by 'flight of fancy'. On the contrary, the

---

[1] Roger North, *The Musicall Gramarian* (London: Oxford University Press, 1925), pp. 11–13: MS. ed. by Hilda Andrews.

early form of the late sixteenth and early seventeenth centuries was more or less strict. Indeed, it proved to be an ancestor of the later Baroque fugue. In manuscripts of the period it is called variously 'fantasia', 'fantasy', 'fantazia', 'fantazy', 'fancie', 'fancy', etc. It was probably so designated because it was the first serious instrumental form to dispense with the regulatory *cantus firmus*. Then too, as the instrumental counterpart of the vocal motet it need not be dependent on words but could follow the dictates of the composer's imagination and skill. To the composer who had been bound to a predetermined line to which all of the other parts had to conform and to the exigencies of the text in vocal music, this was indeed a new-found freedom, so much so that the musician now felt he was at liberty to compose according to his own 'conceit' or 'fancy'.

But the early fantasia was still bound, first and foremost, to the technique of fugal imitation. Formally, these compositions consisted of several sections, each of which amounted to a short fugal exposition with little if any development during its early years. There was no thematic relationship between the sections in the early form and these often overlapped, as in the vocal motet. Unlike the fugue of a century later, the fugal expositions were not strict. A subject need not be fully stated before the entry of an answer or imitation in another voice. The 'points' or 'retorts', to use the contemporary terminology, could enter at any time during the statement of the subject or another imitation, or even after a 'point' had been completed. This *stretto* or *fugato* technique, therefore, could be either very tight or sometimes quite loose. All manner of intellectual contrapuntal techniques were employed in these *fugato* sections, including counter-subjects, inversions, retrograde and invertible counterpoint. While at times quite interesting harmonically, the early fantasia was not especially attractive melodically; the parts containing for the most part scalewise counterpoints with frequently recurring high and low points. Likewise, the sections were often blurred by overlapping parts and stereotyped cadential formulas and rhythm. The classic description of the early fantasia was provided by Thomas Morley in this oft-quoted paragraph from his *A Plaine and Easie Introduction to Practicall Musicke*.

'The most principall and chiefest kind of musicke which is

made without a dittie is the fantasie, that is, when a musician taketh a point at his pleasure, and wresteth and turneth it as he list, making either much or little of it according as shall seeme best in his own conceit. In this may more art be showne than in any other musicke, because the composer is tide to nothing but that he may adde, deminish, and alter at his pleasure. And this kind will beare any allowances whatsoever tolerable in other musick, except changing the ayre & leaving the key, which in fantasie may never be suffered. Other thinges you may use at your pleasure, as bindings with discordes, quicke motions, slow motions, proportions, and what you list. Likewise, this kind of musick is with them who practice instruments of parts in greatest use, but for voices it is but sildome used.'[1]

The instruments for which fantasias were written, and for which William Lawes' five- and six-part works were composed, were the viols *da gamba*. These were built in various sizes and formed an evenly-matched family of instruments, the most important members of which made up a complete 'chest', or, as Thomas Mace points out: 'Your Best Provision, (and most Compleat), will be a Good Chest of Viols; Six in Number; viz. 2 Bases, 2 Tenors, and 2 Trebles: All truly and Proportionably suited.'[2] The tone of the viols is quieter than that of the violin family and more 'reedy' in quality. This is due to the flat back and thinner wood of the instruments. The bow is curved outward and held in an underhand grip which places particular emphasis on the flexibility of the wrist motion in performance. The instrument, in all its sizes, has six strings which are thinner than those of the violin family, and the fingerboard is fretted with cords of gut for the purpose of obtaining greater resonance at all finger stops. All of the viols, regardless of size, were held between the calves of the legs or the knees and played vertically like the violoncello.[3] As a 'consort' for the performance of chamber music these instruments were particularly well suited

[1] (London: Peter Short, 1597), pp. 180–1. Facsimile reprint as No. 14 of the Shakespeare Association Facsimiles (Oxford University Press, 1937).
[2] Thomas Mace, *Musick's Monument* (London: P. Ratcliffe Thompson, 1676), p. 245.
[3] For a more complete description of the viols and their technique see Gerald R. Hayes, *Musical Instruments and Their Music, 1500–1750.* Vol. II, *The Viols and Other Bowed Instruments* (Oxford University Press, 1928).

because of their evenly matched qualities throughout the several sizes. Especially is this true for the performance of the fantasias, inasmuch as the contrapuntal *fugato* style placed an equal importance upon all of the parts and stressed the matter of equal balance between all of the instruments. Each instrument was by turns a soloist and an accompanying contrapuntal part.

William Lawes' fantasias and aires were not published in their own day, and apart from the composer's autographs in the Bodleian Library at Oxford they have survived in only two manuscripts, neither of which contains the complete collection.[1] It is difficult indeed to believe that these works could have been widely known outside of the inner circle of professional court musicians and perhaps a few of their aristocratic patrons. But the fantasias must have been known to Anthony Wood, who frequented the meetings of the Music Club in Oxford, for it was probably his knowledge of these works which prompted the rather naive comment that Lawes' music 'broke sometimes ye rules of mathematicall composition'. Nevertheless, he hastened to add that 'his [Lawes'] things before and after ye restoration' were 'allwaies culled out'.[2]

The consorts for viols include thirty-nine works, comprising fantasias, In Nomines, pavans and stylized aires in four, five and six parts.[3] The four-part works consist of two fantasias and four aires and are to be found only in the Bodleian autograph

[1] These manuscripts are the British Museum, Add. 29410–15, in which the two treble parts are reversed, and the Christ Church manuscript 479–83, which contains only the pieces in six parts. An autograph part-book in the British Museum, Add. 17798, has the bass parts only to the five- and six-part pieces. Only a few of the fantasias and aires have ever been published, and these only in recent years. The Fantasia in Six Parts, from the 'Consort Suite' No. 4 in G minor, and an Aire were printed (as No. 1) in New York by G. Schirmer, Inc., in 1944, edited by Arnold Dolmetsch and Percy Grainger as No. 3 in the series, *The Dolmetsch Collection of English Consorts.* Another piece, The Fantasia in Six Parts, first movement of the 'Consort Suite' No. 1 in C minor, is included in Ernst Hermann Meyer's *English Chamber Music* (London: Lawrence & Wishart, 1946), pp. 265–70.

[2] Anthony Wood, manuscript notes on the lives of English musicians in the Bodleian Library at Oxford (Wood D. 19 (4), No. 106, folio 83r).

[3] Another piece, an aire in five parts, is an arrangement of a piece in the *Royall Consort* and is not included here. (See Chapter III, p. 87.) The two six-part fantasias from the *Royall Consort*, although not strictly viol consorts and therefore not included in the figure of thirty-nine, are so similar to this collection that they will be discussed in this chapter.

score, Mus. Sch. B.2.[1] Of those in five parts there are six
fantasias, three pavans, six aires and one other piece entitled
'On the Playnsong' which is in the style of the In Nomine.[2] The
scores of all the five-part works are also in Mus. Sch. B.2. In six
parts there are eight fantasias, one pavan, two In Nomines and
six aires. These are distributed between the aforementioned
volume and its companion, Mus. Sch. B.3. Also in autograph
are organ reductions of all the compositions in five and six parts
in Bodleian Mus. Sch. D.229.

All of the pieces are arranged into sets of three or four movements. The matter is complicated, however, by the fact that
Lawes' four autographs do not agree, either in the succession
of the 'setts' themselves or in that of their individual movements.
The only constant factor, in all manuscripts, is the arrangement
according to key. The grouping of pieces is also irregular, the
suites consisting of various arrangements, such as fantasia–
pavan–aire, fantasia–fantasia–aire, fantasia–In Nomine–aire,
fantasia–aire–fantasia–aire, etc. Moreover, the positions of the
individual movements do not correspond in any two of the
manuscripts. Nevertheless the two autograph part-books make
it clear that some sort of suite arrangement was intended. In
fact, every one of Lawes' autograph instrumental collections
adheres to a suite form. That large viol consorts were performed
in suites during the middle period of viol fantasia composition
is stated both by Christopher Simpson and by Roger North.[3] It
is Thomas Mace, however, who supplies the description most
like the arrangement of Lawes' fantasias and aires in the composer's autographs:

'We had for our *Grave Musick*, *Fancies* of 3, 4, 5, and 6 *Parts*

---

[1] The four-part pieces are arranged into two suites: No. 1 in C Minor
and No. 2 in C Major. They do not seem to belong to the collection of
consorts in the same respect as do the works in five and six parts since there
are no organ parts for them in the organ autograph and the bass parts are
not included in Br. Mus. Add. 17798.

[2] This piece is erroneously referred to as an In Nomine in E. H. Meyer's
Die Mehrstimmige Spielmusik des 17. Jahrhunderts (Cassel: Barenreiter, 1934),
p. 142.

[3] Christopher Simpson, *The Division-Violist* (London: William Godbid,
1659), p. 49. See also the quote from Roger North in Chapter V,
p. 107.

to the *Organ*; Interpos'd (now and then) with some *Pavins, Allmaines, Solemn and Sweet Delightful Ayres.*'[1]

It will be remembered that the majority of the works included in Lawes' collection are large fantasias and In Nomines. The rest are, as Mace states, pavans and almans or aires. Mace, however, is vague regarding any regular order of movements and implies that the shorter pieces be interspersed between the larger ones 'now and then' which, as Simpson had stated earlier, 'will produce a pleasant variety'.[2] This would indicate a basic difference between the arrangement of movements in suites of '*Grave Musick*' and those in the ordinary dance suite or, as the latter was termed in contemporary sources, the 'suit of lessons', inasmuch as the dance suite followed the middle Baroque sequence of Almans–Corants–Saraband. The difference is indeed similar in some respects to that between the continental *sonata da chiesa* and the *sonata da camera*. In fact, Lawes' instrumental collections do follow these two styles of suite composition. It appears, from a careful examination of the order of pieces in the several autographs and manuscripts, as well as from contemporary references, that so long as the key relationship was maintained, the choice of pieces and their order in the suite was probably left to the performers themselves. This is in keeping with seventeenth-century performance practice. In ordering and numbering these large viol suites in the Catalogue of Instrumental Works given in Appendix B the present author has endeavoured to maintain the closest possible correspondence with the sequence of the works in the autographs. This has resulted in the arrangement of twelve suites for consorts of viols: two in four parts, five in five parts and five in six parts. They will be referred to henceforth as the *Consort Suites*.

In the *Consort Suites* Lawes holds to the tradition of the equally balanced consort; hence the designation 'for y[e] violls'. These large fantasias and aires are in fact the only works, outside of the suites for lyra viols and bass viols, in which the composer does not use violins. For the intense contrapuntal style of these compositions, where each part is of equal importance, the 'scoulding' violins were too powerful, too unrefined, too precocious.

---

[1] Thomas Mace, op. cit., p. 234. [2] Simpson, loc. cit.

The quiet subtleties of a true consort could not admit such 'High-priz'd Noise' as was associated with the music of the violins.[1] The instrumentation of the *Consort Suites*, however, although calling for viols, does not specifically mention which viols are to be used. The melodic compasses of the parts in the two suites for four instruments suggest that these are for two treble viols and two bass viols. Indeed, the four-part works suffer from the absence of a middle register and are certainly not in keeping with Mace's requirements for equal balance. The five-part consorts, on the other hand, seem intended for two trebles, an alto, a tenor and a bass; however, a second tenor viol might easily substitute for the alto. The six-part consorts are for two trebles, two tenors (or alto and tenor), and two basses. Thus the five- and six-part *Consort Suites* are perfectly balanced in the distribution of their melodic compasses. The treble viol, which has a compass ranging from *d* to *d ' ' '*, never descends lower than *a*. In fact, the lowest string is not used at all and the instrument's compass is confined to its upper two octaves. (By this time the two lowest strings of the treble viol had become practically superfluous. Indeed, the treble viol sounds best in its upper ranges.) The alto viol, while upon rare occasions descending to the note of its lowest open string, *c*, also favours a higher compass within a range of two octaves. The tenor viol holds to its middle register but does, on occasion, dip down to its low *G*. Again, about two octaves is its normal compass within these suites. The bass viol, however, vigorously exploits a range of three octaves, from *C* to *c ' '*, and all strings are equally active in the course of the music.[2] This is in keeping with its role as virtuoso of the viol family.

The organ parts to the *Consort Suites* are simply reductions of the other parts. Rarely do they add new material to the work as a whole. They are, however, particularly valuable as an indication of the composer's attitude toward part-writing, for while the string parts seem to move erratically through unresolved dissonances and the like, the organ parts frequently show us the base from which the part-writing is elaborated. In modern

---

[1] Mace, op. cit., p. 236.

[2] The normal tuning of the lowest string of the bass viol was *D*, but it was a common practice to tune down to *C* whenever the music demanded it. Lawes always had his consort basses tune to the lower note.

performances of the *Consort Suites* these keyboard accompaniments had best be omitted, since they interfere with the quality of the consort and are not at all necessary to the music. And besides, they are not very well suited for either the harpsichord or the modern piano, having been designed for a small chamber organ which had the power of sustaining longer note-values.[1] Their texture is altogether sparse as compared with true harpsichord or piano accompaniments and they differ radically from Lawes' really independent and fully written-out keyboard parts in other instrumental collections.[2] In fashioning the organ reductions for the *Consort Suites* the composer included the most important entries and counterpoints of the various string parts and as much else as could be conveniently accommodated by two hands. In cases where all of the parts could not be played on the organ, Lawes used the practice of 'directs' to indicate to the organist the movement of the uninstituted instruments. This points up the *raison d'être* of the organ parts in general, and that is, as an aid or guide for the other instruments. Mace explains this as 'the Chief Office of the Organ in Consort':

'. . . the *Organ* stands us in stead of a Holding, Uniting-Constant-Friend; and is a Touch-stone, to try the certainty of *All Things*; especially the *Well-keeping* the *Instruments* in Tune, &c.

'And in *This service* the *Organ* should be *Equally Heard* to *All*; but especially to the Performers Themselves, who cannot well Perform, without a Distinct Perceivance Thereof.'[3]

During the later Jacobean and Caroline periods it became usual for the organ to accompany a consort of string instruments. Numerous contemporary references to this practice, in addition to the above, may be cited together with the evidence of many works in manuscript. Of particular interest is this statement by Roger North:

'In some familyes organs were used to accompany consorts, but the old masters would not allow the liberty of playing from

[1] For an interesting account of a seventeenth-century table organ see Chapter V, pp. 119–20.

[2] A complete discussion of Lawes' keyboard parts will be found in Chapter V, pp. 118–19.

[3] Thomas Mace, op. cit., p. 242.

a thro' base figured, as harpsichords of late have universally practised, but they formed the organ part express; because the holding out of the sound required exact concord, els the consort would suffer; or perhaps the organists had not then the skill as since, for now they desire onely figures.'[1]

But North is mistaken in assuming that early seventeenth-century English organists could not play from a figured bass. On the contrary, we know, for example, that a theorbo player was even expected to fill in harmonies from an unfigured bass line. Moreover, there is the evidence of printed publications dating from the first half of the century which have figured bass parts for the organ.[2] The real reason for the 'old masters' writing the organ part 'express' was certainly so that it might act as a guide to the performers in bringing in the parts at the correct entries and in keeping the performers reasonably in tune.

William Lawes' fantasias for viols are important landmarks in the formal development of the fantasia in England. The two basic principles of earlier fantasia composition—imitation by stretti and sectional structure—are not discarded by Lawes. They are used as the basis for expansion. What happened to the fantasia in his hands can perhaps best be described by a comparison with the effect of Beethoven upon the early classical sonata form. Without abandoning or attempting to destroy what went before, he proceeded to add to and to alter the existing form to make it suitable for the expression of his more romantic temperament. Thus, the themes were longer and more romanticized, development sections were greatly expanded, rhythms were more varied and interesting, content was richer and the texture more intense. In addition, the instrumental fabric was relieved of a certain monotony by the introduction of contrasting groups of solo instruments, and a specially designed *coda* was added as a climax. By these means the entire work was lengthened and now assumed significant proportions. Moreover, the important element of variety, which had gradually been gaining ground since the turn of the century, became

[1] Roger North, *Memoirs of Musick*, 1728, edited by Edward F. Rimbault (London: G. Bell, 1846), p. 105.

[2] See the discussion regarding the thorough-bass of the *Royall Consort* in Chapter III, p. 81. Henry and William Lawes' *Choice Psalmes* of 1648 were published with a figured thorough-bass.

one of the principal aesthetic considerations in the composition and organization of a musical work.

The new aesthetic principles of the musical Baroque in England paid much attention to what was variously termed 'Humour', 'Conceit', 'Life' and 'The Passions'. In the course of the seventeenth century these concepts became increasingly important to the composer in his search for more expressive melodies and more tuneful 'aires'. 'Humour' especially became one of the three major principles of composition, together with 'Fugue' and 'Form'. Included in this concept of 'Humour' are all of the expressive possibilities of music: gaiety, sadness, passion, nobility, grandeur, serenity—the complete gamut of the emotions, feelings and senses. Naturally, fancy and imagination played an important role in this too, under the concept of 'Conceit'. 'Life' alluded to the spirit or life of the music. Bound up with the concept of 'Humour' also, was the employment of dynamics, the various shades of loud and soft, wherewith expression could be portrayed in its various contrasts. So vital had this principle of 'Humour' become that the several musical keys themselves were stereotyped for different emotional values and moods. According to Thomas Mace, for example, C Major is 'a *Most Noble, Generous*, and *Heroical Key*, fit to *Express* anything of *Magnanimity* and *Bravery* upon', and F major, 'an exceeding *Brisk, Lofty*, and *Sparkling Key*'.[1] Mace, in fact, places more importance upon pure interpretive musicianship than does any of his contemporaries, and in his writing he continually calls the attention of the student to the 'Fugue', 'Form' and 'Humour' of the music. He qualifies these as:

'*The Notion of Fugue, (or Matter;) Form, (or Shape;) Humour, (or Conceit;) . . . . Those 3 Necessary Pertinencies, in reference to Invention, Voluntary-Play, and a Good Composer, viz. Matter, Form, Humour; Life, or Conceit.*

'*And without a due Observance of These, None shall Compose Musick with that Ease, Familiarity, and Certainty, Compleatness, and Pleasure, as Those who do observe Them.*'[2]

Mace defines 'Fuge' as:

'. . . a *Term* used among *composers; by which They understand*

---

[1] Mace, op. cit., pp. 197, 219.   [2] Ibid., p. 138.

a certain intended Order, Shape, or Form of Notes; signifying, such a Matter, or such an Extension; and is used in Musick, as a Theam, or as a subject Matter in Oratory, on which the Orator intends to Discourse.' [1]

'Form' referred to the overall design of the piece, the length and uniformity of phrases and strains and the essential structure of the music. To cite just one of Mace's numerous directions for the correct observation of the 'Humour' of a piece of music, here is one for the *Tattle de Moy*, a form which the theorist himself claims to have invented:

'The *Humour* is *Toyish, Joccond, Harmless*, and *Pleasant*; and as if it were, one *Playing* with, or *Tossing a Ball, up and down*; yet it seems to have a very *Solemn Countenance*, and like unto one of a *Sober, Innocent Condition*, or *Disposition*; not *Antick, Apish*, or *Wild*, etc.

'As to the *Performance of It*, you will do well to *Remember* . . . to Play *Loud, and Soft*, sometimes *Briskly*, and sometimes *Gently*, and *Smoothly*, here and there, as your *Fancy* will (no doubt) *Prompt you unto. . . .'* [2]

Finally, here are Mace's complete instructions for the performance of a corant which he includes in his volume:

'The *Fugue* is seen, in the 3 *first Notes*, and perceptible all over the Lesson.
'The *Form is Even, Uniform*, and *Perfect*.
'The *Humour*, is a kind of *Sorrowing, Pittying*, and *Bemoaning*.' [3]

'Fugue', 'Form' and especially 'Humour' are also important components of Lawes' style. The 'Fugue' is of course evident in his use of the *fugato* style—the imitative entries or 'reports' of the various instruments. But contrary to what one might have expected in the composer's music, there is a decided lack of the more complex contrapuntal devices such as melodic inversion, countersubjects, retrograde, invertible counterpoints, augmentation and diminution, all of which were the standard techniques of the earlier fantasia composers and were regularly employed in the early 'fancy', as they were in the motet. Lawes was dedicated to the aesthetics of the new Baroque and so Renaissance academicisms found little place in his music. 'Form' takes

---

[1] Ibid., p. 116.   [2] Ibid., p. 133.   [3] Ibid., p. 130.

on new significance in his fantasias in the clearly marked and well balanced sections which were larger and fewer in number. The several 'Humours' are especially notable in the variety of these contrasting sections, which range from slow, dissonant laments for the entire consort, to playful interludes for two, three or four instruments. Above all the 'Humour' is reflected in the highly expressive and subjective melodies which invite contrast in both tempo and dynamics to a far greater extent than one would have thought was employed at this early date.

The emotional and introspective character of the *Consort Suites* is boldly announced in the opening subjects of the individual movements, some of which are quoted below:

Ex. 1

1st mov't., "Fantazy",
6 - part Consort Suite No. 1 in C minor

(a)

1st mov't., "Fantazy,"
5 - part Consort Suite No. 3 in C minor

(b)

2nd. mov't., "On the Playnesong,"
5 - part Consort Suite No. 1 in G minor

(c)

3rd mov't., "Aire,"
4 - part Consort Suite No. 2 in C major

(d)

1st mov't., "Fantazy,"
6-part Consort Suite No. 4 in G minor

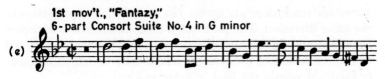

1st mov't., "Fantazy,"
5-part Consort Suite No. 1 in G minor

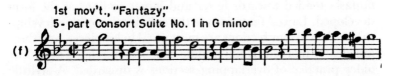

Here, in the fantasias and aires, are the most personal of Lawes' themes. These are not the little scalewise *motifs* often associated with the music of other early instrumental composers. They are romantic melodies of considerable length and breadth, thoroughly and deliciously instrumental in character. Some— for example those of the C minor fantasias—appear eccentric and even extravagant when lifted from their context. The vertical implications of these lines give rise to grinding counter-points and dissonant harmonies. Other melodies are obviously expressions of the most tender romanticism and strikingly like the style of the Italian *bel canto*, such as the opening themes from the C major 'Aire' in four parts and the G minor 'Playne-song'. A third group has a vigorous, rough-hewn cast of a highly instrumental nature. The G minor themes are repre-sentative of this type. Fresh and interesting to our own ears, Lawes' melodies must have appeared extremely daring to pre-Commonwealth music-lovers, who had not the romantic heritage we now possess. In fact, Lawes' music can be better understood and appreciated today in the light of modern linear practices. Such melodies as those of the C minor fantasias are not too far removed from some of our present melodic tendencies. Affec-tive melody is a major element in Lawes' music and, when employed polyphonically, forms the mainspring for his dis-sonant harmonic and contrapuntal technique. The Italianate character of his melody has already been noted. In the works of no other early English composer is the influence of the Italian Baroque so prominent.

Large melodic leaps occur often. Intervals ranging from sixths to as much as two octaves are not unusual. Melodic and harmonic resolutions are ignored in a succession of wide skips in the same direction. The parts often cross and recross each other in pursuance of a full melodic compass, and this without regard to the resolution of dissonances which may be left incomplete or inconspicuously resolved in other voices.

Like the continental *canzona* of the *da chiesa* type, the English fantasia tended towards fewer and larger sections as the form developed. Lawes' fantasias are the culmination of this development. Two to four sections are most usual in his pieces, and these are clearly marked by full middle cadences in related keys. The older practice of overlapping sections is discarded. A stylistic analysis of the composer's fantasias reveals several types of sections of different character, some of longer and some of shorter duration. Those sectional types that appear most often include *fugato* sections with or without development, slow dissonant contrapuntal passages, interludes for small groups of solo instruments, sections in block harmony, *concertante* passages, sections constructed from strings of thirds in the melodic lines, variation or 'division' passages, those containing a continuous interlacing rhythm in syncopations or 'bindings', and extended cadences or codas. These various types had no regular pattern of recurrence. Thus, the composer had a variety of contrasting sections to draw upon as miniature movements for his larger works.

Among these, the *fugato* opening with development becomes especially important, often occupying as much as one half of the entire composition. (Lawes' fantasias frequently achieved the length of one hundred and twenty measures or more.) The entering points of imitation complement each other in subject and answer type 'reports', usually until all parts have completed an exposition. At this point, instead of merely repeating the procedure or moving on to a new *stretti* section, Lawes begins his development. He may use the theme intact and begin his imitations at unusual intervals such as the second and seventh, gradually shifting the tonality. At the same time he may tighten up his *stretti*, or, varying the theme in figurations, he may loosen temporarily the imitative cords which bind the work together. The following illustration is from the opening section of the second movement, entitled 'Fantazy', of the *Six-Part Consort Suite No. 1 in C Minor*:

52

Opening section, 2nd mov't., "Fantazy;"
6-part Consort Suite No. 1 in C minor

Often the theme itself may be modified or even transformed, as in the case of the subject in Ex. 1 (*e*), which, in the development, becomes:

Ex. 3

Development section 1st mov't., "Fantazy"
6-part Consort Suite No. 4 in G minor

Treble Viol I.
Treble Viol II.

Tenor Viol I.
Tenor Viol II.

Bass Viol I.
Bass Viol II.

The working-out of a figure or figures deriving from the opening theme is another feature characteristic of these developments and one of Lawes' most original contributions. A good example of this may be seen by comparing the beginning subject of the first movement, 'Fantazy', in Ex. 1 (*b*) with its transformation in Ex. 6 on p. 57.[1] When the development of a first section has run its course, a clearly defined cadence, frequently in the key of the dominant, completes the section.

The sectional type in which the composer employs smaller instrumental combinations as alternate choirs is another unique feature of the fantasias. Such a passage ordinarily begins after a cadence and towards the middle of the piece. It is usually semi-homophonic in character. Duets, trios and quartets in different blends form short interludes which add a pleasing variety to the concentrated texture of the fantasias. The treatment of pairs of instruments in thirds, tenths and sixths should also be noted here. The use of solo instruments is another illustration of the composer's search for new instrumental combinations and colours and of his penchant for variety. A favourite with Lawes is a passage based upon melodies and counterpoints in ascending and descending thirds. This is the familiar Baroque progression of sequences of third-related

[1] See also the example in E. H. Meyer, *English Chamber Music*, op. cit., p. 184.

Ex. 4

1st mov't., "Fantazy," (excerpt, final section)
5 - part Consort Suite No. 3 in C minor

Treble Viol I.
Treble Viol II.

Alto Viol
Tenor Viol

Bass Viol

Ex. 5

1st mov't., "Fantazy," (excerpt opening section)
5 - part Consort Suite No. 3 in C minor

chords, which were so conveniently used as building blocks for long sweeping passages in which the chords were spread out and often combined with consonant syncopation. These were made possible by the double common tones of the chords themselves. The progression has several variants, all of which are frequently exploited by Lawes, and are particularly well suited for the contrapuntal interplay between the instruments.[1] When the spreading of chords serves as a theme for points of imitation many interesting and often beautiful sections result. One of the best examples is the final section of the first movement, 'Fantazy', of the *Five-Part Consort Suite No. 3 in C Minor* (see p. 55). In the example above the imitations set off successions of third-related chords as the melodic lines virtually sweep downwards in ever-changing colours. By this means Lawes is successful in building climaxes. This fantasia is one of the composer's best

Ex. 6

1st mov't., "Fantazy," (excerpt, 2nd section)
5- part Consort Suite No. 3 in C minor

Treble Viol I.
Treble Viol II.

Alto Viol
Tenor Viol

Bass Viol

---

[1] For an interesting example of this technique by Lawes, see the discussion and illustration in Chapter V, pp. 115–18.

pieces. The *fugato* opening introduces one of his most eccentric themes (see p. 56).

The subject of the second section derives from the large intervals of the first theme (see p. 57). Character and treatment here are far removed from the placid style of the earlier fantasia. Note also the pedal G in the lowest bass, which continues for ten bars, and the free dissonance treatment of the upper parts.

A striking feature of Lawes' fantasias is their cadential treatment. The time-worn but gracious motet formula of the consonant fourth, which at the end of the sixteenth century had been 'as frequent in Musick at the close or conclusion, as *Amen* at the end of a prayer',[1] had long since become a vehicle for sharp dissonances. As far back as 1597 Thomas Morley speaks out against too many harsh discords in cadences, while at the same time acknowledging the practice as fairly common. Referring to an example in which his pupil, Philomathes, included a false relation with the cadential fourth, Morley says:

'... that and many other such closings have been in too much estimation heretofore amongst the very chiefest of our musicians, whereof amongst many evils this is one of the worst.'[2]

In his own cadences Lawes frequently discards the traditional formulas completely. In their place he seeks new and surprising endings in which he intensifies the dissonance practices of his predecessors.

The most interesting of the sectional types are the slow, dissonant passages occuring in the middle of a work or immediately preceding the final cadence. These are among the most exquisite passages to be found in all chamber music and deserve careful attention. To understand them is to understand the very essence of Lawes' technique. The middle section of the first movement, 'Fantazy', of the *Six-Part Consort Suite No. 4 in G Minor*, is for that reason singled out for analysis (see p. 59). The example begins two bars before the close of a spirited development section on the dominant of C minor. A remarkable deception occurs at bar 84, where the E♮ implies the major

---

[1] Christopher Simpson, *Compendium of Practicall Musick* (London: William Godbid for Henry Brome, 2nd ed. 1667), p. 71.

[2] Morley, op. cit., new edition ed. by R. Alec Harman (London: J. M. Dent & Sons Ltd., 1952), p. 272.

Ex. 7

1st mov't., "Fantazy" (middle section)
6-part Consort Suite No. 4 in G minor

chord of the tonic. The parts in the previous bars are left hanging in suspense, cut off by the minim pauses and denied their melodic resolution to the tonic. When the parts do enter the tonic is present, but the expected consonance is shattered by the unprepared entry of the dissonant A♭. This is treated as a

59

suspension and resolved, but the deception is further drawn out by a new dissonant combination occuring between the outer parts in the form of a diminished fifth. The proper resolution of this dissonance leads to the key of F minor. But the new key feeling is immediately weakened in the next bar by the introduction of the major third in the bass, which once more sets up the dissonance of the diminished fourth—this time between the outer parts. This dissonance can hardly be said to resolve at all since the movement of the D♮ to the crotchet, C, acts more as an auxiliary note than as a resolution, especially so since the harmonic rhythm is here governed by minims and the second treble immediately reverts back to the D♭ without any previous preparation in its own part.

Bars 86–8 show the composer's attitude to part-writing. We see here how Lawes employs his instruments in dissonant voice crossings for the purpose of adding pungency to his imitations. The bass of the diminished fourth in bar 87 proceeds upwards as a retardation in the following measure, containing an element of harmonic deception for the imitative entry of the second treble in bar 87 as it proceeds to a B♭ minor chord. The entrance, in bar 88, of the G in the first treble, creates the tritone with the D-flats of the first tenor and second bass. To make matters more dissonant, the D♭ in the first tenor moves to C while the second bass still holds on to its D♭ against the treble G. Even then the bass does not resolve properly but leaps upwards to B♭. The tension is redoubled in bar 89 by a veritable tone-cluster on the second minim as the parts proceed to the dominant of the key. Meanwhile, the second treble makes another unprepared dissonant entry on A♭. Upon the first crotchet of the dominant, in bar 90, Lawes introduces the familiar cadential idiom which combines the four-three suspension with the preceding suspension of the minor sixth over the dominant. This gives us once more the fleeting sound of the augmented triad in first inversion, and coupled with this is the violent, simultaneous cross relation between the E♮ and the E♭. A full-grown tonic six-four cadence results, deflected only by the major third of the tonic in the bass. We are now on our way, via a brief excursion into the subdominant, to the key of G minor.[1]

[1] The complete fantasia is available in print (see footnote 1, p. 42).

The example provides an admirable illustration of Lawes' technique of dissonance. Moreover it enables us to understand the principles by which the composer was guided. Irrespective of the numerous clashes, unprepared and unresolved dissonances, and strange progressions, his technique is based upon the same rules of English harmony that governed all early English masters. The basic tenet of this technique is the principle of the independent movement of the parts. When this principle is applied in the composition of music in the melodic minor scale, with its mobile sixth and seventh degrees, several highly dissonant contrapuntal and harmonic combinations arise inevitably. It will be remembered that it was this scale which emerged from the application of *musica ficta* to the earlier modes, and which formed the basis for the pre-tonal harmony of the early Baroque. Dissonant passages are met with in Lawes' music only in the melodic minor. His work in major keys is singularly bare of bold, dissonant, harmonic ventures. Thus we can understand how it is in the above example, that despite the succession of unprepared dissonances setting off the points of imitation, the augmented and diminished chords, and the unusual melodic leaps, there is not one note which may properly be called chromatic, except possibly the raised third in the bass of bar 87. Diminished and augmented intervals arise naturally from the juxtaposition or succession of the minor third of the scale with the sharped seventh, the raised third with the flatted sixth or flatted seventh, the sharped seventh with the fourth, etc. The familiar cross relation between the raised and lowered seventh degrees may also be mentioned here. All arise when the parts are treated in a logical manner which attaches first importance to linear considerations. But Lawes' dissonance treatment is no mere 'accident' of the English linear practice, as we can judge from the passage from the G minor fantasia. The composer has mastered the style to suit his own preoccupation with jarring counterpoints and pungent harmonies.

It is significant that not one of Lawes' *Consort Suites* was written in a sharp key and that the great majority of the pieces in the collection are in flat minor keys. These were the keys which were used for the expression of sorrow, brooding, laments, deep passion, melancholy, pain, etc. One key especially may be singled out from the others as William Lawes' most favoured tonality, and this is C minor. Indeed, the majority of the composer's finest works, in all collections, vocal as well as instrumental, are set in this key.[1] This fact allows a deeper insight into the innermost feelings and thoughts of the composer. There can be no doubt that despite his debonair appearance, the frivolity and bawdiness of many of his songs and catches, and his general reputation for a 'devil-may-care' existence, William Lawes was essentially a lonely and brooding genius, trapped in the exclusive surroundings of decadent court splendour.

We have recognized in Lawes' fantasias a fusion of both English and Italian styles. That Lawes should have been exposed to Italian influences is not at all surprising. 'Italianisms' had been seeping into English music since at least the last third of the sixteenth century, when the works of Italian madrigalists were introduced to the English musical public. Instrumental as well as vocal music felt the impact from abroad. Thus, Lawes' 'Italianisms' need not have been the result of direct contact, for the tendencies manifested so boldly in his instrumental music had been building up inside England itself for at least half a century before he produced his major works. Significantly, Lawes was a pupil of Coperario (otherwise Cooper), who is said to have spent some time in Italy, and, evidently impressed with the state of music there, to have affected the Italianized version of his name upon his return to England. How much Coperario himself was influenced in his own works by his alleged sojourn into Italy is a subject for another study.[2] We may surmise that Coperario familiarized his pupil with the Italian techniques at least, but to what extent any Italian influences, which may have been brought to England by Coperario, were in turn passed on to Lawes cannot now be determined. We can get some idea of the musical education which Lawes received under Coperario from the latter's important theoretical treatise, *Rules*

---

[1] The key of C minor was not usual in Lawes' day although it was certainly known. In 1597 Thomas Morley was adamant against its use by singers because of the added accidentals, although he admitted that organists often transposed into that key 'for ease of the singers', op. cit., pp. 261–2.

[2] In his introduction to the facsimile edition of Coperario's *Rules How to Compose* (Los Angeles: Ernest E. Gottlieb, 1952), p. [1], Manfred Bukofzer points to the fact that Coperario's music does not, for example, show the influence of the modern recitative of the Florentine opera.

How to Compose.[1] From the *Rules* we may assume that Lawes was introduced to the dissonant style in his childhood, since he was indentured at an early age to the Seymour household, of which Coperario was the chief music master. It may even be that the master wrote the treatise for his highly talented pupil.[2] The date *c.* 1610, which is ascribed to the manuscript by Dr. Bukofzer, is just about the time that Lawes would have been under Coperario's instruction.

The succeeding chapters will illustrate how completely dependent Lawes was upon his teacher for the musical forms in which he worked. We now note, in examining the *Rules*, the similarity between the contrapuntal and harmonic techniques of the two composers. One of the most striking and at the same time most revealing resemblances is a feature of Lawes' harmony which has already been much discussed here—his particular liking for the sound of the augmented triad. In his introduction to the facsimile edition of the Coperario treatise, Dr. Bukofzer repeatedly calls attention to the theorist's propensity for exactly the same type of thing. Characteristically, Coperario himself does not even once refer to the dissonant triad, nor even to the diminished fourth arising from its inversion. We are, oddly enough, more concerned with what we find *en passant* in the theorist's examples than we are with those things he intends to illustrate. Thus we find augmented harmony appearing unprepared, unusual dissonant intervals between the outer voices and dissonant combinations in quick succession, all without a word of comment from the author (see Ex. 8, p. 64).

The cadential use of the augmented triad in first inversion is a hallmark of the early Baroque. Evidence suggests that it first appeared in the sixteenth-century Italian madrigal. Numerous examples may be found in the works of Gesualdo, Giovanni Gabrieli, Anerio, Marenzio, Croce, Monteverdi, and

[1] Ibid.

[2] Bukofzer suggests that the treatise may have been written at the request of John Egerton, Earl of Bridgewater, who owned the only extant copy of the manuscript, for the instruction of Egerton's children. However, since the manuscript in the Huntington Library is not known to be autograph, and since Henry Lawes (who is *not* known to have studied with Coperario) rather than Coperario instructed the Egerton children, this argument is not convincing. (See ibid., intro., p. [3].)

Ex. 8 (a)   folio 21

(b)   folio 22

(c)   folio 23

others. In England, too, examples are present in the works of the late madrigalists, especially in the music of Wilbye and Weelkes. Significantly, many of the compositions of the Italians that were published in England before the turn of the century contain the augmented triad in some form or other, e.g. Nicolas Yonge's *Musica Transalpina* of 1588 and 1597, and Thomas Morley's two collections of songs and madrigals, '*Celected out of the best approued Italian Authors*', of 1598. Coperario, therefore, need not have gone to Italy to have been influenced in this direction. The augmented triad itself arises from the desire to exploit the affective intervals of the melodic minor key, and it thus appears on the mediant and submediant degrees of the scale. Vertically, its earliest application seems to have been to heighten the tension of the cadential formula of the consonant fourth, where, by suspension, it acts as ornamental to the dominant. Both Coperario and Lawes, however, introduce the triad without preparation, recognizing it as an independent harmony. Lawes also uses the submediant variety as ornamental to the final tonic in drawing out a plagal cadence. The augmented triad in second inversion, on the other hand, was frequently used for sudden modulations to subdominant keys—arising as a double suspension, resolving to the diminished triad on the leading note, and concluding in the new tonic (Ex. 8 c). Lawes recognizes even this inversion as an independent harmony and employs it without preparation (Ex. 7). The augmented combination has its theoretical basis in the intervallic harmony of the early Baroque. The two essentially 'chordal' rules that were employed during this period provided that over any given note in the bass it was possible to place, (1) the third and the fifth (root position), and (2) the third and the sixth (first inversion). The composer, meaning to extend his cadence, avoided the fifth of the dominant or tonic and simply used the sixth. Because of the mobility of the parts in melodic minor keys this could give rise to the combination of a major third with a *minor* sixth, which, of course, is our augmented triad in first inversion. The resulting diminished fourth between the upper parts was considered enharmonically as a major third and not as a true dissonance.[1] In theory, therefore, the entire combination could be rationalized, and so it was not proscribed, despite the fact that, all intervals being 'consonant', the result was nevertheless dissonant.

From the foregoing discussion the reader might assume that all or even a major part of William Lawes' work is characterized by eccentric melodies, violent dissonances, strange augmented and diminished progressions, etc. This is by no means true. These more radical features occur only in the slow, dissonant sections and in many of the extended cadences of the larger works in minor keys. While they appear frequently enough to warrant closer examination and to set Lawes apart from his contemporaries, they account for not more than a fraction of the composer's serious production. These same 'radicalisms', which appear so advanced to the modern musician, may be

[1] Christopher Simpson, *Compendium* . . ., op. cit., pp. 94-5.

mistakenly construed to be progressive tendencies in Lawes' music. Certainly, when considered as an extension of late English renaissance techniques, they are indeed very advanced. They appear even more so to us, with our knowledge of the later development of music, for not until more than a century and a half after Lawes' death did such freedom begin to return. But it was exactly this type of dissonant contrapuntal freedom which the new Baroque considered conservative and out-moded in the light of the more progressive and simplified chordal techniques of the new monody. The *Consort Suites* are therefore conservative for their time when compared, for example, with the much more 'progressive' *Royall Consort*. And yet it is the large fantasias and aires which are of far greater worth and interest to us today.

It has been necessary, in the present chapter, to restrict the discussion mainly to the fantasias, which are the major productions of William Lawes' consorts for viols. Even so it has not been possible to do more than single out a few works and to examine some characteristic features of the composer's technique. Several excellent fantasias have not been quoted at all, to say nothing of the stately pavans, the many charming aires, the In Nomine's, the two *Consort Suites* for four viols, and the two excellent six-part fantasias from the *Royall Consort*. The latter are especially important for the opportunity they afford of studying Lawes' early fantasia technique. It is to be hoped that publication of all of these pieces will appear in the near future and so enable the student to examine and above all to perform this exceedingly fine collection.

Ideally the *Consort Suites* should be performed upon the instruments for which they were written. However, since the number of viol consorts active today is pitifully small, even the most severe purist would not have us neglect this great wealth of instrumental music for want of a consort of viols upon which to perform them. Besides, Lawes' fantasias and aires are well suited for performance by violins, violas and cellos. In some pieces the tenor viol may have to be replaced by a cello, or a few notes in the tenor viol part may have to be raised an octave to accommodate the viola. At times a simple transposition will put everything in order, but other than this there is little to impede the successful performance of these works by a group of modern strings.

Modern editions of the *Consort Suites* will require careful and understanding editing. Tempo and dynamic markings, although implied by the character of the music itself, were not generally in use in England before the Restoration. It was not until after Lawes' death that John Jenkins, Matthew Locke and others introduced musical directions in the English language. The need for these indications had of course arisen much earlier with the new aesthetic concepts of the early Baroque. That Lawes' music requires such interpretation is clearly evident from the contrasting moods of the sections. Editorial aids are especially necessary at the beginning of these sections for indicating the character and proper tempo of the music. They are also desirable for setting off the counterpoints and entries, for the indication of proper bowing, for the retarding of extended cadences and for various shades of dynamic expression. Nothing could be more unjustified than the rendering of these fantasias and aires in the vapid, lifeless manner which seems to have become associated with the performance of early chamber music.

III

THE 'ROYALL CONSORT'

Eᴀʀʟʏ instrumental research has in the past mainly concerned itself with the larger composed works of important musical figures. Short secular dances have often been disregarded in the historian's quest for more intellectually contrived works; and yet, on the Continent as well as in England, the leading composers of the seventeenth century wrote prolifically in dance forms. Peuerl, Schein, Scheidt, Rossi, Besard, Froberger, Gibbons, to mention but a few, have left numerous whole collections of such popular dances. In the hands of these learned composers the various dance forms gradually became stylized and ordered into suites which in turn contributed to the development of the *sonata da camera*, the trio sonata and the opera overture.

Within the simple dance forms new instrumental techniques were explored, resulting in the introduction of exciting rhythms, more extended melodic compasses, daring harmonies, more tuneful melodies, new combinations of instrumental colour, various techniques of figuration and a valid style of instrumental writing. These new techniques were carried over into the larger forms of instrumental music as the century progressed. Fantasia, ricercare, canzona and other related forms furnish ample evidence of these influences from the dance.

Like his contemporaries, William Lawes too wrote a great deal of instrumental music of the popular dance type. Much of it undoubtedly was designed for the revels of the aristocracy at the Court of Charles I. Some of it later found its way into many of the printed collections of the seventeenth-century English publisher, John Playford, while other more elaborate dance collections, such as the *Royall Consort*, were never published.

In the library of Christ Church in Oxford are six part-books bound into one volume, the manuscript bearing the title, 'Mr. William Lawes his Royall Consort'. It contains sixty-six pieces of instrumental music for two violins, two bass viols and two theorbo lutes. With the exception of but four works, two fantasias and two 'eccos', all of the pieces are in dance forms, including pavans, almans, aires, corants, galliards and sarabands.[1] As was customary in seventeenth-century manuscripts as well as in published collections of the period, the pieces are grouped according to key, and within the key grouping, into ordered suites. The manuscript is not barred and is in a clear mid-seventeenth-century hand. This volume has hitherto been considered the most complete and authentic extant version of the *Royall Consort*.

In addition to the above manuscript (Ch. Ch. 754–9), at least fourteen other manuscripts contain the *Royall Consort* in whole or in part. In comparing these many versions one is puzzled to find several important differences between them. The number of parts varies from as few as two to as many as six, while the number of pieces comprising the complete collection is anywhere from twenty-five to sixty-six. No two manuscripts correspond in the order of the pieces or suites. Some of the copies are barred differently and others not at all. The two upper parts are often reversed; sometimes they call for violins and at others for treble viols. In some manuscripts no indication of the instrumentation is given at all. In several the inner parts do not correspond. One dares not even attempt to solve the confusion of accidentals. Indeed, it is quite understandable why investigators, from Burney onwards, have been content to accept Ch. Ch. MS. 754–9 as the most authentic copy of the *Royall Consort*.

There is perhaps a touch of irony in the fact that barely a few hundred yards from Christ Church, in the Bodleian Library

[1] The spelling of the titles of these dances varies considerably. I use the most common English spellings found in manuscripts and publications of the seventeenth century.

at Oxford, the autograph of this collection has remained undetected and yet perfectly accessible for at least two centuries; undetected because the *cantus* parts are reversed from the version in Christ Church, because the order and number of pieces are not the same and because William Lawes, in his autographs at least, did not give the collection the title *Royall Consort* or any other title.[1]

With the identification of these dance suites in the Bodleian autograph (Mus. Sch. B.3), many confusing points regarding the collection are resolved. The autograph contains only forty pieces in score for two violins, two bass viols and two theorbo lutes. There are however but four parts and a thorough-bass. The latter, although indicated as such, is not figured and merely furnishes the *continuo* for the two theorboes. The autograph score is also barred throughout and the composer has signed his name to each piece.[2] While the order of pieces is not the same as in the Christ Church manuscript the autograph too is arranged into suites within the larger key groupings.

The absence of a general title in the autograph raises the immediate question whether or not Lawes himself gave the work the name *Royall Consort*. One might even question the existence of the collection as such if it were not for the order and neatly calculated arrangement of the composer's several extant autograph volumes. There can be no doubt that this was meant as a large work. A kind of general heading is in fact given by Lawes when he indicates the instrumentation at the head of the work.[3] But the matter of the title, *Royall Consort*, cannot be dismissed so easily, for although the autograph does not make use of it, the majority of the manuscripts containing the work do. On the other hand, another Christ Church manuscript (Ch. Ch. 391–6), containing the same collection, is designated, 'Mr. Lawes his greate Consort Wherein are Six Setts of Musicke',

---

[1] These autographs were identified as the *Royall Consort* by the present writer during the course of this study.

[2] Rupert Erlebach, in his article, 'William Lawes and his String Music' (*Proceedings of the Musical Association*, fifty-ninth session, 1932–3), p. 108, leaves the impression that none of Lawes' manuscripts are barred. Actually, many manuscripts containing William Lawes' compositions are barred, including all the composer's autographs in score.

[3] In the autographs Lawes indicates each large group by the instrumentation at the beginning of the collection. There are no titles.

and still another source merely indicates, 'William Lawes His Consort'.[1] It appears that there is no positive evidence that Lawes was responsible for the title, but it is also certain that the collection was popularly known by that name, and we may let the title stand. It is interesting to note, however, that the autograph, which is without the attractive title, has hitherto remained unnoticed, whereas the manuscripts bearing the words, *Royall Consort*, have been seized upon by historians as an example of the type of 'conservative' production which pervaded the Caroline Court. No doubt the princely title has also been responsible for the singling out of this collection beyond all others of the period to attempt to prove the historians' point. We shall see, however, that William Lawes' collection, far from being conservative, is one of the most progressive of the seventeenth century and certainly the best produced in England.

The suites of the *Royall Consort* generally follow the arrangement, Alman–Corant–Saraband, with more than one alman and corant (usually two and sometimes three each). A stately pavan or a fantasia often introduces the suite, which in Lawes' autographs consists of six or seven movements. It is probable, however, that the players in conformity with performance practice freely chose the particular pieces they desired from the collection to form their own suites. Evidence of this practice is conclusive in the many manuscripts containing the *Royall Consort*. The inclusion of fantasias and pavans at the head of some of these suites is one of the earliest indications of the developing *sonata da camera*, in which the larger and more serious forms were added as first movements to the dance suites.

The matter of suites during this period must be discussed more fully, since the word 'suite' is not encountered in English manuscripts of this time. The equivalent term is the 'suit of lessons'. In addition we find the designation 'sett', but during the earlier part of the seventeenth century this was not synonymous with the term 'suite' as we understand it. The arrangement

---

[1] Erroneous statements have been published to the effect that the 'Greate Consort' is a separate work. It is, however, a collection of sixty-two pieces from the *Royall Consort*. The confusion has arisen because of the fact that the pieces are not in the same order as in the other manuscripts. Unfortunately the recent edition of *Grove's Dictionary*, in the course of the article on William Lawes, perpetuates this long-standing error.

of dance movements in both manuscript and printed publications of the period was first according to key, and second, within the key grouping, into suites.[1] A 'sett' referred to the entire order of pieces in one particular key and not the suite within the 'sett'. In some instances, however, one finds a single suite in a particular key described, for example, as a 'sett' in *D sol re*. In such a case the words may appear synonymous and have in fact often deceived researchers and cataloguers.

With this difference clearly in mind it is now possible to compare the various manuscripts with a view to determining the exact number of pieces which William Lawes intended for the *Royall Consort* and the correct ordering of the suites. In the autograph volume are the 'setts' in D minor and D major, the former containing twenty-one pieces and the latter nineteen. The additional 'setts' in A minor, C major, F major and B♭ major, found in other manuscripts were probably a continuation. Their absence from the autograph may be explained by the fact that the D minor and D major 'setts' appear at the end of Lawes' volume. They may well have been continued in another autograph which is either lost or as yet undiscovered.[2] From the number of manuscripts containing all six 'setts' it is safe to assume that the original number of pieces in the collection was sixty-six.[3] This conclusion is also justified by the fact that Lawes wrote all of his larger works in collections for specific instrumentation. The twenty-six movements not included in the autograph are most certainly by the composer. As the D minor and D major 'setts' consist of three suites each there is therefore a total of ten suites in the *Royall Consort* and not six. The original order of the suites and the individual movements are to be found only in the autograph in the Bodleian Library at Oxford.

The six part-books in Christ Church, each titled for a separate

[1] This fact has passed unnoticed by many, but will be substantiated by any examination of manuscript or published collections of the period. The arrangement by key applies to vocal as well as to instrumental music.

[2] Precedent for this claim is established by the continuation of the five- and six-part fantasias and aires in two autograph volumes. I am firmly of the opinion that perhaps as many as a dozen or more autograph volumes by William Lawes are either lost or not yet discovered. See the discussion in Chapter I, pp. 32–3, concerning these.

[3] Further to this in footnote 1, pp. 75–6.

instrument, have misled some historians as to the correct number
of parts in which the work was written. A comparison of the
two theorbo parts shows that these are merely doubled. The
autographs confirm this and add the fact that they are the
thorough-bass.[1] Furthermore, closer examination of the two

Ex. 9   5th mov't., "Alman," (first strain) from the
"Royall Consort" Suite No. 3 in D minor (Later version)

[1] In the autograph score the lowest staff is indicated as a 'through base'
for two theorboes. It is unfigured. There is not a single instance in any of
the composer's nine extant autograph volumes where Lawes has supplied

bass viol parts in both manuscripts reveals a peculiar switching of parts between these two instruments, as illustrated in Ex. 9. In the first phrase, while the second bass viol has a genuine third part, the first viol doubles the thorough-bass line and is in effect acting as a *continuo*. In the second phrase the viols exchange parts with the first bass viol now playing the third part and the second bass viol doubling the theorboes. In reality therefore, it appears that the *Royall Consort* was written in three real parts plus thorough-bass, despite the fact that the instrumentation calls for six instruments. This arrangement is curious, particularly for the contrivance of the inner part between the two bass viols. The foregoing technique is in fact described by Christopher Simpson in his *Compendium: or Introduction to Practical Musick* (1667 ed.):

'Many Compositions are said to have two *Basses* (because they are exhibited by two Viols or Voices) when, in reality they are both but one *Bass* divided into several parcels; of which, either *Bass* doth take its Part by turns, whilst the other supplys the office of another Part, Such are commonly design'd for Instruments.'[1]

Fortunately, the discovery of a notation in another Bodleian manuscript (Mus. Sch. D.236), which also contains part of the *Royall Consort*, explains both the autograph and the Christ Church arrangements. On the reverse side of *folio 1* of this manuscript is the following paragraph:

'The followinge Royall Consorte was first compos'd for 2 trebles a meane & a Base, but because the middle part could not bee performed with equal advantage, to bee heard as the trebles were, Therefor the Author involved the Inner part in two breakeinge bases: which I caused to be transcrib'd for mee in the Tenor and Counter-Tenor Bookes belonging to thes. & soe bound, Wher the two breakinge Bases are to bee found & soe many figured as agree with thes in Order.'

The entire picture now becomes clear. Even the Bodleian auto-

the figures for the thorough-bass. Indeed, the unfigured *continuo* is a characteristic feature of the early baroque.

[1] Christopher Simpson, *A Compendium: or Introduction to Practical Musick* (London: 1667 ed.), p. 73.

graph is not the original version of the so-called *Royall Consort*. Apparently, William Lawes first composed the work in the four parts as noted above, for while the autographs of this original are not extant, the four-part original does exist in at least two of the extant manuscripts containing the collection and confirms the authenticity of the paragraph quoted above.[1] Following is the original of Ex. 9 as taken from the Bodleian manuscript, Mus. Sch. F.569:

Ex. 10   5th mov't., "Alman;"(first strain) from the "Royall Consort" Suite No. 3 in D minor (Early version)

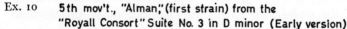
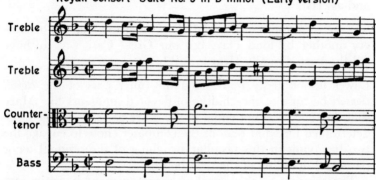

---

[1] The manuscripts in question are Bodleian, Mus. Sch. E.431–6 and F.568–9. The latter is incomplete and contains only the second violin and tenor viol parts. A note in this manuscript indicates that the first eighty-nine pieces are by William Lawes. I have been unable to identify nos. 39–61 as being by the composer except for the aforementioned note. In addition, five other pieces, which I have identified as by Lawes, are also not from the

The paragraph quoted from Mus. Sch. D.236 also clarifies the reason for the composer's later arrangement in his autograph score. Undoubtedly, it was because the polarity and brilliance of the two *concertante* violins on the one hand and the strong *continuo* on the other, did not allow the middle part to be heard 'equally' with the others. Here is perhaps the earliest evidence for the famous statement by Thomas Mace in which he laments the decline of both the viols and the equal balance of the old consort. In his criticism of the 'High-Prized Noise' of the 'Great Idol' (the violin), he recalls the chamber music of his youth and asserts:

'. . . we would never allow Any Performer to Over-top or Out-cry another by loud Play; but our Great Care was, to have All the Parts Equally Heard. . . .' [1]

Lawes undoubtedly rearranged the inner part of the *Royall Consort* because of the chiding of devoted amateurs like Mace that the tenor was not equal to the other parts. It is now to be determined for what reasons the composer chose to engage the two bass viols in this peculiar switching of the original tenor parts and doubling of the theorbo line.

The solution to this puzzling rearrangement is again suggested by the very valuable paragraph from Mus. Sch. D.236, which furnishes the information that the tenor part was 'involved', (i.e. broken up), for two 'breakinge' basses. [2] The seventeenth-century term 'breakinge base' referred to a certain type of variation or 'division' practice whereby, on the repeat of the dance strains, the original bass line was involved in certain figurations which displayed the skill of the violist in *ex tempore* playing. [3] Here then is the reason for the treatment of the two

Royall Consort. Furthermore, this manuscript does not have the title, and if authentic, indicates that there were at least ninety-four pieces in the original version of the *Royall Consort*. If this be so, then Lawes may have chosen the sixty-six best works for the later arrangement.

[1] Thomas Mace, *Musick's Monument* (London: 1676), p. 236.
[2] Several of the *Royall Consort* manuscripts indicate 'breakinge bases'.
[3] The bass viol was the virtuoso of the viol family. English violists in particular were famous for their skill in *ex tempore* playing and were much in demand at European courts. The bass viol itself was built in a smaller size and termed the 'division viol' or 'breakinge base viol' in order to facilitate the performance of swift variations. The various types of variations are

bass viols in the *Royall Consort: in the later autograph version the two instruments took turns in performing variations upon the original bass and tenor parts*. Moreover, in comparing the original tenor part with the later version one finds that many of these variations are in fact written out by the composer himself. This rearrangement not only bolstered the inner part but satisfied the English penchant for 'divisions'. Instead of one bass viol being bound to the *continuo*, the two players took turns in displaying their skill. Following is an illustration of Lawes' own 'breakinge base' parts taken from the 'Aire' of the second suite in D minor. The original middle part from Mus. Sch. F.569 is given on the fifth staff of the score for comparison (see pp. 78–9). Oddly enough, the importance of this discussion is to be noted in the light of the continental development of the trio sonata. In his original version, Lawes wrote the *Royall Consort* in four real parts as a series of dance suites. This arrangement must have been a very early work, perhaps *c.* 1620, and was most likely written for four instruments, probably viols for the lower parts and violins for the upper ones. At this time the composer was not yet ready to give up the middle part of his compositions, even though he made use of the new *concertante* techniques in his upper parts. Later, finding his middle parts weak and out-moded he compromised by inserting 'divisions' for two bass viols, treating the tenor as a 'descant' to the bass in a technique which was common at the time in compositions for two bass viols and organ.[1] In the latter the viols frequently exchange parts, one holding or 'breakinge' the bass while the other performs 'descant' division to it. In the later version also the new thorough-bass technique was added by the composer to bolster the bass part. This Lawes did by designating the original bass line for two theorboes.

The transformation which took place in the *Royall Consort* from a four-part consort work to a three-part form bearing marked resemblances to the developing trio sonata is an exciting find, for it shows the problems which confronted the composer

discussed in detail in Chapter IV, pp. 96–102, and the 'division' viol is described more completely in Chapter VI, pp. 126–8. Lawes was one of the great 'division' composers of the seventeenth century.

[1] This technique is discussed fully in the section dealing with Lawes' own suites for two bass viols and organ in Chapter VI, pp. 139–46.

Ex. 11

Second mov't., "Aire"(first strain) from the
"Royall Consort" Suite No. 2 in D minor

in the face of new developments from abroad and it is a striking illustration of how one important master actually reworked an entire collection of suites in an attempt to meet these innovations and at the same time satisfy popular taste. In several respects the later version of the suites in the *Royall Consort* reflects strong influences from across the Channel. The two violins are *concertante*, imitating, crossing and recrossing each other at equal pitch. These lively upper parts, to use Mace's description, 'Out-top and Out-cry' the others. The continental *basso continuo* is also a very real part of these suites. Another characteristic of the trio sonata evident in Lawes' collection is the more homophonic treatment and the absence of learned contrapuntal techniques. Then too, there is the fact that Lawes' dances are stylized and arranged into suites. Unlike the older practice of dance 'couples', these dance movements are not in pairs and bear no thematic relationship to each other as is the case in the much more conservative collection by Johann Hermann Schein, for example the *Banchetto Musicale* of 1617. It appears, in fact, that apart from the presence of the 'breakinge' bass part, the suites of the *Royall Consort* might very well be taken for some of the earliest examples of the Baroque trio sonata. That the collection was actually recognized as such in contemporary sources is evident from a manuscript of the *Royall Consort* which is now in the British Museum in London, Add. 31,431. The title of the work as given there is as follows:

> Consorts of 3 parts, viz. 2 trebles and 1 Bass.
> with a Bas. contin. also A tenor parte for the
> royall consort from No. 1 to No. 66.
> The Royall Consort by William Lawes
> 3 parts.

The arrangement described is of course that of the trio sonata, and yet the copyist acknowledges the existence of a tenor part which he does not use. The unique treatment accorded the original tenor part in the later version of the *Royall Consort* also provides a clue for estimating the date of that version, for in a later collection of *sonata da camera* the composer discarded the tenor part completely and thus broke away from his early concept of the equally balanced consort.[1] This together with other considerations of form, harmonic content, melodic treatment and some further evidence makes it clear that the *Royall Consort*

---

[1] Lawes did this in his violin sonatas. See the discussion of these works in Chapter V.

could not possibly have been a late work.[1] Its date can hardly be later than about 1630.[2]

The employment of two theorboes for the thorough-bass in the later version of the *Royall Consort* to support the 'breakinge base' of the viols is also interesting as an example of the use of that instrument in consort. The theorbo was indicated as an optional instrument for the realization of the thorough-bass, together with the virginals and harpischord, until about the end of the eighteenth century. The instrument of Lawes' day was a double-necked lute about three and a half feet long. The extra neck and peg box anchored up to seven 'courses' or pairs of diapason strings which were tuned in octaves and ran outside of the fingerboard. They were therefore not fingered but plucked 'open'. The diapasons descended diatonically to low GG below the bass staff. The six 'courses' of strings which ran over the fingerboard employed the normal lute tuning, G–c–f–a–d'–g', and each pair of strings was tuned in unison.[3] Because of the tension produced on the highest string, due to the largeness of the instrument, this string was usually tuned an octave lower. The theorbo, therefore, had a range of more than four octaves, when the highest string was not lowered. When the instrument was written for as a thorough-bass instrument it dispensed with the usual lute tablature and played from ordinary notation. Early theorbo parts, as those in the *Royall Consort*, were not figured and yet the player was expected to be able to furnish the harmonies as he went along. Since Lawes specified his theorboes as a 'through base' in the *Royall Consort*, it is clear that the players were to furnish harmonies upon the unfigured bass line.

Some analysis of the dances in vogue in England prior to the middle of the seventeenth century is essential for an understand-

---

[1] See the discussion on p. 87 concerning the arrangement of the 'Alman' from Suite No. 6 in D Major as a five-part 'Aire'.

[2] E. H. Meyer, *English Chamber Music* (Lawrence and Wishart, 1946), p. 181, gives the date *c.* 1640, but offers no explanation for his claim. Rupert Erlebach, op. cit., p. 109, would have us believe the *Royall Consort* to be a late work because it calls for violins. Violins were written for in England long before Lawes' time by the Lupos and others, including Coperario, who died in 1626.

[3] This tuning is among those given on p. 131.

ing of the dance forms of the *Royall Consort*. By far the over-
whelming majority of dances found in extant manuscripts of the
period are in four major types: pavans, almans, corants and
sarabands. The all-inclusive term 'aire' could be used for any
of these dances in their stylized forms but was more often an
interchangeable term for the alman.[1] By Lawes' time the pavan
was no longer a member of the dance pair, pavan-galliard,
which was so popular during the last half of the sixteenth
century.[2] The pavan had dropped its *nachtanz* and had become
stylized in several respects. In fact, only the fantasia was more
important than the pavan form as a serious and larger vehicle
for the instrumental composer's art.[3] The pavan consisted of
three strains in duple metre. Each of these was repeated, and
most often, during the repeats, 'divisions' or variations were
performed. The variations could be either extemporaneous or
written out. The underlying rhythmic feeling is that of the
dactyl, although pavan melodies of this period are by no means
bound strictly to that metre. Since a complete pavan step,
which contained two singles and a double, required four bars
of music, phrases of this length are most common and dominate
the structure of the piece.[4] In William Lawes' pavans the strains
are anywhere from sixteen to thirty-two bars in length. Imitation between the parts is also a characteristic feature in the
composition of these dances, but this imitation is not carried
through for long periods as it is in the fantasia. The stately
rhythm of the pavan lends itself well to the employment of
daring harmonies and counterpoints, and Lawes took advantage
of this form for some of his most beautiful dissonant writing.
Aside from its use as a slow and dignified court dance the pavan
was also used in processions at various public functions. Like

[1] Any piece of instrumental or vocal music might be called 'aire' in
seventeenth-century England.

[2] The galliard was superseded in the dance suite by the saraband, q.v. on
page 84. It was still used, however, in more serious forms, such as the chamber
sonata, as a last movement in a highly stylized form. Lawes does this in his
violin sonatas, q.v. p. 122.

[3] Thomas Morley, *A Plaine and Easie Introduction to Practicall Musicke*, 1597,
p. 180. Also see the quote by Roger North on p. 107.

[4] For a more complete discussion of the dance steps see Mabel Dolmetsch,
Dances of England and France (London: Routledge and Kegan Paul Ltd.,
1949), Chapter V.

the fantasia, the pavan could either stand alone as a finished work or be employed as the first movement of the dance suite, preceding the almans.

The alman of the second quarter of the seventeenth century seems to differ in some respects from the earlier form described by Thomas Morley in 1597 and again by Thoinot Arbeau in 1588.[1] According to these sources the dance consisted of three strains in duple metre. Arbeau explains the third strain as being lighter and quicker than the first two. Morley allows the alman to have two or three sections. Both authors indicate that the dance is set in phrases of four bars each. William Lawes' almans, on the other hand, are without exception composed in two strains and they do not adhere strictly to the four-bar structure. Moreover, while the alman is variously described as a rather simple, 'heavie' dance, 'fitly representing the nature of the people whose name it carrieth' (Morley), Lawes' compositions make use of running figures and diminutions which suggest a much faster tempo. In the process of stylization the pace of the alman had probably quickened, and too, the length of the strains increased, for while Morley gives the normal alman strain the time of eight semibreves, Lawes' sections average sixteen. Like the pavan each strain of the alman was repeated and usually formed the basis for variations. The dance steps consisted of the same doubles and singles used in the pavan but could be varied to permit phrases with odd numbers of bars. The character of this type of alman afforded the composer the opportunity to employ the livelier *concertante* principle imported from the Continent.

The third movement of Lawes' suites is a corant in fast triple time and is based upon the iambic metre. The dance step of the corant is basically that of the pavan (two singles and a double), but it is danced at a much faster tempo with a skipped or hopped step before the first beat of every bar. This skipping coincides with the anacrusic character of the iamb. Unlike the alman or the pavan, each step of the corant falls upon the first beat of a bar. The complete corant figure therefore consists of eight bars. The very nature of this dance step proves the tempo to be quite rapid, since even at a moderate tempo the dancer would be

[1] Morley, op. cit., p. 181. Thoinot Arbeau, *Orchesographie*, new ed. trans. by Mary Stewart Evans (New York: Kamin Dance Publishers, 1948), p. 125.

left suspended in mid-air. Running figures are a characteristic of this dance and portray the traversing manner in which it was executed. Like the alman, the corant was fashioned in two repeated strains. Often a corant strain was repeated three and even four times in various types of 'division'.[1] The length of the strain varied from ten to twenty-eight bars, the greatest number of the corants in the *Royall Consort* averaging about twenty bars to a strain. The corant, because of its livelier tempo, was treated by Lawes in a more homophonic setting than either the pavan or the alman. In his larger suites the composer used two corants in succession for third and fourth movements.

The English dance suite of this period invariably ended with a saraband. Unlike the slow and solemn saraband on the Continent the English variety was a light, fast movement which was performed even more quickly than the corant. Thus Mace says, '*Serabands* are of the Shortest Triple-Time; but are more Toyish and Light, than Corantoes'.[2] Superseding as it did the very nimble galliard, it is possible that, in England, the saraband acquired some of the characteristics of the former dance. Both were based upon the trochaic metre and thus it would have been quite natural for the faster tempo of the one to influence the other, transforming the saraband into a fast dance. As stated above, the underlying metre of the saraband is trochaic. The dance may, in fact, be quickly identified by the trochee which often appears in the last measure of a strain. Lawes' saraband consists of two or three strains treated homophonically as in the corant. The strains are of a standard eight bars in length and each may be repeated several times with variations. The saraband was a newcomer to England in comparison with the other dances of the suite, but it quickly gained favour. Neither Morley nor Arbeau mentions it in their treatises.

A truly representative cross-section of the *Royall Consort* cannot be presented here, but it is possible to mention a few of the pieces which will serve not only to illustrate William Lawes'

[1] The variations which were performed during the repeats of the dance strains consisted of several definite types which were ordered in certain general sequences. A complete discussion of these types and the 'ordering' of 'division' will be found in the next chapter for all of the dance forms of the suite.

[2] Mace, op. cit., p. 129. See also Mace's description of the other dances, loc. cit.

style, but also to add to the repertory of modern chamber-music players. The first of these pieces is the excellent pavan from the second suite in D minor. Possessing little of the daring of Lawes' later style, as exemplified in the larger fantasias and aires and in the violin sonatas, this piece is nevertheless a good example of the composer's melodic gifts and a fitting testimony to his mastery of the new *concertante* style of violin writing.

Some hint of Lawes' later style can be observed better in the introductory aire to the third suite, which is again in D minor. This charming piece embodies several techniques which can be associated with William Lawes' style. (Cf. Appendix D.) One is immediately introduced to a short disjunct melody based upon the spreading of tonic and dominant chords. This melody is a harbinger of Lawes' later melodic and contrapuntal lines. As yet it does not display the angularity of the later melodies, such as that of the fantasia (first movement) from the *Consort Suite No. 3 in C Minor for five viols,* but one can see the composer almost preparing to dispense with the broken chord patterns and strike out in search of bold, new lines for his music. As has already been seen, this technique developed with Lawes into an intensely personal and subjective invention of melody which at times achieves a fascinating, elongated beauty which has been likened to the eccentric figures of the painter, El Greco.[1]

In contrast to the foregoing is Lawes' fondness for descending and ascending scale lines in thirds and sixths, employing crotchets and quavers. Entering in close *stretti* the parts pair off in thirds to form as it were a cogwheel descent in the first strain. Later, in the second strain, the same technique is used again, but this time in an ascending scale line. The opening of the second strain illustrates another of the composer's propensities, and this is the 'working-out' of a short figure between all the parts in true *concertante* fashion. While the technique is quite simple and direct at this stage, we shall meet it later on in more complex applications by the composer.

The closing measures of the D minor 'Aire' are once again a portent of the later Lawes in the beautiful melodic line of the *continuo* as it falls by ever widening diminished intervals to the sharp third of the key and then rises to the close. The introduction of the sharp third in the bass sets off a series of clashes

[1] By E. H. Meyer, op. cit., p. 187.

which finally resolve upon the dominant as it proceeds to its tonic. In the second bar before the last, the sharp third proceeding upwards coincides for the space of a crotchet with the minor third of the key proceeding downwards. This produces a simultaneous cross relation.[1] Continuing upwards the altered third moves to a passing note, which this time produces a minor seventh between outer voices. When the dominant is reached in the bass, the note F is suspended in the topmost part. The drop of a seventh in the second violin part sets up the even more dissonant minor ninth and this is reiterated by the first violin before the resolution to the dominant triad. This example is one of the most extreme applications of dissonance writing in the *Royall Consort*. It results from the mobility of the parts in the melodic minor, but is mild compared with Lawes' later dissonant style in the fantasias and aires and his other instrumental and even vocal collections.

In the *Royall Consort* Lawes' dissonances are almost always prepared and resolved, but there is often a certain restlessness, as if the composer wished, even at this time, that he could break through the ordinary conventions and step boldly forward on his own. This is noticeable, e.g., in the use of ornamental resolutions for which Lawes seems to have had a particular affinity in his earlier works.

Aside from the dance forms discussed in the present chapter four others are included in the *Royall Consort*. The most important of these is the fantasia, of which there are two examples. These are the only pieces in the entire collection which are in genuine six-part writing. They are both solid works and are of particular interest as examples of the composer's early fantasia style. In the *Royall Consort* they are the introductory movements to Suites No. 1 in D Minor and No. 6 in D Major. Two other pieces in the collection are entitled 'Ecco'. These portray their title exactly, the instruments echoing each other in short fragments in pure *hocketus* technique. Another dance, from the second suite in D Minor, is called 'Aire' by Lawes but is in reality a charming galliard of the type later found in the composer's violin sonatas. The last of the four divergent forms is a lilting morris dance, a fine illustration of its type.

[1] See the previous chapter for a discussion of the cross relation as a logical by-product of the English linear techniques in the melodic minor, p. 61.

In only one instance does a piece from the *Royall Consort* occur in another of Lawes' major collections. The popular Alman from the sixth suite is found rearranged by the composer as a five-part Aire in Bodleian, Mus. Sch. B.2. To the present study this particular Alman is of great importance, inasmuch as it furnishes conclusive proof that the *Royall Consort* was written before the five-part fantasias and aires. From internal evidence it is certain that the five-part arrangement was fashioned from both the original and later versions of the Alman in the *Royall Consort*. None of the composer's other five-part aires are contrived in this manner.

The evidence presented in this chapter proves beyond any doubt that the *Royall Consort*, far from being a conservative work, is in reality a very progressive one, possessing all of the characteristics of middle and even late Baroque instrumental music. The many manuscripts in which it is still extant testify to its immense popularity, not only in its own day but in later times as well. The *Royall Consort* is in many ways a unique collection and most certainly occupies an important position in the mainstream of the development of the dance suite, the *sonata da camera* and the trio sonata.

I.V

THE 'HARPE' CONSORTS

O NE of William Lawes' most interesting and attractive collections of instrumental music is that which he wrote for violin, bass viol, theorbo and harp. This set of stylized dance suites is one of the few extant collections of music for a 'broken' consort and contains some of the earliest known completely written-out parts for the harp. Even more important is the fact that the 'Harpe' Consorts are a key to the performance practice of the seventeenth-century English dance suite, inasmuch as they include fully written-out variations or 'divisions' for the repeated dance strains. These sets of variations show not only the manner in which dance suites were performed but also the different types of 'divisions' and their sequences in the repeated strains of the various dance forms. Aside from their historical significance the 'Harpe' Consorts represent some of Lawes' finest work, indeed some of the best instrumental music of the century.

Like the composer's other major works, these pieces were never published in their original and complete form.[1] That they

[1] As far as the writer has been able to determine, no notice of the existence of the 'Harpe' Consorts as a collection or otherwise has appeared in print prior to now. E. H. Meyer, *English Chamber Music* (London: Lawrence & Wishart, 1946), pp. 271–7, confuses these suites with the violin sonatas. The latter collection was designated expressly for organ and not for 'Organ or Harp' as Meyer states. Rupert Erlebach makes no mention of the 'Harpe' Consorts at all in his article, 'William Lawes and his String Music', *Proceedings of the Musical Association*, fifty-ninth session (1932–3), pp. 103–19.

enjoyed considerable popularity before and after Lawes' death, however, is proven by their presence in several contemporary manuscripts and by the fact that John Playford included sixteen of the dance movements from the collection in four of his early publications: *A Musicall Banquet* (1651), *Court-Ayres* (1655), *Courtly Masquing Ayres* (1662), and *Musick's Hand-maide* (1663). The dances in these printed books, however, are arranged for only two instruments, a treble and a bass, and unfortunately, none of the variations are included. These simplified arrangements or 'lessons', as Playford calls them, were designed primarily for amateurs and learners and in that capacity they served admirably for didactic purposes. But the original *'Harpe' Consorts* with their elaborate variations could hardly have been performed by beginners. Hence the market for such a publication would necessarily have been confined to a limited number of advanced players and professionals. These apparently did not form a large enough clientele to warrant the printing of such a large and complex work. In fact, both John Playford and Christopher Simpson, author of the *Division-Violist* (1667), stated that the larger and more significant collections of instrumental music with written-out 'divisions' could not 'enter into the light' because the cost of their publication would be prohibitive.[1]

The complete collection of *'Harpe' Consorts* consists of thirty individual dance movements with written-out 'divisions' for the violin and bass viol. There is, however, no single manuscript which contains the complete work. The main source is a set of three part-books in William Lawes' autograph in the Bodleian Library, Mus. Sch. D.238–40. These are the separate parts for the violin, bass viol and theorbo only and are clearly numbered from one through thirty by the composer himself. They are the only manuscripts which contain the violin and bass viol 'divisions' for the entire collection. The first twenty-five dances are ordered into six suites, each containing four movements: alman (aire)–corant–corant–saraband, except for the last suite which has an additional alman. The pieces numbered twenty-six through thirty are five larger works of much greater musical interest than the suites proper. These comprise an 'Aire', three 'Pavens' and one 'Fantazy'. The three pavans in

---

[1] Christopher Simpson, *The Division-Violist* (London: 1667 ed.), p. 61. Lithographic facsimile (London: J. Curwen, 1955).

particular are the highlights of the collection. Fortunately the five individual consorts are laid out, together with their divisions for violin and bass viol and the complete harp music, in William Lawes' volume of autograph scores, Bodleian, Mus. Sch. B.3.

The complete harp music to the first six suites, however, is not extant. Lawes began copying the harp parts into his organ book, Bodleian, Mus. Sch. D.229, but only incomplete harp scores to the first eight dances are to be found there. They include only the treble and bass lines of the original, as suggested by the five completed harp parts in the autograph score. That they are not merely reductions of the other instrumental parts for thorough-bass, however, is proved by the fact that the treble line is not a duplicate of the violin part, but a new and vital component of the score.

The task of reconstructing most of the remaining harp scores is facilitated by another manuscript, this time in the library of Christ Church, Ch. Ch. 5. This manuscript, which is not autograph, contains the harp parts to the first twenty-one pieces. The first two suites in this folio, when compared with those in the Bodleian organ book, reveal slight variants in the treble line, but for the most part the versions are substantially the same. There is no reason, therefore, why the Christ Church manuscript, in the absence of an autograph, should not be accepted as reasonably authentic for the remaining harp scores. In this manuscript also the harp music is less bare, containing an inner part in the tenor range, but this line is simply the violin part which has been put down one octave. Judging by the five completed harp parts in the Bodleian Library it is doubtful whether this type of filler was Lawes' original intent. The real significance of Ch. Ch. MS. 5 is that it supplies the new treble parts for the harp scores to numbers nine through twenty-one. There remain but four dances, the major portion of the sixth suite, for which no trace of the harp music has as yet been uncovered.

In the Bodleian autograph score of the five larger consorts William Lawes has expressly indicated the instrumentation for violin, bass viol, theorbo and 'harpe'. The question whether the composer intended 'harpe' as an abbreviation for harpsichord or truly for harp is solved by an examination of the music itself.

The spacing of the chords in the bass staff of the harp score often encompasses as much as two octaves. Even allowing for the smaller dimensions of the keys on seventeenth-century keyboard instruments these parts would not have been playable upon a harpsichord, whereas a chromatic harp could perform the music quite comfortably. The argument that the chords may have been arpeggiated on the keyboard instrument in accordance with Baroque practice falls to the ground also when the harp parts are compared with the keyboard parts in Lawes' other instrumental collections. The wide spacings are present only in the harp scores.[1] Lawes' spelling of 'harpe' may also come under scrutiny here, for in his autographs the composer has written out the names of the instruments several times, and in each case the spelling is the same, with no marks of punctuation present to suggest an abbreviation. Throughout his autograph manuscripts Lawes seldom uses a shortened word, and when he does so, a colon indicates the abbreviation. Moreover, the same spelling by Lawes for harp is to be found in the composer's vocal autograph in the British Museum, Add. MS. 31432, where, in the charming vocal 'trialogue' between Orpheus, Alecto and Euridice, Lawes writes, 'my *harpe* is out of tune'. While the argument of spelling is certainly not conclusive in the light of the variable spellings of the period, the combined evidence presented here should leave little doubt that the collection was intended for the harp and not the harpsichord. It is significant in this respect also that at least two noted harpists were colleagues of William Lawes in the King's private music at Court. These were John de Flelle and Philip Squire, both 'musicians in ordinary' for the harp.[2]

Two types of harp were in use in England at the time, the Irish harp or clarsech, and the Welsh or Gaelic harp.[3] The former was strung diatonically and was distinguished by a curved front pillar and a swelling soundbox, whereas the Welsh harp had a straight pillar, a flat sound box and was fitted with three

---

[1] Compare, for example, the harp score of Ex. 13, p. 103, with the organ part of Violin Sonata No. 8 in Appendix D.

[2] Henry Cart de Lafontaine, *The King's Musick* (London: Novello and Co. Ltd., 1909), passim. Philip Squire began his career 'for the lutes and voices', but ended up as a harper.

[3] Francis W. Galpin, *Old English Instruments of Music* (London: Methuen & Co. Ltd., 3rd ed., 1932), p. 15.

rows of strings. The two outer rows were tuned diatonically and in unison while the centre row produced the chromatic notes. This instrument was usually set in the key of G and had a chromatic compass of four octaves.[1] Undoubtedly this was the harp intended for these consorts by the composer.

The six dance suites in the Bodleian autograph part-books are arranged according to key. Nos. 1 and 2 are in G minor, No. 3 in G major, No. 4 in D minor and Nos. 5 and 6 in D major. The five larger works at the end of the collection are in the same keys as the suites themselves and may have been designed as the first movements to them.[2] Fantasias and pavans often served this purpose, as has already been noted in the five- and six-part fantasias and aires and in the *Royall Consort*.[3] The importance of these five large movements is manifest in the greater independence of the parts, in their greater length and by the fact that Lawes himself copied them into his volume of autograph scores. There is, in fact, a basic difference in the style of composition between the large consorts and the dances in the suites proper. In the unvaried strains of the latter the violin has the predominant melody while both the bass viol and theorbo play the thorough-bass line. The harp serves primarily as an accompaniment. In the varied strains of the suites the violin either repeats the 'aire' or melody, or 'divides' upon it. The bass viol abandons the thorough-bass, but makes use of it in its own variations, while the harp again furnishes the accompaniment and the theorbo maintains the thorough-bass. In the five large consorts, however, the parts are more intricately woven. Both the 'Fantazia' and the 'Aire' are in four real parts in the characteristically imitative style. In the unvaried strains of the 'Pavens' the main pavan melody is in the treble register of the harp score, while both the violin and bass viol perform beautifully contrived slow counterpoints to it, and the theorbo doubles the lowest notes of the harp. In the varied strains the violin takes over the pavan melody from the harp or 'divides' upon it, while the bass viol performs its 'divisions' upon the bass line

[1] Loc. cit.

[2] In the appended Catalogue of Instrumental Works the five individual consorts are listed as '*Harpe*' Consorts Nos. 7–11.

[3] See also the discussion of the first movements of the violin sonatas and the bass viol suites in Chapters V and VI.

which is held by the theorbo. Often, both the violin and bass viol engage in variations together. The function of the harp in the varied repeats, however, presents another problem. In the autograph scores Lawes copied the harp music in with the unvaried strains only. The 'divisions', which follow the main body of the pavans in each case, do not include the harp parts. From the directions given by Christopher Simpson in the *Division-Violist* it is nevertheless clear that in the composition of 'divisions' for two or three instruments to the organ, the latter did play during the varied repeats and even performed variations of its own 'if he had the ability of Hand'.[1] The harp (which here takes the place of the organ) was therefore probably meant to accompany the violin and bass viol in the varied strains, and simply repeated its part as long as the divisions lasted, or may even have improvised strains of its own.

The place of the theorbo-lute in these compositions is an extremely interesting one, since its delicate plucked harmonies blend beautifully with the graceful pizzicato of the harp accompaniment. Lawes has not expressly indicated the theorbo as a thorough-bass in his autographs as he did for the two theorboes in the *Royall Consort*, and yet the single bass line suggests that a realization of the harmonies was in order. Theorbo players were well schooled in thorough-bass realization and usually performed this function both in instrumental consort and in the accompaniment to vocal music.[2] While it is true that at times the theorbo did not act as a thorough-bass, these instances were rare and occurred only when a true part was written for the instrument, as in the case of the two six-part fantasias in the *Royall Consort* and the single 'Fantazia' of the '*Harpe*' Consorts themselves.

A few observations may be made here in respect to the suites of the '*Harpe*' Consorts as compared with those of the *Royall Consort*. The sequence of dance movements in both collections follows generally the same pattern, i.e. Alman–Corant–Saraband. But whereas the *Royall Consort* suites contain six or seven movements (allowing for more than one alman or corant), the harp suites have only four or five, the extra movement being a

[1] Simpson, op. cit., p. 58.
[2] Thomas Mace, *Musick's Monument* (London: P. Ratcliffe Thompson, 1676), p. 217.

short corant. The dances in the harp collection are therefore shorter by one-third in the number of movements comprising a suite. They are also shorter by one-third in the length of the individual strains, except for the saraband which has the standard eight-measure section. The same proportion holds true for the number of instruments employed. The significance of this observation lies in the recognition of the principle that compositions of more parts were to be of greater length in direct proportion to the increased number of parts.

In many respects the two collections are quite similar. The second strains of the dances (excluding the saraband) are longer than the first and the key schemes are the same. Either tonic, dominant or mediant modulation is used for the close of first or middle strains. But one of the salient features of the *Royall Consort*, the *concertante* interplay between the parts, is not present in the *'Harpe' Consorts*. The former combined the variation technique in a modified form with the all-important *concertante* activity of two dominating violins, whereas the *'Harpe' Consorts* are designed primarily for their variations.

The seventeenth century has been called 'the century of the variation.'[1] The phrase is particularly apt in regard to developments in England during this time; for while the English instrumental art of the seventeenth century is represented in its highest form by the fantasia for strings, no less importance must be attached to the practice and art of variations, or as the English termed them, 'divisions'. England, in fact, had the particular distinction of developing the first important school of variation composers and virtuosi.[2] English virginalists in the persons of John Bull, Peter Phillips, William Byrd, Giles Farnaby, Thomas Tomkins, Orlando Gibbons and others were developing an art for the keyboard which was to shape the course of instrumental music for some time to come. Some of the English virtuosi, like Phillips and Bull, carried this art to the Continent where it was enthusiastically received

[1] Wilhelm Fischer, 'Instrumentalmusik von 1600–1750', *Handbuch der Musikgeschichte*, 2nd ed. edited by Guido Adler, 2 vols. (Berlin, 1930), Vol. I, p. 558.

[2] Robert U. Nelson, *The Technique of Variation* (University of California Press, Berkeley and Los Angeles, 1948), p. 29.

and later became absorbed into instrumental technique there.[1]

But at the same time that English keyboard players were achieving such fame at home and abroad, English violists were developing a school of their own. Encouraged by the patronage of Henry VIII during the first half of the century viol technique had developed considerably and was now borrowing verbatim the figurations and musical forms perfected by virginalists. Since many virginal composers wrote for the viol as well it is not at all surprising that strong influence is traceable from one to the other, just as the vocal composition of the madrigalists influenced their own writing for consorts of viols. Indeed, a detailed study of these early influences might prove to be a valuable area of research. Here, however, one can only point to the parallel techniques used by virginal composers represented in such important collections as *The Fitzwilliam Virginal Book*, *The Mulliner Book* and *Lady Nevell's Book*; to such men as Thomas Tomkins and Orlando Gibbons, for example, whose writing for the viols is so evidently imitative of their keyboard 'divisions'. As the virginal art diminished towards the middle of the seventeenth century the viol emerged as the leading solo and ensemble instrument of the period. The noble heritage left behind by the virginal school, however, was still very much alive in the solo and ensemble 'divisions' of the violists. The technique naturally had to adapt itself to the limitations and possibilities of the bowed strings but in this it succeeded admirably. From here developed the art, which in the following decades brought the English 'division' technique to its summit.

It is fitting that the most distinguished treatise ever written upon the variation art was the labour of an Englishman. So well did Christopher Simpson deal with the subject in his *The Division-Violist* (1659), that none of his contemporaries would dare a discussion of the rules for 'divisions' in print. Thomas Mace, for example, quotes Simpson extensively in his directions for playing the viol in *Musick's Monument* (1676).[2] *The Division-Violist*

[1] For a detailed study of the virginal art see Charles Van Den Borren, *The Sources of Keyboard Music in England* (London: Novello & Co. Ltd., and Oxford University Press, 1913).

[2] Mace, op. cit., pp. 248–9.

was republished in a second edition in 1667 and again as
late as 1712. The author himself was a violist, composer and
teacher of international repute. In his youth he was contemporary with such famous violists as Alfonso Ferrabosco II,
Giovanni Coperario, John Jenkins (who remained his life-long
friend and even helped him with his *magnum opus*), and William
Lawes. Simpson had seen, heard and performed with the greatest
virtuosi not only in England, but abroad as well. An outstanding
performer and improviser himself he was therefore in an excellent position to sum up the contributions of more than half
a century of 'division' practice.

The Division-Violist is especially valuable for understanding
the 'division' technique used by William Lawes in the *'Harpe'
Consorts*. So accurately do Simpson's rules for 'division' mirror
Lawes' style of writing that one might suspect that Simpson had
arrived at his precepts through a thorough study of Lawes'
music. The latter's early death therefore establishes the fact that
viol 'division' technique reached its maturity long before
Simpson wrote his treatise. A comparison of Giovanni Coperario's directions for 'divisions' in the *Rules How to Compose*, upon
which Lawes was nurtured, with Simpson's rules written half a
century later, shows how far Lawes had gone in perfecting the
art. Coperario limits the intervals which may be divided upon
to thirds, fourths and fifths; his rules for descanting are elementary and his prescribed rhythms are limited.[1] In addition, no
mention is made of multiple stops or the mixture of the various
'division' types.

Simpson, on the other hand, classifies the art of 'division' into
three major types. The first he calls 'Breaking The Ground';
the second, 'Descant Division'; and the third, 'Mixt Division'.
'Breaking the Ground' consists of 'dividing its notes into more
diminute notes' and this may be done by note repetition, by the
use of neighbouring tones, by scalar transitions, by chordal
figuration, or by a combination of the last two.[2] In faster tempi
the latter was often referred to as 'running division'. *'Descant
Division'*, as its name implies, employs figuration above the
'ground' only, avoiding the notes of the theme itself in favour of

[1] See also the comments of Manfred F. Bukofzer, *Rules How to Compose*
by Giovanni Coperario (Los Angeles: Ernest E. Gottlieb, 1952,) intro., p. [8].
[2] Simpson's rules for 'division' are to be found on pp. 27–61 in his **book**.

its concordances. This type could be fast or slow. The slow variety formed the basis for some of Lawes' finest 'division' writing. '*Mixt Division*' combines the techniques used in the first two and adds rules for disjunct figuration, multiple stops, and the use of dissonance. The combination of 'Descant Division' and 'Breaking the Ground' in 'Mixt Division' results in a kind of disjunct figuration which presents two parts to the ear instead of one. This type of variation will be recognized as a characteristic of Baroque music and was known in England by the name 'Skipping Division'. Another type mentioned by Simpson is 'Tripla Division'. This is purely rhythmic and employs whole strains in triplets. It may include all of the other 'division' techniques. Examples of all of these are profuse in Lawes' '*Harpe*' *Consorts*. Below and on succeeding pages are some short excerpts. In the larger varied strains, where the violin engages in a veritable 'contest of division' with the bass viol, the technique of 'driving a point' was considered the *ne plus ultra* of the 'division' violist's art. This consisted in the improvisation of a motive or 'point' by one of the players and its imitation by the other in an improvised fantasia-type *fugato* strain.[1]

The varieties of 'division' described above furnished the composer or performer with an assortment of techniques whereby the repeated strains of the dance movements could be made

Ex. 12   **(a)**   **"running division" of the "breaking bass" variety from the "corant" of the "Harpe" Consort No. 2.**

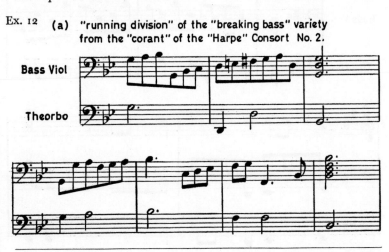

---

[1] For Simpson's description of this type see paragraph 15 in Appendix A.

(b) "descant division" upon the first strain of the "Alman" from the "Harpe" Consort No. 1

(c) "skipping division" from the "Almane" of the "Harpe" Consort No. 6

(d) "tripla division" from the "Paven", "Harpe" Consort No. 9

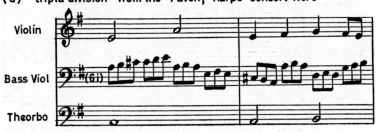

(e) "driving of a point" from the "Paven"in G minor,
"Harpe"Consort No. 10, (excerpt)

interesting and exciting. In this respect the *'Harpe' Consorts* are
historically important inasmuch as they reveal the formal plan
for the dances of the period, together with their repeated and
varied strains. They also enable us to determine the proper
sequence in which 'division' types were used within the formal
scheme of the dances themselves. The schemes employed most
often by Lawes are as follows:

Pavan	‖ : A : ‖ : B : ‖ : C : ‖ A′ ‖ A″ ‖ B′ ‖ B″ ‖ C′ ‖ C″ ‖
Alman or *Aire*	‖ A ‖ A′ ‖ B ‖ B′ ‖
Corant	‖ : A : ‖ : B : ‖ A′ ‖ A″ ‖ B′ ‖ B″ ‖
Saraband	‖ A ‖ A′ ‖ B ‖ B′ ‖ C ‖ C′ ‖

The length of the movements alternates between long and short.
The tempo begins fairly slow with the pavan and increases in
speed with each successive movement. This concept of the dance
suite appears purely English in character since continental
models concentrate upon the alternation of slow and fast dance
movements.

In his treatise Simpson also devotes a section to what he calls
the 'ordering of division'.[1] Here again we see how closely his
rules mirror Lawes' practices, with the important exception that
Simpson's point of departure is the '*Ground*' or single bass theme,
whereas Lawes based his variations on both the bass and the
treble lines of his dances. Simpson's 'ordering of division' provides us with detailed instructions for the sequence of the various
division types and these may be traced closely in the fully
written-out variations of Lawes' consorts. Thus, in the *alman* or
aire, which usually varied a strain but once, Lawes sets his
divisions in crotchets and quavers for each repeated strain. This
corresponds with Simpson's account which calls for the first
variation to be slow enough to permit the identification of the
theme and at the same time allow the performer to gain some
familiarity with his 'ground'. Lawes' first variations of a strain
usually employ either 'descant division' or a mixture of 'descant'
and 'breaking bass'. This is another example of a practice used
by Lawes and later codified by Simpson:

'. . . in playing or composing *Division to a Ground*, we may either
continue any one way (perhaps a whole Strain together) or
change from This [breaking bass] to That [descant], as frequently as we please; insomuch, that sometimes *part* of the
same Note is broken in one sort of Division, and *part* of it in
another, . . .'[2]

In Lawes' corants, which vary each strain twice, the first
variations are treated like those of the almans, but the second
are in 'running division'. Again, this holds true to Simpson's

---

[1] See paragraph 12, Appendix A.   [2] Simpson, op. cit., p. 46.

directions for divisions 'of a quicker motion' for the second varied repeat. Another characteristic here is the short-phrase structure, similar to the end-stopping of lines in Lawes' songs. The 'divisions' are arrested at intervals of from two to six bars by cadence-like pauses on minims or dotted minims. The latter are frequently multiple stops in the bass viol part.

The saraband, which usually consists of three strains, normally varies each strain but once. The 'divisions' are of the slow 'breaking bass' variety, probably because the fast tempo of the English saraband did not easily allow of thinking in terms of semiquavers or 'descant'. In sarabands of two strains the varied repeats are frequently in pairs, as in the corant, and they make use of the same 'ordering' of 'division'. Some of these are strongly suggestive of Lawes' 'ballad' songs. The saraband from the *'Harpe' Consort No. 4 in D Minor*, for example, is in reality one of the composer's most celebrated part-songs, 'O My Clarissa'.[1] Undoubtedly, these dance songs were danced to as well as sung.

As delightful as the first seven *'Harpe' Consorts* are, they do not compare in quality with the three outstanding pavans at the end of the collection. Within the confines of the larger pavan form Lawes pours forth a lush romanticism of majestic serenity. In the unvaried strains in particular the pavan melodies and their interweaving counterpoints reveal the composer in some of his finest linear writing. Indeed, these last works must be accorded a lasting place besides such landmarks in the pavan form as Ferrabosco's 'Dovehouse Pavan', and Dowland's 'Lachrymae'. An example is provided in the opening strain of the G Major Pavan, *'Harpe' Consort No. 8*. The counterpoints in the violin and bass viol parts are slow 'descant' division to the main theme, which is in the treble of the harp part. This theme later becomes the subject for extensive variations. The beginning excerpt is printed opposite.

In the remaining pavans Lawes borrows his main themes from other composers. This practice remains even today one of the most accepted ways in which the composer may pay tribute to great contemporaries or masters of the past and at the same time display his complete mastery of the variation

---

[1] This song with its original variations will be found in Appendix D. It is also discussed in Chapter VII, p. 167, at greater length.

Ex. 13   "Harpe" Consort No. 8 in G major
          Pavan: (opening strain, excerpt)

technique. In the G Minor Pavan, 'Harpe' Consort No. 10, Lawes acknowledges his own teacher, Giovanni Coperario. The theme has been identified by the author from among Coperario's works and, fortunately, it is to be found in print as No. 101 in the excellent collection of *Jacobean Consort Music* included as Volume IX (1955) of the *Musica Britannica* series. Lawes uses only the first eight measures of Coperario's bass (the time value of which has been halved by the editors of the above publication). Coperario's piece is for two bass viols and organ, and in the printed score it is entitled 'Fantasia'. It is, however, a pavan, for it is neither in the *fugato* style common to the fantasia nor does it employ any of the other techniques which distinguish the form. In fact, Coperario's composition closely resembles Lawes' pavans in his suites for two bass viols and organ.[1] One bass viol either doubles or 'breaks' the bass while the other 'descants' to it. Coperario's piece, however, is divided into only two strains and these are without divisions, whereas Lawes' pavans are in three strains and the divisions are fully written-out. A comparison of the two works is of value, in that both teacher and pupil may be compared through their treatment of the same theme. Coperario's work, while not without merit, lacks inspiration. In Lawes' pavan, on the other hand, the contrapuntal and melodic treatment is richer and more interesting, the general proportions are more expanded and technique is more developed. Coperario, the master craftsman, is too academic. Industry there is aplenty but that rare and most vital spark is missing.

The last of the pavans, *'Harpe' Consort No. 9 in D Major*, is set to a bass theme by 'Cormacke'. This piece contains some of Lawes' most elaborate 'division' writing. Long passages in semiquavers and demi-semiquavers are not unusual here and these place great demands upon the performer's technique. Passages of this sort had to be written by one who himself had this technique at command, or as Simpson puts it:

'. . . no man is fit to Compose *Division* to a *Ground* (how great a Master in Musick soever he be) unless he know the neck of the Instrument, and the Method of Fingering belonging unto it.'[2]

The D Major Pavan abounds in flourishes of written-out ornamentation, including 'relishes' and 'shaked turns', the English equivalent of the Italian *groppi*, which had been adopted earlier by the virginalists in their own highly florid figurations. Also included in this pavan are excellent examples of what may be termed the 'division cadence', in which the full time of the final

---

[1] Lawes' suites for two bass viols and organ are discussed in Chapter VI, pp. 139–46.

[2] Simpson, op. cit., p. 57.

THE 'HARPE' CONSORTS

breve is occupied in extending the divisions in one or more of
the parts in order to produce the gradual retardation necessary
after such a display of virtuosity.

In the performance of these pavans, as well as in the other
dances, the keynote is variety; not only in the choice of 'division'
types but also in the employment of dynamics and tempo
changes. One has only to read the paragraph (12), by Simpson
from the *Division-Violist*, printed in Appendix A, p. 261, to
understand that the use of contrast, dynamics, tempo changes
and emotional expression was an integral part of this music.
Simpson's concern with maintaining the attention and interest
of the listener is also noteworthy here. It belies the statement,
which has often been repeated, that this music was solely for the
enjoyment of the performer. The absence of tempo, dynamic,
and expression markings in Lawes' music must not be interpreted to mean that they were not used in performance. The
very character of the music defies this senseless interpretation.
Within the bounds of good taste, based upon a thorough knowledge of the period, these works may be edited for modern
performance. They will provide an interesting and delightful
addition to our repertory.

V

THE VIOLIN 'SONATAS'

T HERE is a chapter in the history of instrumental music
which is yet to be written. It concerns the development of a
genre of violin music in England during the seventeenth century
which parallels the rise of the Baroque trio sonata in Italy.
Curiously, this violin music has managed to elude historians and
remains even today almost totally obscure, mainly due to the
fact that it was never graced with publication. Because contemporary manuscripts do not employ a uniform terminology
for these works they are referred to here as early English
examples of the Baroque chamber sonata, the counterpart of the
Italian *sonata da camera*. They are in reality stylized fantasia-
suites or 'setts' for one or two violins, bass viol and organ, consisting of three movements: a fantasia, an alman and a galliard
plus *coda*. This early type of chamber sonata was cultivated in
England from about the beginning of the second decade of the
century and possibly even earlier. Thus a direct line may be
traced from the more than twenty 'setts' by Coperario to the
sixteen by William Lawes, at least an equal number by
Christopher Simpson and several by John Jenkins, Matthew
Locke and others.[1] At the end of the century the form merged

---

[1] It is unfortunate that the catalogue of English chamber music in Ernst
Meyer's *Die Mehrstimmige Spielmusik des 17. Jahrhunderts* (Cassel: Barenreiter,
1934) lists the first movements of chamber sonatas by some of these composers as individual fantasias. Meyer in general seems to have missed the
existence of this instrumental form, even in his latest work, *English Chamber
Music* (London: Lawrence & Wishart, 1946).

with formal elements borrowed from the early Italian sonata to culminate in the famous violin sonatas of three and four parts by Henry Purcell.

This early English sonata was in fact described with fair accuracy by Roger North early in the eighteenth century. Referring rather nostalgically to the first decades of the previous century North writes:

'During this flourishing time, It became usuall to compose for Instruments in setts that is After a fantasia, an aiery lesson of two straines, and a tripla by way of Galliard, wch was stately; courant or otherwise not unsuitable too, or rather imitatory of the Dance. Instead of the fantasia they often used a very grave kind of Ayre, wch they called a padoana or pavan; this had 3. straines, each being twice played went off heavyly, especially when a rich veine failed the master. These setts altogether very much resembled ye design of our sonnata musick Being all consistent In ye same Key; but the Lessons had a spice of ye french from whom we had the lute. . . .'[1]

North's observation that the 'setts' closely resembled the sonatas of his own period suggests that the earlier form merely lacked christening and supports the undeniable evidence of the music itself that in the seventeenth century at least, England developed a chamber sonata which was mainly of its own making.

In the manuscripts containing these works the sonatas are for the most part without any general title.[2] Lawes, for example, simply designates his 'setts' 'ffor one violin, base violl and organ', or 'ffor two violins, base violl and organ'. Each of the individual movements, however, was entitled with the name of the dance upon which it was modelled, or in the case of the first movement, 'fantasia'. The title 'Aire' or 'Ayre' was used interchangeably with either the alman or the galliard by many

---

[1] Roger North, *The Musicall Gramarian*, MS. ed. by Hilda Andrews (Oxford University Press, 1925), pp. 20–1.

[2] In some MSS. the title 'sonata' evidently does exist alongside others for similar pieces which are simply entitled 'fantasia'. See the article by Peter Evans, 'Seventeenth-Century Chamber Music Manuscripts at Durham', *Music and Letters*, Vol. XXXVI, No. 3 (July 1955), pp. 205–23.

composers to signify a stylized dance.[1] Thus Coperario writes his sonatas with one violin in three movements which he names 'fantasia', 'alman' and 'ayre', while those for two violins received the titles 'fantasia', 'alman' and 'galliard'. Lawes on the other hand calls his sonata movements 'fantasia', 'aire' and 'aire'.

It was probably owing to Lawes that the chamber sonata became an accepted form of composition in the aristocratic musical circles of seventeenth-century England. To Coperario, possibly, must go the credit of being one of the most important, if not the most important innovator of the form, but the older composer's sonatas are clogged with reminiscences of the already antiquated style of his individual fantasias. Though exhibiting solid craftsmanship they are not successful in their attempt to blend the new variation techniques into the old contrapuntal idiom.[2] Lawes received the chamber sonata from his master but poured into it the strength, vigour and romanticism of a superior creative temperament. As in his large viol fantasias so here too he does not discard the old, but rather expands and adds to the already established form. Strong, romantic melodies, larger developments, rich and dissonant harmonies and counterpoints, extended solo interludes and *codas*, idiomatic instrumental writing, a remarkably independent treatment of the keyboard and greater insight into the technical and expressive potentialities of the violin distinguish William Lawes' chamber sonatas from the mediocre production of many of his colleagues and successors.

The contemporary popularity of Lawes' chamber sonatas may be gleaned from the fact that several manuscripts containing the collection are today extant in the British Museum, the Bodleian Library and the Library of Christ Church in Oxford. One English manuscript, containing among other things the sonatas for two violins, has even found its way into the archives of the Paris Conservatory.[3] The chief sources for Lawes' sonatas,

[1] See the discussion of this term in Chapter III, p. 82. When used in context 'aire' simply meant the tune or melody and 'aiery' meant tuneful as in the last quote from Roger North above.

[2] Four of Coperario's chamber sonatas are available in Vol. IX of *Musica Britannica*, edited by Thurston Dart and William Coates. They are Nos. 98a, b, c; 99a, b, c; 102a, b, c; and 103a, b, c.

[3] Paris Conservatory, MS. Res. 770. This MS. also contains works by Coperario, Gibbons, Locke, Jenkins, 'Farabosco' and Ward.

however, are his own autograph volumes, which are in the Bodleian Library at Oxford. The separate parts for the violin sonatas are in the autograph part-books, Mus. Sch. D.238–40, and in the organ book, Mus. Sch. D.229. Only one fantasia, that of Sonata No. 8 in D Major for one violin, is represented in the autograph score, Mus. Sch. B.2.[1]

Unlike the composer's other large instrumental collections there can be no question here as to either the order or arrangement of the sonatas and their movements. As in the case of the 'Harpe' Consorts each movement is numbered consecutively, despite the fact that they are clearly 'setts'. There are eight sonatas for one violin, bass viol and organ and eight sonatas for two violins, bass viol and organ. Both groups follow the same order of keys: No. 1 in G minor, No. 2 in G major, No. 3 in A minor, No. 4 in C major, No. 5 in D minor, No. 6 in D major, No. 7 in D minor, and No. 8 in D major. Although Lawes himself does not distinguish numerically between the 'setts' in the autographs, other manuscripts definitely number each group of three movements from one to eight. Moreover, in all manuscripts, including the autographs, the order of movements is identical. There can be no argument contrary to the fact that these pieces were written as serious works in the three-movement chamber sonata form described by North.

It is best to approach an analysis of the violin sonatas through an examination of the treatment accorded the individual instruments in the music itself. Each instrument can be identified with certain techniques of writing which will at the same time explain the formal and stylistic characteristics of the sonatas and point up the most significant works in the collection as well. That this should be true is in itself a striking indication of how far removed the chamber sonatas are from the older fantasia form. No longer are the instruments to be 'equally-matched' and the parts to be 'equally-heard'. The instruments of the sonatas have definite roles to fulfil within the contrasting textures and open fabrics of the new style. Sometimes one or the other takes the spotlight or recedes into the background, but there can be no denying the fact that the 'scoulding' violin is the undisputed leader of the group, even over the still-venerable viol.

[1] For the major sources of the sonatas other than these, see the Catalogue of Instrumental Works, pp. 269–70.

Lawes' death in 1645 dates his violin music before the Commonwealth. Moreover, at least seventy-five per cent of his instrumental music includes prominent parts for violins. In fact, only the five- and six-part fantasias and aires employ the full consort of viols exclusively. Thus Lawes, whose fame as an instrumental composer has hitherto rested mainly on his music for viols, was at least equally prolific in writing for the violins. His is one of the largest and most impressive collections of violin music written in England before the Civil War. It is certainly the largest body of specified violin music extant from that period.

The date of the serious employment of the violin in England may actually coincide with the earliest examples of chamber sonatas. Its use was specified in consorts prior to that time as well, but mainly as a substitute for the treble viol. Violins had been accepted in English court circles by at least the beginning of Queen Elizabeth's reign.[1] Their early function was in popular dance music, in which they gradually replaced the rebecs at court revels. The violin had, in fact, become the symbol of homophonic music, and so when popular dance tunes invaded the serious music of the viols toward the turn of the century the violins went right along. With the changing ideals of the new Baroque, in which beauty of melody figured prominently together with dance rhythms and variation techniques, the violin found a fertile field for its powers. It rode the popularity of the dance suite into the chamber sonata and emerged during the last half of the century a full-grown *prima donna*, with full title to the Baroque *trio sonata*.

The all too common notion that the violin made its English *début* in the band of twenty-four violins set up by Charles II in imitation of the *vingt-quatre violons* of Louis XIV must be most assiduously repudiated. Violins played at the funerals of Queen Elizabeth in 1603 and James I in 1625.[2] The Lupo family of musicians had been playing and composing music for the violins at Court since before about 1600, and by 1621 Thomas Lupo junior was appointed the first official court composer for the

[1] See the discussion by Walter L. Woodfill, *Musicians in English Society from Elizabeth to Charles I* (Princeton University Press, 1953), p. 183n.

[2] Henry Cart de Lafontaine, *King's Musick* (London: Novello and Co. Ltd., 1909), pp. 45, 57.

violins.[1] He was succeeded in 1627 by Stephen Nau. In fact, from the year 1558 all bowed string players in the service of the English Court were listed as 'viols or violins'.[2] In the light of this evidence it is difficult indeed to attach any credence at all to the account given by Anthony Wood in which he claims that the violin was not used in the private music meetings which he attended at Oxford because it was esteemed 'by Gentlemen' to be 'an Instrument belonging to a common Fiddler'.[3] The weekly music gatherings in Oxford numbered among their participants Dr. John Wilson, William Ellis, Edward Lowe and other prominent musicians and composers, all of whom were not only friends and admirers of William Lawes but were known to have possessed copies of his works. These men were most certainly familiar with his violin sonatas as well as with those of Coperario and others. The violin may well have remained the instrument of 'common fiddlers', but by about the second decade of the century serious composers were writing specifically for the instrument, and the violin had become firmly entrenched at the English Court.

By about 1630 the intrusion of the violin upon the serious instrumental forms of the consort of viols had resulted in the remodelling of the fantasia from a composition of equally balanced parts in *fugato* style into a vehicle of expression for the sparkling tones of the violin. Except for the characteristic *fugato* opening there are few resemblances to the older fantasia form. In Lawes' hands the fantasia is transformed into a unified movement, beginning with a strong melodic section containing lengthy expressive subjects, assuming definite direction, introducing development by means of various instrumental techniques, employing several means of contrast, and consciously working towards a definite conclusion. Paramount is the individual treatment accorded the different instruments. The composer is fully aware of the inherent differences between the conversant viols and the animated violins, aware also that the

---

[1] Ibid., p. 53. In 1612 Thomas Lupo is listed as violinist to Henry, Prince of Wales and after the Prince's death, to his brother, the future King Charles I. See Woodfill, op. cit., pp. 302–3, also pp. 300–1.

[2] Ibid., pp. 299 ff.

[3] Anthony Wood, *The Life of Anthony à Wood from the year 1632 to 1672* (Oxford: Thomas Hearne, 1772), pp. 96–7.

Ex. 14

Violin Sonata No. 1 in G minor
1st mov't., "Fantazia", (beginning excerpt)

musical style and forms of the former must be altered to suit the particular qualities of the newcomer. Thus he could write fantasia openings of heroic proportions as on pages 112 and 113.

The most characteristic feature of Lawes' violin style in his sonatas is the *concertante* interplay between the instruments, which has already been noted in the *Royall Consort*. This swift dialogue-like *repartée* may take place between the violin and bass viol in the sonatas for one violin; between the two violins in the second set of sonatas; or between all of the instruments at once. For the first time the *concertante* technique invades not only the stylized dance movements, but the fantasia itself. Thus the first movements of the violin sonatas, unlike those of the five- and six-part fantasias and aires, no longer can be distinguished by clear-cut fugal sections or other characteristic passage types. Instead it is the *repartée* of the instruments themselves, often growing out of a beginning fugal exposition and mingled with various 'division' techniques, which assumes dominating importance. Typical instrumental figures are bantered about in close imitation or in clear alternation for development purposes. At the base of this is the short thematic fragment which is treated in a lively, kaleidoscopic fashion.

'Division' technique is another prominent feature in the violin parts. This is often combined with the *concertante* style itself to produce a gradual heightening of tension as the added figuration gathers momentum in the tightly interlaced fabric of the development. An excellent example of the employment of 'divisions' by the violin may be seen in the first movement of the *Violin Sonata No. 8 in D Major* for one violin, bass viol and organ.[1]

It has already been noted that the chamber sonata, or at least the first movement, was a fusion of many styles of writing. Nowhere is this more evident than in the treatment of the bass viol. It is in fact possible to distinguish six distinct types of writing for the instrument. They are: (1) as an independent contrapuntal part, (2) as a *basso seguente*, doubling the lowest bass of the organ part, (3) as a 'division' viol, performing variations on the bass part, (4) as a partner to the violins in *concertante* passages, (5) as *tacet* while the keyboard plays a solo interlude or accompanies the violin in a solo passage, and (6) as a soloist in its own right accompanied by the organ. Thus Lawes employs every type of

[1] This piece is printed in Appendix D.

technique, blending the old and the new into one unified work. But most prominent in the writing for the bass viol is the influence of the English 'division' skill. The following example from the first movement of *Violin Sonata No. 6 in D Major* for two violins, bass viol and organ is a good illustration of this art. In the autograph the composer provides an alternate part for the difficult divisions, this alternate being the bass line of the organ part:

Ex. 15   Violin Sonata No. 6 in D major
1st mov't., "Fantazia, (excerpt)

The effect which Lawes achieves from the variation of a simple scale line, employing all of his instruments, is extremely interesting. The sequential design of this variation-development is carried through to the very end of the movement. The entire passage is a good example of Lawes' architectural planning. Above a rising, 'broken' bass line the composer builds an interlaced network of patterns, all based upon the rising and descending D major scale. The technique employed is the familiar Baroque device of consonant syncopation whereby, in the terminology of intervallic harmony, the sixth alternates with the fifth to produce a succession of chords in root position and first inversion.[1] On the way down, the same technique is used but this time the harmonic rhythm eases the parts by thirds over the interlaced descending scales. This technique was a favourite of viol composers, since the consonant syncopation produces successions of thirds, enabling the use of long double-stop passages which are easily fingered on the viol. It is one of Lawes' favourite devices in building up intensity.[2] And as for the viol, one may

[1] Coperario gives the complete rules for this technique in his *Rules How to Compose*, *c.* 1610 (Los Angeles: Ernest E. Gottlieb, 1952), f. 22r, 32 v. Also see the introduction to this by Manfred F. Bukofzer, pp. [11] and [13], where he discusses the implications of this technique in the evolution of the II_5^6.–V–I cadence.

[2] See also the vocal example to the words 'Build up thy walls' in the example and discussion in Chapter X, pp. 245-6.

see it employed here on the one hand in doubling the bass of the organ and on the other as a genuine 'division' viol, making use of the three familiar categories of 'division': 'breakinge base', 'descant', and 'mixt'. Note particularly this last, in which the double-stops necessitate the use of the higher positions. The appearance of such a passage as Ex. 15 in a movement entitled 'fantasia' shows the insertion of the variation technique of the repeated dance strain into a more serious artistic medium, and is valuable evidence of the influence of the variation form of the dance suite upon the evolution of the sonata.

The treatment of accompanying chordal instruments, such as the organ, theorbo and harp, in Lawes' instrumental collections falls into three types: (1) as an unfigured thorough-bass, (2) as a reduction of the instrumental score, and (3) as an independent and integral part of the music itself. The first type will be remembered from its use in the *Royall Consort*, where an unfigured bass line serves as the thorough-bass for two theorboes and as a *basso seguente* for the bass viol as well. Related to this is the treatment of the harp part in the lesser dances of the *'Harpe' Consorts*, in which only the unfigured bass and a treble are present for the harpist to use as the basis for filling in the harmony. The last was a customary practice of the middle baroque. The second type of accompaniment noted is that which has been discussed in the chapter dealing with the five- and six-part fantasias and aires, which is largely a reduction of the other parts of the score. In fashioning these organ parts Lawes included the entrance points of the most important counterpoints and as much else as could be conveniently accommodated by two hands. The third type of keyboard part, in which the accompanying chordal instrument is an equal partner with the other instruments, is a distinctive feature only of the violin sonatas and the large *'Pavens'* of the *'Harpe' Consorts*. The degree of independence of these organ parts particularly excites our attention.

There is, indeed, little resemblance between the keyboard accompaniments of the sonatas and the *continuo* or thorough-bass practices of the period. As a matter of fact, the organ parts of Lawes' violin sonatas are closer by far to the role of the keyboard in sonatas of the eighteenth and nineteenth centuries than they are to that of their own date.[1] This can be seen from the numerous ways in which Lawes employs his keyboard accompaniment: as a solo introduction before the entrance of the other instruments, as an equal partner in *concertante* passages, as *tacet* during a solo passage by other instruments, for its own solo interludes, in adding additional contrapuntal parts of its own such as new points of imitation or 'retorts' in *fugato* sections, for duets with the other parts, sustaining and filling in harmonies, accompanying another solo part or being accompanied by the other instruments as a solo part itself. At times the organ also serves as a reduction of the other parts, but never consistently or for long periods of time. It is interesting to note here that in none of his instrumental works does the composer employ the division technique for the keyboard, as if tacitly acknowledging the supremacy of the virginalists in that medium.

For modern performance these organ parts pose a problem. The sustaining character of that instrument was recognized by Lawes, and the music is therefore fashioned expressly for the particular qualities of the organ. Thus, the keyboard parts are sometimes sparse in texture and employ long sustained notes without complementary motion in other parts. This is particularly evident in some solo introductions or interludes, which consist of but two real parts. These, while perfectly suitable for the organ, are not successful when transferred to the harpsichord or modern piano. On the other hand it would be equally impossible to attempt these works upon a large modern organ since the latter would be too powerful against the other instruments and foreign to the true character of the music. A good idea of the proper type of organ required for these sonatas may be got from the writings of Thomas Mace. This author, writing in 1676, describes a table organ which he claims to have invented for the purpose of performing chamber music

[1] The remark by Peter Evans in his article 'Seventeenth-Century Chamber Music Manuscripts at Durham', *Music and Letters*, Vol. 36, No. 3 (July 1955), that William Lawes' 'Fantazyas', in effect, do not contain new material in the keyboard parts, is probably based on the writer's familiarity with the five- and six-part fantasias and aires only. Evans, probably, was not fully aware of the existence of the chamber sonata and its line of development when he wrote his article, although he came close to it in his examinination of the Durham manuscripts. See also, Cecily Arnold, 'Early 17th Century Keyboard Parts', *Music and Letters*, Vol. 33, No. 2 (April 1952), pp. 151-3.

in consort, and furnishes an illustration of it.[1] The instrument is
three feet and one inch high, seven feet and five inches long and
four feet and three inches wide. The keyboard is at the width
end of the table and the bellows are operated either by the feet
or by a cord at the far end. The surface of the table is entirely
smooth and polished, and cut into it are eight music racks or
leaves which lift up at an angle to hold the music. These also
serve to control the volume of tone, so that the greater the
number of instruments participating in the consort the louder
the organ would sound. The performers sat around the table,
as was customary in the performance of early chamber music as
well as in madrigals—a very neat arrangement. It is doubtful,
however, that table organs of this type were known to Lawes'
generation. More likely a small chamber organ of the upright
positive kind, containing both flue and reed pipes, was the
original instrument for which Lawes wrote. It must have had a
range of at least four octaves, similar to the large regal built in
1650 by John Loosemore and now preserved in the castle at
Blair Atholl.[2] The best modern substitute for this early chamber
organ might be a small console, which admittedly cannot
approach the quality of tone of the original, but may serve at
least to represent the particular characteristics of the organ
parts in modern performance and still not overpower the other
instruments.

One of the most outstanding compositions of the two sets of
violin sonatas, and one more deserving of the title 'sonata' than
perhaps any musical work written during the first half of the
seventeenth century, is the *Sonata No. 8 in D Major* for one
violin, bass viol and organ. The complete work is printed in
Appendix D. It is a fine example of the composer's writing for
violin and bass viol, as well as his independent treatment of the
keyboard. We note the ten-bar organ introduction, which com-
mences the beginning fugal exposition, and we note also the
organ-like character of the theme, which is so sparsely treated
for the keyboard. The theme soon breaks into *concertante* figuration after the entrance of the violin and bass viol and is even

---

[1] Thomas Mace, *Musick's Monument*, pp. 242–5.
[2] See a photograph of this instrument in Francis W. Galpin, *Old English
Instruments of Music*, 3rd ed. (London: Methuen & Co. Ltd., 3rd ed. 1932),
plate XLVII.

joined in this *repartée* by the organ itself. All parts, thus far, are completely independent. At bar 35 the keyboard engages in a duet with the bass viol, with both hands adding contrapuntal parts to the three-part writing. Then, at bar 46, the organ accompanies the violin in its rapid figurations. The broken chord work in rapid semiquavers at bar 50 furnishes an example of what Lawes could do in this vein. The 'divisions' become more intense at bar 53 where the three instruments rejoin in *concertante* division interplay and lead into an interesting section at bar 61. Here, all three instruments engage in a delicate interlaced *concertante* fabric which has all the traits of the old *hoketus* technique discussed in the previous chapter. The 'broken-work' of this section is a remarkably advanced example of concerted chamber music. In its turn it leads into a lively section in fast triple time, one bar of the new section equalling the minim of the old. This new passage is entirely dance-like in character and evidences once again the influence of the dance upon the evolving sonata. At bar 103 the tempo reverts to 4/4 and the organ takes over in a new dance-like section with a particularly fine solo for 11 bars. It subsequently recedes to allow the bass viol to enter with figurations. The violin re-enters at bar 118 and performs its own 'divisions' while the bass viol drops out completely. Once again all instruments join at bar 125 in difficult virtuoso elaboration which builds up intensity as it drives towards the conclusion of the movement and finally bursts out into a striking theme in the violin part. This is solidly supported by double stops in minims in the bass viol part and in the left hand of the organ. Note in particular the crossing of registers of these stops in 'see-saw' fashion and the imitation of the violin theme in the right hand of the organ in bars 141-2. The final theme, moreover, is a definite outgrowth of previous figuration, as may be seen for example in the violin part of bar 128 and in the bass viol part of the second half of bar 136. One is amazed at Lawes' employment of such an advanced principle in preparing this heroic close for the D major fantasia.

An important observation must be made here concerning the second set of sonatas, those for two violins, bass viol and organ. It concerns the violin writing, which contains some of the most expressive dissonant contrapuntal lines in all of Lawes' music.

These are characterized by lengthy melodies in piquant inter-woven counterpoints between the two violins. They also make use of the *concertante* style, but are minus any elaborate figura-tions. In particular, the first and sixth sonatas of this set are worthy of special mention.

The 'almans' or second movements of the sonatas are in the traditional bipartite form. They are often similar in character to those of the *Royall Consort* and of approximately the same length or slightly longer. The workmanship of these 'aires', however, appears more mature. The *concertante* technique is especially well conceived and we note certain subtleties begin-ning to appear. The keyboard does not revert to the role of a *continuo* in these movements, but is used effectively for adding new interest. Many of these charming second movements deserve mention here but unfortunately space does not permit.

The galliards, which make up the third movements, and which Lawes calls 'aires' in their stylized form, are not to be confused with the nimble and quick galliards of the Elizabethan period.[1] The latter will be recognized as the familiar *nachtanz* of the pavan, which was set in triple metre and wrought from the same thematic material as the pavan itself. Together they were known as the dance pair and paved the way for the dance suite. There is no thematic relationship, however, between the move-ments of Lawes' sonatas, and his galliards are of a much slower variety. In outward appearance they are similar to the earlier type, being in 3/2 time with a preponderance of semibreves and minims. The basic dance step of the galliard was the *cinq pas*, which gave to the music the characteristic rhythm of the tribrach followed by the trochee, (♩ ♩ ♩ | o ♩). Lawes employs this galliard rhythm, or some modification of it, in all of his last movements. Thomas Mace describes the stylized galliard as follows: '*Galliards*, are Lessons of 2 or 3 Strains, but are per-form'd in a Slow, and Large Triple-Time; and (commonly) Grave and Sober.'[2] Lawes' galliards are all in bipartite form, and, as in the first and second movements, the *concertante*

---

[1] For the performance of this dance step see Mabel Dolmetsch, *Dances of England and France* (London: Routledge and Kegan Paul Ltd., 1949), Chapter VI.

[2] Mace, op. cit., p. 129.

technique plays a dominant role. Following the last movement, and after a first and second ending, Lawes adds a 'close' or *coda* in 4/4 metre. The length of this coda varies from five to eighteen bars, the majority being ten or twelve bars long. Undoubtedly the function of the *coda* was to balance the sonata by returning to the original rhythm of the beginning of the fantasia and to a more serious vein. Like the extended cadences of the large fantasias and aires for viols, after which these endings are modelled, the 'closes' are reserved for slow dissonant contrapuntal writing. The *coda* was not new with Lawes but, like almost all of the formal features of the composer's music, was handed down to him by his teacher, Coperario. The latter's *codas*, however, are considerably shorter and are not at all as convincing as his pupil's. It is interesting to note here that these 'closes' are the same type of endings which were later indicated by the markings 'slow' or 'drag' by Jenkins, Locke and Purcell.

The same features of Lawes' contrapuntal style which were found in the extended cadences of the five- and six-part fantasias and aires are in evidence in the *codas* of the violin sonatas. In particular, the mobility of part writing resulting in augmented and diminished triads or dissonant chords in various inversions is especially pronounced. The augmented triad is the most frequent of the dissonant combinations and may be found in a majority of the *codas* in some form.[1] One new and significant element which the composer introduces into some of the endings is the dominant seventh. The *coda* of the G major sonata is a fine illustration of Lawes' endings, for in it several of the composer's favourite progressions may be pointed out. The rare instance of an augmented triad in root position appears almost immediately, in the second bar of the 'close'. The harmonic rhythm has slowed to that of the semibreve and this sometimes gives rise to veritable clusters, like that in the second half of bar 4. As a result of suspensions the augmented triad in its second inversion appears in bar 8 and following this the introduction of a chromatic line in the bass leads to the familiar unprepared augmented triad in first inversion, which in its turn sets off the otherwise traditional four-three suspension cadence. But, not being satisfied with this, nor yet in the position to come to a full

---

[1] For an explanation of Lawes' use of the augmented triad see Chapter II, pp. 63–5.

close because of the key, Lawes prolongs it by taking the deceptive submediant, which in turn acts as a pivotal chord of the subdominant in returning to the original key of G major. He then continues into another consonant fourth, in the midst of which the dominant seventh is introduced, producing a second dissonance with the bass. The seventh holds in the penultimate bar as the fourth is resolved and then itself resolves as a true dominant seventh to the final tonic.

There naturally arises the temptation to compare Lawes' chamber sonatas with the *Twelve Sonatas of Three Parts* and the *Ten Sonatas of Four Parts* by Henry Purcell.[1] The comparison indicates how Purcell was endeavouring 'a just imitation of the most fam'd Italian Masters', as he himself wrote in the preface to the 1683 set. We know now, and most certainly Purcell knew, that the basis did exist for a characteristically English variety of the trio sonata. Even assuming that Purcell was not familiar with Lawes' music—and this assumption seems unlikely—there were the chamber sonatas of Purcell's fellow composer and good friend, Matthew Locke, besides those of other contemporary musicians. But Purcell, by his own evidence and that of his music, deliberately turned his back upon the already established tradition in favour of what he termed 'the power of the Italian Notes'. He also gives as his reason for composing the violin sonatas in the Italian vein, 'principally, to bring the seriousness and gravity of that sort of music into vogue'. Now, just a cursory examination of the sonatas of Coperario, Lawes, Jenkins, Locke and others shows more 'seriousness and gravity' than even the overall design of Purcell's sonatas indicates. Undoubtedly, Purcell was referring to the slight and frivolous dances so much in favour with Charles II, which the latter had grown accustomed to during his exile in France. Hence Purcell's admonition that it was high time 'our Country-men . . . should begin to loath the levity and balladry of our neighbours'. And yet, instead of seeking out and continuing the already established English tradition, which his genius could have greatly enhanced, Purcell sought further afield, finding his own model in the works of the Italians. Thus, he adopted Italian

[1] In *The Works of Henry Purcell* (London and New York: Novello, Ewer & Co.), Vol. V, ed. by Maitland, Vol. VII, ed. by Stanford, 1893 and 1896. The sonatas were first published in 1683 and 1697.

nomenclature, even to the substitution of the fantasia (now respectably English) by a canzona, and he imbued his works with the very spirit of the Italian art. While in his formal scheme and outward appearances Purcell capitulated to his weakness for 'the Italian Notes', in his contrapuntal and harmonic practices at least he remains essentially English. How much he was influenced by developments in the English chamber sonata during the seventeenth century will not be determined until a comparative study of several seventeenth-century sonata composers is attempted. Likewise, until the entire chapter dealing with the growth of the chamber sonata in England is written it will be impossible to determine the exact stature or importance of Lawes' sixteen sonatas. We may well suspect, however, and with good reason, that they deserve an important niche in the history of early instrumental music. Certainly, their worth as performance repertory for the present is considerable. They will without doubt be welcomed by chamber music lovers and players everywhere when finally they receive the light of publication.

VI

LYRA VIOL AND BASS VIOL SUITES

Notwithstanding the increasing popularity of the violin, the bass viol *da gamba* remained the leading solo instrument of the early Baroque. In his *Introduction to the Skill of Music*, Playford described three different sizes of these bass viols and as many styles of writing:[1]

'There are three sorts of *Bass-Viols*, as there are three manner of ways in playing. First, a *Bass-Viol* for *Consort* must be one of the largest size, and the strings proportionable.

'Secondly, a *Bass-Viol* for *Divisions* must be of a less size, and the strings according.

'Thirdly, a *Bass-Viol* to play *Lyra-Way*, that is by *Tableture*, must be somewhat less than the two former, and strung proportionably.'

The most common of the three types mentioned by Playford was the first, which was also known as the 'consort bass'. Its place was in the consort or full chamber group for the performance of *fancies* and *ayres* in parts. There, its large size was a decided advantage, providing depth for the group as a whole and adding a quiet richness to the music. Such an instrument would have been used in the performance of Lawes' five- and six-part fantasias and aires. While the music written for the consort bass sometimes attained a degree of virtuosity, it was for the most part restricted to moderate technical demands upon the performer and seldom exploited the higher registers or positions

---

[1] (1672 ed.), p. 93.

of the instrument. Thus, it was mainly confined to fugal imitations and low bass counterpoints, for which, of course, it was particularly well suited.

The 'division' bass viol, on the other hand, was used for a special type of solo or limited consort work. This instrument is best described by Christopher Simpson:[1]

'I would have a *Division-Viol* to be of something a shorter *size* than a *Consort-Basse*, that so the Hand may better command it; more or less short, according to the reach of his Fingers who is to use it: but the ordinary size, such as may carry a String of thirty Inches from the Bridge (duely placed) to the Nutt. The *Sound*, quick and sprightly, like a *Violin*; and *Viols* of that shape (the Bellyes being digged out of the Planck) do commonly render such a Sound. It must be *accomodated* with six strings; and seven Frets, like those of a *Lute*, but something thicker. The *Strings*, a little bigger than those of a *Lyra-Viol*, which must be laid at the like nearness to the Fingerboard, for ease and convenience of Stopping. The *Bridge*, as round as that of a *Consort-Basse*, that so each several String may be hit with a bolder touch of the Bow. The *Plate* or *Finger-board*, exactly smooth, and even. Its *Length*, full two parts of three from the Nutt to the Bridge. It must also be of a *proportionate* roundness to the Bridge, so that each String may lie at an equal nearness to it.'

The 'division' bass was especially popular for the performance of dance suites, in which, as we have already noted, there were usually several sets of variations upon the dance strains. These were sometimes written out by the composer, but more often performed *ex tempore*. After the middle of the seventeenth century the stylized dance was largely superseded by specially composed bass themes or '*grounds*' which served as the basis for the 'divisions'. In Lawes' music the 'division' viol would have been used for the *Royall Consort*, the '*Harpe*' *Consorts*, the *Violin Sonatas* and the *Bass Viol Suites*, in fact, for practically all of the composer's instrumental music, excluding the five- and six-part fantasias and aires and the *Lyra Viol Suites*. Because of its smaller size and the thinner strings, which lay close to the fingerboard, the 'division' viol was better suited than the consort bass for quick divisions and virtuoso passages in the higher reaches of the

[1] *The Division-Violist* (London: 1659), p. 2.

instrument. Since it was often paired in consort division with the violin it had to compete with it, and therefore, as Simpson observes, 'division' viols were often made in the shape of large violins or violoncellos in order to obtain a livelier tone.[1]

The third member of the bass viol group, the lyra viol, was perhaps the most demanding in technical skill. Its special sphere was the performance of polyphonic music in 'full stops' or chords, employing two or more strings at the same time. It is distinguished not only by its smaller size, which is about mid-way between that of a consort bass and a tenor viol, but also by the fact that it did not play from ordinary musical notation, resorting instead to the musical tablature of the lute family for greater ease in performance. Like the 'division' viol, for which it often substituted, it too found its literature in the dance suite of the period. The classic account of the lyra viol is given by Thomas Mace in his oft-quoted provisions for a complete 'chest' of viols. After enumerating the instruments which make up the usual viol consort, Mace calls for the addition of violins and theorboes, and then adds:[2]

'And now to make your store more *Amply-Compleat*; add to all these 3 *Full-Sciz'd Lyro-Viols*; there being most *Admirable Things* made, by our *Very Best Masters*, for *That Sort of Musick* both *Consort-wise*, and *Peculiarly* for 2 and 3 *Lyroes*. Let them be *Lusty, Smart-speaking viols*; because, that in *Consort*, they often *Retort* against the *Treble*; *Imitating*, and often *Standing instead of that Part*, viz. a *Second Treble*. They will serve likewise for *Division-Viols* very Properly.'

In order to facilitate the playing of double stops and chords the strings of the lyra viol were made thinner than either those of the consort bass or the 'division' viol, and like the latter, they lay closer to the fingerboard for ease in fingering. At the same time the bridge and fingerboard were somewhat flatter so that the bow might play on more than one string without too much pressure. Mace's reference to the fact that the lyra viol often took the part of a second treble clearly indicates the importance

---

[1] In the beginning of *The Division-Violist* Simpson gives an engraving of this type of 'division' viol besides one of the standard variety, and he states that the former is better for 'divisions'.

[2] Thomas Mace, *Musick's Monument* (London: 1676), p. 246.

of the highest string and the use of the high positions thereon. Nevertheless, the lyra viol employed all compasses, rapidly changing from the lowest notes on the bottom string to its extreme high register. In fact, the sudden shift of registers is a characteristic of lyra viol consorts, brought about by the fact that the instruments frequently trade parts, or as Christopher Simpson put it, 'the Parts do frequently mix and pass through one another'.[1] Thus, in the course of a single piece of music, or even a single melody, several abrupt permutations may occur permitting each part to shift suddenly and successively from treble to alto to tenor or to bass in any of a number of groupings. Whatever the part of the moment, the instrument was treated as such.

Just as at the beginning of the seventeenth century the lute experimented with new tunings to facilitate the playing of chords and technical passages and to explore new possibilities for added string colours and harmonies, so did the bass viol. According to Playford, it was because of the several tunings or *scordatura* that the lyra viol was so named:[2]

'The Lero or Lyra-Viol, is so called from the Latin word *Lyra*, which signifies a *Harp*, alluding to the various Tuning, under the name of Harp-way, etc. This way of playing on the *Viol*, is but of late invention, in imitation of the Old *English Lute* or *Bandora*, whose Lessons were prickt down by certain Letters of the Alphabet, upon six Lines or Rules; which six Lines did allude to the six course of strings upon those instruments, as they do now unto the Six single Strings upon the Viol.'

As Playford's account would seem to suggest, it was probably because of the various tunings as well as to facilitate the fingering of full stops that tablature was found more practical than regular notation. So that an unfamiliar tuning of the strings would not interfere with the technical execution of the music the performer was merely presented with a graphic picture of the finger positions and rhythm. Consequently, whatever emanated from the instrument was apparently just as much a

---

[1] Christopher Simpson, *A Compendium of Practical Musick* (London: 1667 ed.), p. 121.

[2] John Playford, *Musicks Recreation on the Lyra Viol* (London: 1669 ed.), preface.

Common Viol and Lute Tunings (1600 - 1650)

Consort Viols (old tunings)

Treble Viol

Alto Viol

Tenor Viol

*Bass Viol

Lyra Viols (new tunings)

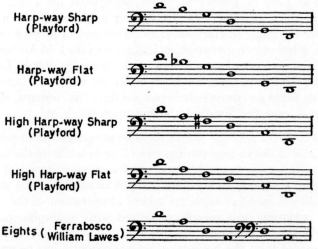

Harp-way Sharp
(Playford)

Harp-way Flat
(Playford)

High Harp-way Sharp
(Playford)

High Harp-way Flat
(Playford)

Eights (Ferrabosco
William Lawes)

*The Violone was tuned one octave lower than the Bass Viol

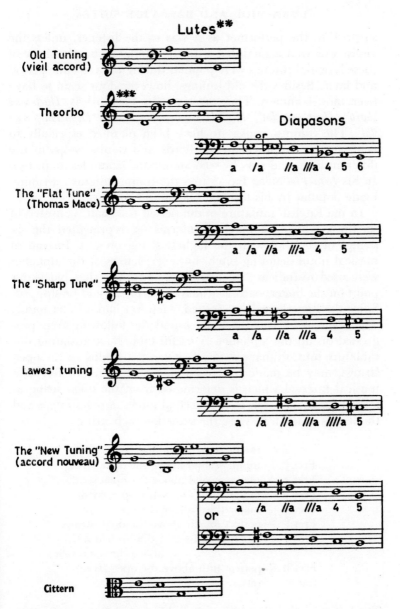

Lutes**

Old Tuning
(vieil accord)

Theorbo* ***

Diapasons

a /a //a ///a 4 5 6

The "Flat Tune"
(Thomas Mace)

a /a //a ///a 4 5

The "Sharp Tune"

a /a //a ///a 4 5

Lawes' tuning

a /a //a ///a ////a 5

The "New Tuning"
(accord nouveau)

a /a //a ///a 4 5

or

Cittern

** The Lute tunings are based upon the tuning of the diapason strings
which are given in ordinary notation by Thomas Mace.

*** The first string of the theorbo was often lowered an octave.

131

surprise to the performer as it was to the listener, unless the violist was well acquainted with the tuning at hand. Many of these lyra viol tunings were popular during the Caroline period and later. Besides the old tunings, however, four seem to have been most common. They are given by Playford as '*Harp-way sharp*', '*Harp-way flat*', '*High Harp-way sharp*', and '*High Harp-way flat*'. The tunings appear to have been planned especially to facilitate the employment of chords and double stops in the different keys, and may be seen among the examples on p. 130. In his *Lyra-Viol Suites* Lawes uses the tuning 'Eights', a tuning made popular by his teacher, Giovanni Coperario.

In the English tablature of the period the 'staff' consisted of six lines, which, as Playford informs us, represented the six strings of the viol with the highest string on top. Instead of musical notes denoting pitch, however, letters of the alphabet were used to indicate the fingering, or rather, that particular point on the fingerboard at which the string should be stopped. Since the fingerboard was fretted, each fret had a letter name. The open string was the letter *a* and the following frets progressed on up the alphabet. A useful table for translating this tablature into ordinary notation, given the tuning of the open strings, may be made by considering each letter or fret as a musical interval which is determined from the open string as follows (*N.B.* The frets were spaced at intervals of half steps and the letters of the frets were the same for each string):

> — a — the open string tuning.
> Fret b — minor second above the open string.
> Fret c — major second above the open string.
> Fret d — minor third above the open string.
> Fret e — major third above the open string.
> Fret f — perfect fourth above the open string.
> Fret g — augmented fourth (diminished fifth)
> above the open string
> Fret h — perfect fifth above the open string.
> (etc.)   (etc.)

The letter *j* was omitted from the tablature alphabet and *y* was sometimes substituted for *i*, as in lute tablature. The tablature staff was divided into bars by bar lines in the same manner as ordinary notation and the rhythm was placed above the staff in the form of musical notes denoting rhythm only. A time value, once placed above a letter on the staff, remained in effect for all following letters until a new rhythmic symbol was necessary. A time value with no letter on the staff below denoted a pause for that amount of time. For the performance of double stops and chords the letters were written vertically or under one another on the staff and a line under two or more letters could mean either a slur or a tie. (See Ex. 16, pp. 134-5, for an example of Lawes' tablature and its solution.)

In the preface to *Musick's Recreation on The Viol, Lyra-way* (1669 ed.), John Playford paid tribute to William Lawes as one of the 'famous masters' whose 'inventions and Skill' had helped to develop and to perfect the lyra viol notation and manner of performance. Exactly how Lawes contributed to this development is difficult to determine at this late date, but it is certain at least that in the field of lyra viol composition, as in practically all others of the period, the composer was intensely prolific. Significantly, Lawes' lyra viol pieces in Playford's publication are not at all representative of his major works for the instrument. Playford's book is a hodge-podge of transcriptions for the lyra viol of popular ballads, dances and common tunes of the period, made easy, as the publisher himself owns, for 'young Practitioners'. Consequently, although William Lawes is represented by ten pieces (1661 ed.), none of these is characteristic of the composer's true lyra viol style. One is merely a transcription of the song, 'Gather Y^e Rosebuds'; another, No. 71, is a transcription of a piece in the *Court-Ayres* of 1655 in which little if any adaptation for the lyra viol is present. The rest are short dance tunes, not unattractive, but not at all typical of Lawes' mature lyra viol works in manuscript. Likewise, the music by Lawes in Playford's *Musick's Delight on the Cithren* (1666) consists simply of popular and easy transcriptions of the composer's best known songs. They were not written expressly for the cittern. It is, in fact, doubtful that Lawes ever wrote music for that instrument. The cittern, however, was popular in England throughout the sixteenth and seventeenth centuries. Its literature was the common tunes, dances and ballads of the people. With but four pairs or 'courses' of wire strings it was simple to play and could be found hanging on the wall of many a London barber shop for the amusement of patrons. The instrument had an odd tuning which is included among those on p. 131.

William Lawes' lyra music falls rather into the category mentioned by Thomas Mace, i.e. '*Peculiarly* for 2 and 3 *Lyroes*'. Indeed, a complete volume of these larger works for the lyra viol is still extant in autograph.[1] However, a good indication of the contents of this autograph volume is furnished by a manuscript now in the library of Christ Church in Oxford. This manuscript, Ch. Ch. 725–7, contains three suites for '3 *Lero Vyalls*': the first, a 'Fantazia' and 'Serabrand'; the second, a 'ffantasie' and 'Almaine'; and the third, a 'Pavin' and an unnamed piece which appears to be an alman. These 'setts' are among the very best of Lawes' production, and in them one may catch an excellent view of true lyra viol writing: the frequent employment of double stops and chords, the use of the extreme high register, and the sudden shifting of parts between the instruments resulting in wide skips from one compass to another.

The most interesting of these pieces is the second 'ffantasie', which opens with a slow fugal section in the traditional manner:

Ex. 16

Lyra Viol Suite No. 2 in D minor
"ffantasie : second" for 3 Lyra Viols

---

[1] Unfortunately, this manuscript is not yet available for study.

Note here the employment of double stops and chords in which Lawes' dissonance technique figures prominently. The tablature is given above, inasmuch as it is not one of the common lyra viol tunings described by Playford but a tuning which Lawes calls 'Eights'. (For its solution see p. 130.) Another characteristic technique to be observed here is the use of unisons in double stops. Whenever open strings are indicated in the tablature they are almost always doubled in the unison by a stopped finger on an adjacent string. By this it may be seen how the violist endeavoured to achieve the utmost in resonance and power from his instrument. As the D minor fantasia progresses, contrasting *fugato* sections are introduced and beautifully contrived counterpoints weave a closely knit texture spanning the complete range of the instruments. This fantasia, in its formal scheme, is similar to the *Violin Sonata No. 8 in D Major* for one violin, bass viol and organ. It has three large sections in contrasting tempi and key signatures which are marked off by double bars. The middle section is in 3/4 and begins after an interesting half-cadence in D minor:

Ex. 17

136

The cadence is distinguished by an unusual polytonal combination in the penultimate measure of the first section, where a full G minor chord is suspended over the bar line while the pivotal chord of A major is introduced against it for the space of a minim leading into the second section in D major. In contrast to the opening *fugato* section the centre one is semi-homophonic. The tempo is fairly rapid and to all intents and purposes it is simply a stylized corant strain. Once more the intrusion of dance rhythms upon the fantasia is evident.

At the head of the composer's volume of autograph songs in the British Museum, Add. 31432, there are three pieces, apparently for one lyra viol, in the tuning of 'harp-way sharp'. Two are sarabands and the other, a corant. These are simple dance tunes and of no great significance. The first saraband, however, does contain a set of 'divisions', and thus substantiates the statement by Thomas Mace that the lyra viol might also substitute for a division viol. There are four additional pieces in tablature for lyra viols in manuscript in the Bodleian Library in Oxford, but these again are short dance tunes and warrant no further discussion.

In Lawes' autograph score in the Bodleian Library, Mus. Sch. B.2, are three pieces in tablature for two lutes. They consist of an alman and two corants and are the only pieces for the lute by William Lawes that the author has been able to locate. And yet, these works suggest a mature technique of lute composition. The tuning of the strings is not specified by Lawes but the process of decoding the tablature has resulted in the *accordatura* shown on p. 131. This tuning is interesting, since it is neither the 'sharp tune' nor the 'flat tune', both of which were most commonly employed during this period. Lawes' tuning is in fact a compromise between the two last. Its possibilities are evident in the seventh chord produced by the four highest strings, which Lawes uses to good advantage. These lute pieces are quite attractive and rather delicate, especially the first, entitled 'Alman'. The opening of this work together with its tablature is given overleaf.

In view of the maturity of technique and expression one wonders if this was the sum total of Lawes' writings for the lute. Is it possible that more of Lawes' music for lutes is still extant?

137

Ex. 18 First mov't, "Alman" (beginning excerpt)
from the Suite for Two Lutes

Or could there possibly have been another autograph volume containing the composer's lute works, just as there is one for the lyra viol suites?

The Suites for Two Bass Viols and Organ

William Lawes' debt to Coperario for the instrumental forms in which he wrote, is evident once again in the three suites for two 'division' basses and organ.[1] These bear a close resemblance to the large '*Harpe' Consorts* discussed in Chapter IV. Like the latter, their keyboard parts are fully written out and largely independent, and all of the pieces include 'divisions' of the most complex sort. In these Lawes reaches towards the very summit of viol virtuosity. Indeed, they are the most technically demanding of all of Lawes' music. The formal arrangement is the same

[1] Two of Coperario's pieces for two bass viols and organ are printed in *Musica Britannica* (London: Stainer and Bell Ltd.), Vol. IX, 1955, edited by Thurston Dart and William Coates. They are Nos. 100 and 101. Although entitled 'Fantasia', the second of these is in reality a pavan. See this piece discussed in Chapter IV, pp. 103–4.

as the *'Harpe' Consorts*, in that the first movement is in pavan form. However, in the ordering of movements there is no definite sequence as in either the suites of the *'Harpe' Consorts*, or those of the *Violin Sonatas*. The use of the pavan form instead of the fantasia may be explained by the fact that the former offered a greater opportunity for the composition of 'divisions', and, as has already been shown, the pavan was often substituted for a fantasia at the beginning of a chamber suite, especially when variations were intended.[1]

The order of the suites is as follows: Suite No. 1 in G Minor, consisting of a pavan and two aires; Suite No. 2 in C Major, a large pavan with but a single aire; and Suite No. 3 in C Major which appears to be incomplete, inasmuch as there are only two short aires, the first of which is minus a complete organ part. All of these pieces, together with their 'divisions', are in Lawes' hand in the Bodleian autograph score, Mus. Sch. B.2. They are also in autograph in the Bodleian part-books, Mus. Sch. D. 238–40, and in the organ book, Mus. Sch. D. 229. Suite No. 1 seems to have been fairly popular, since it has survived in several manuscripts in addition to the autographs, and in various arrangements as well. Interestingly enough it was re-arranged in two of the most important manuscript sources (though not in the autograph) of the *Royall Consort* and was actually included in those manuscripts as one of the collection. The latter arrangements, however, do not include the 'divisions' which are to be found only in the autograph. Opposite is the beginning excerpt of the original version of this pavan.

The final aire of this suite seems to have been especially well known and is, in fact, a charming example of the instrumental stylization of a dance. The middle movement was equally popular and was included by John Playford as No. 17 in the *Court-Ayres* of 1655. In that publication, however, there are only a treble and a bass, which are but the outside parts of the original organ score. Here once again we observe that what appear in Playford's collections as simple dance tunes 'of two parts, Treble and Basse, for Viols or Violins', are in reality mere skeletons of the composer's larger works which the publisher does not mention.

The title of the second suite is given by Lawes as follows:

[1] See the quote by Roger North in Chapter V, p. 107.

Ex. 19   First mov't, "Paven," (beginning excerpt) from the
         Suite No.1 in G minor for two Bass Viols and Organ

'*Paven and Alman of Alfonso—sett to the Organ and 2 Division Base Viols by W. L.*' 'Alfonso' is none other than Alfonso Ferrabosco junior, who was affectionately known by his Christian name in manuscripts and publications of the period. As in the large pavans of the '*Harpe*' Consorts, where Lawes uses bass themes by Giovanni Coperario and 'Cormacke' so here too Ferrabosco's bass line supports an elaborate set of variations for the viols. If the fact that Lawes employed a bass theme by 'Master Alfonso' is a sign that the two were good friends, it is difficult to say. There is as yet no definite proof to that effect. However, it does seem probable that Lawes should have known and even worked with Ferrabosco before the latter died, in 1627. Lawes' music shows the older master's influence to a marked degree, even as it does that of his teacher, Coperario. Furthermore, since all three were active in or about court circles at the same time, they could hardly have been unknown to one another.

The formal scheme of the 'division' viol suites adheres almost identically to the instructions set forth by Christopher Simpson in his *Division-Violist*. The full text of these is given in Appendix A, paragraphs 15 and 16. Likewise, it should be noted that the 'division' types, i.e. 'breakinge base', 'descant', 'mixt', 'skipping division', 'running division', 'tripla', etc., are the same as those in the *'Harpe' Consorts*, as are the 'ordering' of these types in the repeated strains discussed in Chapter IV. The chief

Ex. 20 **First mov't.,"Paven" from Suite No. 1 in G minor**
for two Bass Viols and Organ (repeat of 2nd strain with variations)

difference between the two collections is in the addition of the violin in the *'Harpe'* Consorts, where it is concerned primarily with 'descant', and not with 'breaking the ground', nor with 'breaking' the treble pavan melody of the harp part. Here all figuration upon the bass line was reserved for the bass viol since the bass was its 'proper sphere'. In the *Bass Viol Suites*, however, one of the two 'division' viols is often active in descanting to the bass, especially in the unvaried strains, while the other viol 'breaks' the 'ground' for it.[1]

The 'divisions' of the *Bass Viol Suites* are technically more difficult to perform than those of the *'Harpe'* Consorts. For the first time in Lawes' music the full compass up to d″ is exploited, and in rapid passages of semiquavers and even demisemiquavers. (The note d″, fourth line on the treble staff, is at the half-way mark between the bridge and the nut of the fingerboard. An additional fret was often tied at this point.) The complexity of this technique may be observed in the excerpt from the *'Paven'* of the first suite on pages 142–5.

The 'division' suites will be welcomed by modern cellists as well as bass violists and *gamba* players since the music is easily adaptable for the violoncello and will, moreover, present a challenging addition to the literature.

Miscellaneous Instrumental Pieces

In the course of the present work William Lawes' instrumental music has been presented exclusively under the headings of the original collections for which the music was intended. There are, however, well over two hundred additional instrumental pieces by the composer, mostly in dance forms, in various manuscripts and early publications of the period. Almost half of these are incomplete fragments. In addition, in the Bodleian Library, the library of Christ Church and in the British Museum, as well as smaller libraries, there are scores of manuscripts which contain hundreds of anonymous pieces. Many of these have been identified by the present author, in comparing manuscripts and autographs, as compositions by

---

[1] This is the same technique which Lawes used for the two bass viols in the *Royall Consort*. See the quote by Christopher Simpson in Chapter III, p. 74.

Lawes, though undoubtedly many anonymous pieces which I have not been able to identify are also by him.

One of the most popular instrumentations used in these miscellaneous dance pieces is that for two trebles and a bass. Sometimes the treble parts are indicated for violins and at others the instruments are not mentioned at all. Apparently, either treble viols or violins could be employed. This is of course the instrumentation of the Baroque trio sonata—equally popular in England as in Italy—which we have already seen employed in an arrangement of the *Royall Consort*, as well as in the *Violin Sonatas*. Twenty-one of Lawes' dances in this form are contained in the British Museum Add. MS. 31429.[1] Others are to be found in Add. 18940–44, Add. 31423 and in the library of St. Michael's College in Tenbury, MS. 302.

Several other pieces, in the original four-part version of the *Royall Consort*, but not actually a part of the latter collection, are also extant. Many of these have already been discussed in Chapter III as possibly belonging to the *Royall Consort* before it was rearranged. Twenty-three incomplete pieces, containing second treble and tenor parts only, are in the Bodleian, Mus. Sch. F.568–9, and six pieces in the same arrangement, but complete, are in Mus. Sch. E.431–6. In the latter set of manuscripts are similar pieces also by John Jenkins, Charles Coleman, Christopher Simpson, Benjamin Rogers and others.

The largest group of miscellaneous pieces are the familiar two-part, treble and bass dance arrangements, many of which were published by Playford in his simplified collections, especially in the *Court-Ayres* of 1655 and the *Courtly Masquing Ayres* of 1662. A large part of these, however, are not new but merely simplified transcriptions of Lawes' major works: several are from the composer's court masques or instrumental arrangements of his ballad songs. In all, about four score of these were printed by Playford. The bass part only to forty-six additional pieces, which were apparently in two parts, is also extant in the Bodleian, Mus. Sch. D.220, and twelve more bass parts are in

---

[1] The statement by Rupert Erlebach, 'William Lawes and His String Music', *Proceedings of the Musical Association*, 59th session, 1932–3, p. 111, that only two of these pieces are by Lawes must be set aside in the light of the positive identification of most of the pieces with the same music attributed to the composer in other manuscripts.

both Mus. Sch. E.451 and D.233-6. The latter also contains copies of pieces from the *Royall Consort* and twenty-five two-part pieces, most of which are duplicates of dance tunes in the above publications.

The few remaining pieces are mostly keyboard arrangements of dance tunes which were originally intended for viols and violins. Eight of these are contained in Playford's *Musick's Hand-maide, Presenting New and Pleasant Lessons For The Virginals or Harpsycon*, 1663. Included is the very popular suite entitled *Golden Grove* which may also be found in Oxford, Christ Church, MSS. 1236 and 1003. Finally, in a manuscript now in the Paris Conservatory, Res. 1185, is another charming suite arranged for keyboard and containing a set of variations.

VII

THE SONGS

IT is certainly in the field of chamber music that William Lawes has made his greatest contribution. Yet, he is chiefly remembered for his delightful setting of Robert Herrick's 'Gather Y^e Rosebuds While Y^e May'. It was, in fact, as a musician in ordinary 'ffor ye lutes and voices' that Lawes received his court appointment in 1635. His vocal output was second only to that of his brother, Henry, who was six years William's senior and outlived him by seventeen years. William's songs, dialogues, catches and glees were a favourite of the many Playford publications which appeared after the middle of the century. They were known and beloved by the great diarist, Samuel Pepys, and were accorded a prominent place in song books as late as 1678, when Henry Purcell was almost a lad of twenty.[1] Like Henry Lawes too, William worked in close association with the foremost poets and wits of the age: Robert Herrick, Thomas Carew, James Shirley, William Davenant and the rest, many of whom continued to celebrate his obsequies long after his demise. This extended popularity in the face of musical developments which occured after his death accords to William Lawes an important position in the vocal music of the century.

The bulk of Lawes' songs has never been published. The chief

---

[1] Sixteen of William Lawes' songs were included in the *New Ayres and Dialogues*, edited by John Banister and Thomas Low (London: 1678). Samuel Pepys refers to Lawes' songs and psalms several times in his *Diary* (see Chapter I, p. 38).

source for these is his vocal autograph in the British Museum, Add. 31432, which is from the same set of autograph volumes as those in the Bodleian Library in Oxford.[1] The famous John Gamble Commonplace Book and the Drexel manuscript 4041, both in the New York Public Library, are the other major sources. If we add to these the autograph of John Wilson's songs in the Bodleian Library, the Beaconsfield autograph of Henry Lawes' works and the British Museum, Add. 11608, we have all of the important manuscript sources for Caroline song. It is from these and the many English song books published by Playford and others after the middle of the century that a composite picture of the various forms, styles and characteristics of vocal music composed during the reign of Charles I may be formed.

Caroline song was dominated by an intellectual creation, the declamatory style, or, as it was called in contemporary musical and literary circles, 'recitative musick'. It would be a mistake, however, to overemphasize the mass popularity or appeal of the declamatory song, even in its hey-day. It was an exclusive art form designed for a small *coterie* of intellectual nobility, poets, wits, musicians and artists who adorned the sophisticated chambers of the Court. Indeed, several distinct types of song were equally, or even more popular with the middle and upper classes of English society. A gentleman had occasion to sing the bawdiest of catches, glees or drinking songs at his favourite ale-house, or to hum a composed 'ballad' while at work, to sing part-songs and psalms with his family as well as to listen to the performance of 'dialogues' and solo 'recitative musick'. Madrigals too were still beloved and rounds, canons and religious songs were always in fashion. All of these made up the vocal music of the period and were the stock-in-trade of every composer.

The declamatory and other forms of English song were the result of several forces at work during the first decades of the century. They were not, as Milton states, the invention of one man, Henry Lawes.[2] William Lawes, John Wilson, Simon Ives,

---

[1] See the discussion of Lawes' autographs in Chapter I, pp. 29–33.

[2] In his commendatory verse 'To my Friend Mr. Henry Lawes', in the *Choice Psalmes* of 1648, by William and Henry Lawes (London: Printed by James Young for Humphrey Moseley).

Charles Coleman, John Gamble and many others were setting verse in precisely the same manner at precisely the same time.[1] All were subject to new styles emanating from the humanistic revivals in France and Italy, to the great heritage bequeathed by the English madrigal and lutenist schools, to the changing ideals and dominating position of English poetry in the wake of Will Shakespeare and Ben Jonson, and to the demands of the society in which they lived and worked.

The reign of Charles I (1625–49) roughly bridges the gap between the last of the lutenist publications (John Attey's *Ayres*, 1622) and the first printed editions of the declamatory song-writers (Henry Lawes' *Select Ayres and Dialogues*, 1652). During this time no lute-song literature was published in England, despite the fact that poets and musicians were undergoing a period of intense productivity. The object of this productivity, however, was not the lutenist 'ayre', but the newer forms—declamatory songs, 'ballads', dialogues, catches and glees. Playford's many song books published after Charles' death are, in fact, a reflection of the fertility of this period, and the declamatory style itself is a product of this age, although it extended well into the Restoration. Since William Lawes' vocal works fall entirely within this period, they are important for any study of Caroline vocal music.

As the vogue of the lutenist 'ayre' sharply declined at the beginning of the second decade of the seventeenth century, the relationship of music and poetry was undergoing a radical change. In the madrigal, music had been the most important element; in the lute-song an almost perfect balance between the music and the text was achieved; and now, in the declamatory song, it was the poetry which dominated the music. This underlying shift in the relative importance of the text reflects the increasing stature of the poet in the artistic circles of the time. It represents as well a fundamental difference between the circumstances of song composition in the Renaissance and in the Baroque. Lutenist, as well as madrigal, composers largely composed their own lyrics. Indeed, many were known as musical-poets and the lyric itself had always been considered the natural

[1] See, for example, the comment by Ernest Walker, *A History of Music in England*, 3rd ed., revised and edited by J. A. Westrup (Oxford University Press, 1952), p. 162.

province of the musician. Lyrics were intended to be sung.[1] But with the increased interest on the part of literary men in Classical and Roman lyric forms during the Baroque, a gradual process of specialization set in. A generation of minor poets and dramatists, who were non-musicians, assiduously cultivated the now-popular lyric style. Many of these poets were well aware of the need for good musical settings of their works. Even an aristocratic public, apparently, might be influenced by the fact that some reputable musician had thought enough of a particular lyric to set it to music. Consequently, when poets published editions of their works they often included the name of the musical composer either under the title of each poem or on the title page of the publication itself, although no music was included.[2] Musicians rarely included the names of their poets, either in their manuscripts or in their publications.

The close association of musicians and literary men through the conditions of their employment at the great manor houses of the nobility and at Court undoubtedly had much to do with the emergence of the declamatory style. In a new era of Court splendour and hyperculture, with its influences from abroad, both poet and musician sought a new approach which would satisfy the intellectual tastes of their sophisticated patrons. Many of the aristocrats were themselves poets of some skill. Fewer were real musicians. The art which they paid for was one which suited their own particular talents. Ever anxious to please his patron, the Caroline musician did not hesitate to subject purely musical considerations to the new literary ideals. These same circumstances account for the 'horseloads' of 'lessons' or short dance tunes of little consequence which clutter up the manuscripts of the period. Only in the larger forms of instrumental music could the composer give free reign to his creative imagination. Only these rise above the demands of the occasion and are certain to outlast the superficiality of those sophisticated years. Henry Lawes is himself the perfect example of one who worked almost entirely to satisfy the tastes of

[1] For an interesting account of lyric poetry and its association with music see Bruce Pattison, *Music and the Poetry of the English Renaissance* (London: Methuen & Co. Ltd., 1948), p. 19 and passim.

[2] See, for example, Richard Lovelace's *Lucasta* (London: 1649), Edmund Waller's *Poems* (London: 1645) and Milton's *Poems* (London: 1645).

Jacobean and Caroline culture. For his efforts he was lauded
and eulogized by the foremost poets of the age, and raised to a
pre-eminent position in Court circles—but he wrote no serious
instrumental music.

Just as the madrigal and the lutenist 'ayre' could no longer
satisfy the delicate, pseudo-intellectual refinement of the aristocracy, so too Elizabethan poetry had to be abandoned as a
model for the Caroline poet and as a source for the Caroline
musician. With the ascendancy of Herrick, Carew, Davenant,
Shirley and a host of others, the lyric came into its own in new
forms and with new content. The predominant theme of Caroline poetry was love—love embellished by allegory and meta-
phorical reference to Greek and Roman mythology. Pastoral
themes were also popular and shepherds and shepherdesses often
converse with Charon, Orpheus or Venus in the many dialogues
of the period. Literature of the Augustan Age in particular was
the great source to which the English men of letters turned for
their inspiration. Horace, Ovid and Virgil were avidly studied
and copied. Their works were translated anew and paraphrased
in simplified forms by such scholars as Caxton and Lydgate and
widely disseminated in cultural circles. But although the Caroline poets used these models for their lyrics, the tone of their
writing is not the same. Themes are slight and the poetry takes
on a frivolous character as the myths succumb to courtly
sophistication and humour. Love, in the person of Cupid
(chaperoned by Mother Venus), runs rampant and the pro-
verbial arrow is dulled through overuse. Thus, mythological
hyperbole mars the success of many lyrics which might otherwise be tolerable. Indeed, the best lyrics of the period are those
which employ the least reference to Greek and Roman deities.[1]

The Caroline poet no longer followed the rigid metres and
stanzaic forms of his predecessors, and the musician, playing a
subordinate role, was faced with the problem of meeting the
aesthetic requirements of the new poetry. The content of
Caroline verse in particular posed a serious problem since it
allowed little scope for the composer's imagination. Many of the
lyrics of this period are too well thought out and tightly packed

[1] For a good account of the influence of mythology on English poetry of
the period see Douglas Bush, *Mythology and the Renaissance Tradition in English
Poetry* (University of Minnesota Press, 1932).

to allow room for musical interpretation. Each word seems to have been carefully weighed for its narrative, descriptive or emotional effect. The logical and continuous character of the verse often led to its being incorporated entirely into one large stanza and necessitated some form of through-composition rather than strophic treatment in the musical setting. Declamatory songs, however, were set both ways, depending upon the degree of logical continuity involved. Poems in regular metre, and in stanzaic form, containing a high degree of self-sufficiency between the stanzas, were made into composed 'ballads' in strophic form.[1]

English declamatory song was an attempt on the part of the Cavalier composer to portray to the fullest possible extent the meaning of his poet's words in a single declaimed musical line, and to imitate as closely as possible the oratorical nature of their delivery in actual recitation. It was frankly modelled after the declamatory principles of the Italian recitative and influenced by earlier developments in France, but it was beset with problems of its own in matters of technique, temperament, metre, style, stress, language, form and subject matter. Indeed, it differed from its foreign counterparts in being a more intellectual attempt at declamation, concerned more with the 'sense' of the words than with their emotional impact. The *meaning of the text* was at the very core of the declamatory song-writer's aesthetic considerations and it determined the composer's choice of techniques as well. Interesting melody was of less importance. To bring out the meaning of his text the Caroline musician employed two basic techniques. The first of these was the use of various types of stress or emphasis on important words, paying particular attention to the degree of stress required. This was accomplished through the use of (1) greater or lesser duration of note values, (2) varying degrees of pitch, especially large leaps in the melody, (3) the effective employment of pauses or rests, (4) the repetition of words, (5) affective melodic intervals, and (6) bar-accented notes. Any combination of the foregoing might also be employed for added stress. Harmonic emphasis as well as other forms of complementary emphasis in the accompaniment was rare.

[1] Further to this see Eric Ford Hart, 'Introduction to Henry Lawes', *Music and Letters*, Vol. XXXII, No. 3 (July 1951), pp. 222–4.

The second means by which the Cavalier song-writer attempted to portray his poet's meaning was through pictorial expression of motion, emotion and dimension. This was conveyed *via* 'word-painting', or as it is sometimes called, 'eye-music'. Caroline composers were especially fond of this technique. Indeed, it was their heritage from the great madrigal school. Madrigal composers were very careful about 'framing' music 'to the life of the words', as Byrd states in his introduction to the *Psalmes, Songs, and Sonnets* of 1611. Thomas Morley devoted considerable space to the same subject in his *A Plaine and Easie Introduction to Practicall Musick* in 1597:[1]

'Moreover you must have a care that when your matter signifieth "ascending", "high", "heaven", and such like you make your music ascend; and by the contrary where your ditty speaketh of "descending", "lowness", "depth", "hell", and others such you must make your music descend.'

Morley also has much to say about the emotional character of various musical intervals, melodically as well as harmonically. According to the theorist, diatonic notes and progressions signify 'cruelty, tyranny, bitterness, hardness, and such others'. Chromatic intervals 'may fitly express the passions of grief, weeping, sighs, sorrows, sobs, and such like'. The pictorial representation of motion is also treated:

'Also if the subject be light you must cause your music go in motions which carry with them a celerity or quickness of time, as minims, crotchets, and quavers; if it be lamentable the notes must go in slow and heavy motions as semibreves, breves, and such like; and all this you shall find examples everywhere in the works of the good musicians.'

Finally, he goes on to give his views regarding accentuation and presents us with a pretty sound English basis for this principle:

'We must also have a care so as to apply the notes to the words as in singing there be no barbarism committed; that is that we cause no syllable which is by nature short be expressed by many notes or one long note, nor no long syllables be expressed with a short note.'

[1] New edition edited by R. Alec Harman with a foreword by Thurston Dart (London: J. M. Dent & Sons Ltd., 1952), pp. 290–2.

All of the foregoing techniques are essentially those of the Caroline declamatory song-writer applied horizontally rather than vertically. Morley, it seems, was as much a prophet of the new age as he was a historian of the old.

Complementary to the composer's efforts to express the meaning of his poet's words was his attempt *to represent the oratorical nature of poetic delivery*. This was accomplished through the somewhat strict observance of four regulatory principles which placed restrictions upon the free flow of both the rhythm and the melody of declamatory song. The first and most important of these is the close patterning of the musical rhythm after the natural rhythms of declaimed speech. Thus, the syllabic rhythm follows closely that of the declaimed text, attributing longer note-values to accented syllables and shorter note-values to weak syllables. It often takes precedence over the metre of both the poetry and the music, and sometimes gives rise to a syncopated treatment of certain words which is a hallmark of the style.[1] The second regulatory principle is the musical approximation of the natural intervals of voice inflection, co-ordinated, wherever possible, with speech rhythm, metre and stress. It is this principle at work which is responsible for the lack of direction and somewhat angular character of the melodic line, and which therefore restricts the tunefulness of the music. Contributing to this lack of interest on the part of the melody is the third regulatory principle, the incisive marking or punctuation of phrases by long note-values and frequent cadences. It is this which Tovey had in mind when he criticized Henry Lawes' declamatory songs for tending to 'overpunctuate the words and interrupt the flow of the music'.[2] The 'end-stopping' of phrases or lines is practically mandatory, especially on the last words of rhyming verses, and leads to the perfunctory introduction of stock cadences which close with a minim or semibreve, thus cutting a work up into many small segments which may not be at all regular. Often one feels that something interesting is about to happen musically and suddenly finds his expectations frustrated by the 'overpunctuation' of a line or

[1] See, for example, the setting of the words 'lover', 'move her', 'win her', 'sinner', etc., on Ex. 31, pp. 201–2.

[2] Sir Donald Tovey, 'Words and Music', in *Seventeenth Century Studies Presented to Sir Herbert Grierson* (Oxford University Press, 1938), p. 350.

phrase, much in the manner in which the elementary school boy pulls up at the end of his lines in recitation.

Finally, the fourth regulatory principle is the metre of the poetry itself. Ideally, this was to coincide with that of the music, and with the demands of stress, speech rhythm, voice inflection and the marking or 'punctuation' of phrases. This was indeed a large order for the composer to fulfil. It was further complicated by the demands of the recent introduction of bar-lines in music of the period, resulting in the added restriction of the bar-accent.[1] The bar-accent, although it had not yet become rigid, did introduce a new problem for the declamatory song-writer. Lutenist and madrigal composers had only to observe the metre of their poetry. Now the composer had to consider the metre of the music as well, and still prove true to the principles of accentuation. One must not, however, overestimate the influence of the bar-accent at this time. Bar-lines and barring were not regular in the manuscripts and publications of the period. Many 'ballads', for example, were written in double-length bars when introducing a *hemiola* rhythm which necessitated the absence of a bar-accent. The metre of the poetry was also an important factor in determining whether or not a song was to be set as a declamatory piece or as a 'ballad'. Dactylic metres were favoured for the latter as were many of the poems containing some metrical variety. Declamatory song was almost always fashioned from verses employing iambic or trochaic feet. All of the foregoing principles and techniques will be shown in application as we enter into a discussion of William Lawes' songs.

One hundred and thirty-six of William Lawes' secular vocal works have thus far been identified. This number does not include any of the music for the composer's masques, nor does it incorporate the many anonymous works in manuscripts and publications of the period, which so closely resemble Lawes' style.[2] Vocal styles during this period are so similar that guessing is a hazardous game at best. It would therefore be better to await positive identification before attributing anonymous

[1] Eric Ford Hart, op. cit., p. 225. See also the discussion by H. C. Colles, *Voice and Verse, a Study of English Song* (Oxford University Press, 1928), pp. 61–5.

[2] The masque music is discussed in Chapter IX.

works to certain composers.[1] Of the total figure quoted above, sixty-nine songs are for solo voice and a thorough-bass, the latter presumably intended for the theorbo-lute or bass viol. Eleven songs are 'dialogues', one is a 'trialogue', and five are part-songs in madrigal style for from three to five voices. Of the remaining pieces, five are glees of two parts, seven are three-voice drinking songs and thirty-six are catches or rounds in from two to six parts. For two additional pieces the words only are extant.[2] Moreover, three of the madrigals and one of the solo songs are incomplete. Of the sixty-nine solo songs with *continuo*, thirty are in declamatory style, twenty-one are composed 'ballads' and dance songs, and eighteen are in a bipartite 'recitative-ballad' form, beginning in declamatory style and ending as 'ballads'.

Lawes' autograph volume of secular songs in the British Museum, Add. 31432, contains sixty-one of these works, including forty-nine solo *continuo* songs, six dialogues, the lone 'trialogue' and five of the three-part drinking songs.[3] The autograph in the Bodleian Library at Oxford, Mus. Sch. B.2, has the

---

[1] Such is the case, e.g., with the song 'Balow my babe' suggested as Lawes' by Vincent Duckles, 'The Gamble Manuscript as a Source of Continuo Song in England', *Jnl. of the Am. Musicol. Soc.*, Vol. I, No. 2 (Summer 1948), p. 37. Also the anonymous song 'Come, come away . . .' in Playford's *A Musicall Banquet* (1651), part iii, No. 10, claimed to be by Lawes by J. P. Cutts, 'British Museum Additional MS. 31432, William Lawes' writing for Theatre and Court', *The Library*, Fifth Series, Vol. VII, No. 4 (December 1952), p. 231. I have found neither of these two songs attributed to William Lawes in any of the manuscripts or publications of the period. John Stafford Smith, in his *Musica Antiqua* (London: 1812), p. 207, wrongly attributes Henry Lawes' 'If My Mistress Fix Her Eye' (*Ayres and Dialogues*, 1653, p. 18) to William.

[2] Richard Lovelace, in his *Lucasta* (London: 1649), indicates under the titles of three of his poems that the music was set by William Lawes. The music to one of these, ascribed to William Lawes, the 'Sonnet', 'When I By Thy Faire Shape', is in the New York Public Library, in the John Gamble Commonplace Book (1659). The other two are those referred to above. See Appendix C, p. 278, for titles.

[3] The Hughes-Hughes *Catalogue of Manuscript Music in the British Museum* lists in all sixty-two songs in Add. 31432. The first two pieces in the manuscript, however, are one and the same song, 'A hall a hall' from John Suckling's *The Tragedy of Brennoralt*. Unfortunately, J. P. Cutts, while noting the identification, has insisted on numbering these items separately in his list of the autograph's contents, op. cit., p. 227.

madrigals and fourteen of the catches.[1] In addition, fifteen of
the composer's songs not found elsewhere are in the Drexel
manuscript 4041 in the New York Public Library. Also in New
York are five additional works, in the John Gamble Commonplace Book. The rest of Lawes' songs are distributed among
minor manuscript sources and in several of the Playford miscel-
lanies published after the composer's death. Many of the
catches, dialogues and songs are in Hilton's *Catch that Catch Can*
(1652) and in the various editions of John Playford's *A Musicall
Banquet* (1651), *Select Ayres and Dialogues* (1652), (1653), *Musick's
Recreation on the Lyra Violl* (1652), (1661), *Musick's Delight on the
Cithren* (1666), *The Musical Companion* (1667), (1673), and *The
Treasury of Musick* (1669).[2] The last-named work is devoted
largely to Henry Lawes' songs, but William also figures prominently with nineteen works. Of the latter, two appear anonym-
ously and three are wrongly attributed to Henry Lawes, as are
one each to Nicholas Laniere, Simon Ives and Alphonso Marsh.[3]
Apparently, Playford's memory was failing, for among the
anonymous and wrongly-attributed songs are some of William
Lawes' finest vocal works, including the beautiful 'Amarilis',
Herrick's 'On The Lillyes', Ben Jonson's 'Still to bee Neate, Still
to bee Dresst', and the very fetching, 'Upp Ladies Upp'. The last
publication to contain Lawes' songs in any quantity was the
New Ayres and Dialogues of 1678, edited by John Banister and
Thomas Low. In it are sixteen of Lawes' choice songs.

Thus far, the texts to only forty-seven of the total one hundred
and thirty-six secular songs have been identified with their

---

[1] Twelve catches by William Lawes are printed in score by Edward
F. Rimbault, *The Rounds, Catches and Canons of England* (London: 1865),
pp. 30–5.

[2] For further discussion of all of these publications see the remarks in
Chapter I, pp. 33–38.

[3] The songs attributed wrongly to Henry Lawes are 'Amarilis', 'Pleasure's
Bewty Youth Attend Yee' from John Ford's *The Lady's Trial* (1639), and
'That Flame is Born of Earthly Fire'. Erroneously ascribed to Nicholas
Lanier is Herrick's 'On the Lillyes'; to Simon Ives, 'Love's Affection' ('Be
Not Proud Pretty One') and to Alphonso Marsh, 'Cupid's Progress' ('Upp
Ladies Upp'). The two anonymous works which are really by William
Lawes are 'Faith Be Noe Longer Coy' and 'On A Proud Lady' ('Still to bee
Neate, Still to bee Dresst') from Ben Jonson's *Epicoene: The Silent Woman*
(1609).

poets.[1] Moreover, eighteen of the identified texts are from the drama of the period. They and their music will be discussed in the next chapter. Of the remaining twenty-nine identified texts, seven are from Robert Herrick's *Hesperides* (1648), four are from James Shirley's *Poems* (1646); three poems are by William Davenant, one from *Madagascar* (1638), and two are found in his *Works* published in 1673. Three poems also are from Richard Lovelace's *Lucasta* (1649),[2] two from Thomas Carew's *Poems* (1640), and one each from John Tatham's *Ostella* (1650), William Herbert's *Poems of Pembroke and Ruddier* (1660), John Suckling's *Fragmentea Aurea* (1646), Henry Glapthorne's *Argalus and Parthenia* (1639), Edmund Waller's *Poems* (1645), and William Cartwright's *Comedies, Tragi-Comedies, with other Poems . . .* (1651). Additional poems are by Thomas Cary, Andrew Marvell and William Browne.[3] One text also is apparently by William Lawes himself, that of the elegy, 'On The Memory of My Friend, John Tomkins'.[4] It is possible too that many of the texts of the catches in particular are by the composer, but this is not known for certain.

The identification of these texts is of some literary importance. The death of William Lawes in 1645 places the composition of the poetry prior to that date, thus enabling literary scholars to approximate the composition dates of some of these poems more closely. Such is the case, for example, with Marvell's 'A Dialogue between Thyrsis and Dorinda', Shirley's 'To His Mistress' ('I would The God of Love Would Dye'), and all seven of the Herrick poems. It has been pointed out that the period between 1632 and 1651 is a difficult one for scholars engaged in the study of poems and their settings. Since 1632 is the latest date covered by E. H. Fellowes in his work on madrigal verse, and the bibliography of the English Song Books by Day and Murrie does not begin until 1651, Lawes' settings are all the more important even from a purely literary point of

---

[1] Coincident with my identification several were identified by J. P. Cutts, op. cit. The list in Appendix C, however, supersedes that printed by Mr. Cutts.

[2] The music to only one of these is extant. See footnote 2, p. 158.

[3] For the titles of all these poems, see Appendix C.

[4] Tomkins, brother of Thomas Tomkins and organist of His Majesty's Chapel Royal, was a close friend of Lawes' and died in 1638.

view.[1] A further and perhaps more important significance of the texts used by Lawes concerns the matter of earlier textual variants. Many of the poems used by the composer differ slightly in their reading from those in published collections by their poets. A few even differ to some great extent, immediately raising the question as to whether or not these texts are, in fact, early versions of the poets' works. This matter has been treated at some length in an exchange of articles between Miss Margaret C. Crum and Mr. John P. Cutts, wherein several of the texts in British Museum, Add. 31432, and their variants in published editions have been presented and discussed.[2] It is certainly true, as Miss Crum has shown, that in many cases slight textual changes were made by the composer himself for purely musical reasons. As Miss Crum also indicates, other variants may be the result of careless transcription or faulty memory. Nevertheless, a few undoubtedly represent earlier versions of the poetry than have hitherto been known. Still others may well be entirely spurious. It remains for the literary scholar to sort these poems out and to assimilate this new information into any future writings concerning them, and their poets.

In his vocal works William Lawes was undoubtedly influenced by the Italian monodists, but the intense emotional and expressive *affeti* of the latter are not one of his most characteristic features. At least one of his declamatory songs, however, is equal to the best of its Italian models and is certainly the most successful English attempt in that vein. This is probably the composer's finest song, 'Amarilis'. The author of the text of this piece is unknown, but the words are particularly well suited to the affective style. Neither Caccini nor Monteverdi exceeded the depth and pathos of its expression and the beauty of its phrases. Here is a song 'well worth an Englishman's transcribing':

[1] Margaret C. Crum, 'Notes On The Texts of William Lawes' Songs in B.M. MS. Add. 31432', *The Library*, 5th Series, Vol. IX, No. 2 (June 1954), p. 122. The works referred to are E. H. Fellowes, *English Madrigal Verse 1588–1632* (Oxford, 1920), and C. L. Day and E. B. Murrie, *English Song Books, 1651–1702* (London: 1940).

[2] Crum, op. cit., and Cutts, op. cit. Miss Crum's article is especially good.

Ex. 21

Amarilis

Am-a-ril-is teare thy haire, beate thy brest sigh weep dis-
-paire, cry, cry, Ay mee, Is Daph-nis dead I see a
pal - nes on his brow and his cheeks are drownd in snowe whither
whith-er, whith-er are those ros- es fled,—— O 'my hart how
cold, how cold he's growne, sure his Lipps are turn'd to stone,

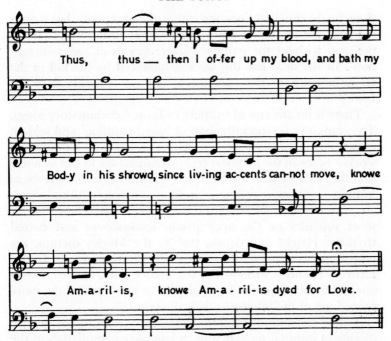

Thus, thus — then I of-fer up my blood, and bath my Bod-y in his shrowd, since liv-ing ac-cents can-not move, knowe — Am-a-ril-is, knowe Am-a-ril-is dyed for Love.

'Amarilis' is a fine illustration of the employment of several declamatory techniques. The opening phrase immediately mirrors the natural speech-rhythm and voice inflection of the words and the leap of a large seventh on a strong beat excellently serves the purposes of added stress and of pictorial as well as emotional representation. Pauses are used with telling effect to frame the words 'cry', 'whither' and 'thus'. The last is heightened further in being combined with repetition, another means of added stress. The standard Italian exclamation, 'Ay mee', receives the 'affective' interval and this is lengthened to a minim for added emphasis. Speech-rhythm is also neatly captured in words like 'Amarilis', 'whither', 'dis-paire', 'palness'. Note also the consistent treatment in voice inflection of 'Amarilis'. The pictorial and emotional elements in 'beate thy breast' and 'living accents', the hardness of the diatonic run in A minor at the words 'sure his lipps are turn'd to stone', the shivering of 'cold', the actual reproduction of a sigh—all are vividly realistic in creating a spellbinding aura of grief and icy death. The incisive marking of phrases is evident here too, but these finely chiselled lines are rather the exception that proves the rule, for the music flows convincingly from one phrase to the next without the irritating interruptions of 'overpunctuation'. In the final bar the work is balanced by the fall of the major seventh to the conclusion, 'knowe Amarilis dyed for Love'.

There is no attempt at subtlety in Lawes' declamatory songs. The composer is especially fond of 'word-painting' and seldom misses an opportunity to indulge in it, even in his religious works.[1] Some of the pictorial representations are in fact so naive that they call forth a chuckle. Such obvious locomotion verbs as 'running', 'flying', 'rolling', 'rocking', 'tossing', 'thundering', etc., are temptations which he can never resist. These call for short roulades in the appropriate semiquavers and dotted rhythms. Height and depth, true to the Morley dictum, are subject to ascending or descending intervals respectively. In this Lawes is simply a successor of the madrigalists. Indeed, it was one of the techniques of late polyphonic music which the more refined art of the lutenists rebelled against.[2]

A chief criticism of English declamatory song will always be its lack of inspired melody and its complete capitulation to the poetry. In his efforts to portray to the utmost the meaning of the words the Caroline composer frankly abandoned melody as an important criterion. William Lawes was no exception. Often, as in his 'O Let Me Still and Silent Lye', a song is begun with an interesting melodic phrase only to wander off in stereotyped clichés. Cavalier poetic practices, such as 'end-stopping', generally require a cadence at the end of each line or phrase. These, being short and often irregular, produce the sensation that one has barely begun a musical phrase before it is arrested by cadence. There is no musical development from one short phrase to the next, since each line has its own problems of stress, pictorial content, speech-rhythm, voice inflection, metre, etc. Then too, the well-developed thought, description and

[1] See, e.g., Chapter X, Ex. 41, pp. 253–5.
[2] Already in 1601 Thomas Campion and Phillip Rosseter, in the preface to *A Booke of Ayres*, criticized music in which '. . . everie word is precisely expresst in the Note, like the old exploded action in Comedies, when if they did pronounce Memeni, they would point to the hinder part of their heads, if Video, put their finger in their eye'.

action of each line leave little for the imagination of the composer or for purely musical considerations. The product was already moulded in the poetry. The musician had but to brighten it—if he could.

In his efforts to emboss the text Lawes reduced the accompaniment to a single unfigured bass line. This was an abrupt departure from the highly elaborate and integrated accompaniments of the lutenists, but in keeping with the practices of Italian monody. It was followed by all of the declamatory song-writers, even in their 'ballads' and other vocal forms. While Lawes does not specify which instrument shall play the *continuo*, there is little doubt that the theorbo was first choice. The Playford publications often call for songs 'to be sung to the Theorbo-Lute or Bass Violl'. From the instrumental accompaniments of songs in such printed collections as *Musick's Recreation on the Lyra Violl* (1652), (1661) and *Musick's Delight on the Cithren* (1666) it is also clear that the realizations of these bass lines were kept as unobtrusive as possible, with but one or two chords to a bar and little movement in the inner parts. The *continuos* themselves indicate the simplest of harmonies and contain little motion or imitation of the vocal line. Thus, the accompaniment merely sets the mood for the declamation.

It is in the composed 'ballad' or 'air' that we recognize Lawes' melodic gifts. The seventeenth-century 'ballad' is the exact counter to the declamatory song. In its lilting rhythm and straightforward tunefulness it is a stylized imitation of the authentic folk song. Thurston Dart has neatly summed up the distinction between 'ballad' and declamatory song as follows:

'Take away the words of an air and you are left with a tune; a declamatory song without its words is a mere string of notes.'[1]

The 'ballad' usually employed triple metre and consisted of two or more quatrains in a regular strophic setting. In the spirit of its namesake it has a simple tune and does not bother overmuch with problems of accentuation. It is meant to be tuneful, light and charming, and so it is. Many of Lawes' 'ballads' might be quoted from here. One of the most popular is his setting of Thomas Carew's 'Ask Me Noe More Where Jove Bestows':

[1] In *Grove's Dictionary of Music and Musicians* (5th ed.), vii, p. 931.

Ex. 22 Ask Me Noe More Wher Jove Bestowes

Ask me noe more wher Jove be - stowes when June is Past the fad-ing Rose, for in your bew - ties Or - -ient deepe, These flowers as in their caus - es sleepe.

A device frequently encountered in Lawes' 'ballads' is the use of the *hemiola* rhythm. This is a familiar feature of Baroque vocal music which introduces a shift in accent or metre from 6/4 or 3/4 time to 3/2, as for example:

The *hemiola* is characteristic of both French and English *courantes* (corants) and betrays the 'ballad's' descent from the dance-song of the turn of the century. There is, in fact, convincing proof that many 'ballads' were danced to as well as sung, just as we today dance to composed 'popular' music or jazz.[1] Some of Lawes' songs, for example, are found in instrumental dance arrangements in which the names of the dances and not of the songs are specified. Such is the case with one of the composer's most beloved 'ballads', 'O My Clarissa', which appears as a saraband—although it is in reality a corant—in Playford's *Court-Ayres* (1655). It was also used, and designated as a saraband, by Lawes himself in the autograph of '*Harpe*' *Consort No. 4 in D Minor* (last movement), where it is to be found with its original variations.[2]

A fine example of the employment of the *hemiola* is Lawes' setting of the anonymous lyric, 'Dearest All Faire':

Ex. 23   **Deerest, All Faire** (beginning excerpt)

It should be noted that not only the rhythms of the corant, but those of the galliard, alman and saraband influenced the composition of song, just as they did the serious instrumental music of the period.

Although most of Lawes' ballads are in triple metre a few are in duple, including his very popular setting of 'Gather Yᵉ Rosebuds While Yᵉ May'. Herrick's lyrics express the well-worn classical theme of the enjoyment of life in the present. This is the same theme which so absorbed the leader of the French *Pleiade*.

[1] See the remarks of Thurston Dart in *Musica Britannica*, Vol. VI, pp. xii–xiii.

[2] The dance-song is No. 95 in Playford's collection. It is included in Appendix D complete with variations. See also Chapter IV, p. 102.

'*Cuiellez des aujourd'hui les roses de la vie*', sings Pierre Ronsard.[1] In fact, this thought runs through much of the poetry of the late sixteenth and seventeenth centuries and is partly explained by the humanistic interest evinced in the Latin poets and Horace in particular. Such titles as 'Enjoy Life While It is Here', 'Seize the Day', 'Enjoy the Present' are evidence of Horace's preoccupation with this Epicurean philosophy. A comparison of Herrick's popular treatment of the subject, however, as charming as it is, with the more learned style of the Roman poet, is a good example of the lighter treatment accorded classical models as mentioned earlier in the chapter. For his part, Lawes has beautifully captured the spirit of the Cavalier poet's lines. Scarcely a publication or manuscript of the period exists in which this song does not figure prominently. 'Gather Ye Rosebuds' as well as 'O My Clarissa' and another of Lawes' favourites, 'Come Lovely Cloris', are also found in contemporary manuscripts as three-part 'ballads' and as instrumental dance-song arrangements.

Another group of Lawes' *continuo*-songs is composed in what may be termed a bipartite 'recitative-ballad' form. In these, the declamatory style is used for all but the last two lines of a stanza. The latter are set in 3/2 rhythm and in 'ballad' style. This mixed form is not peculiar to Lawes alone but is common in manuscripts and publications of the period. It seems to have escaped notice until now and may well have been an effort on the composer's part to make the declamatory song more palatable to less sophisticated listeners by finishing the piece off with a good tune. In some cases the change from common to triple metre seems to reflect a change in the mood or emphasis of the poem, separating the more continuous thought from general or moral speculation.

One of the most curious forms which came into vogue in England about the third decade of the seventeenth century was the dialogue. Despite its novelty, this type of Baroque song has received little attention. It was evidently modelled after the *dialoghi* of the early Italian monodists which so greatly influenced the development of the chamber cantata, and paved the way to the dialogue-like recitatives of later opera. Its importance today, however, is mainly historical. In England it seems

[1] In the poem '*A Helene*'. See also Ronsard's '*Mignonne, Allons Voir Si La Rose*'.

to have enjoyed a greater popularity than on the Continent and usually occupied a section of its own in song books of the period. By its very nature the dialogue is essentially a dramatic form, consisting of alternating question-and-answer-type recitative between two voices, usually a treble and a bass. These join together at the end of the composition in a short concerted duet in 'familiar' (note-against-note) style. By far the larger number of dialogues occur between mythological subjects, pastoral characters or both. Once again the theme is love and the most favoured setting—the infernal shores of the river Styx, the boatman Charon, ferrier of dead souls, and Hades beyond. Thus, not only do we find in this form the essential musical-dramatic elements from which opera was evolving, but we note as well a preoccupation with the identical literary and mythological themes which furnished the texts for some of the great landmarks in opera—the same themes which were so popular in Italy and France. There was, however, this difference in the English approach to these subjects; their treatment was lighter, at times even frivolous, interposing love situations and humour on the most gloomy of scenes. One of Lawes' most interesting and unusual compositions in this setting is that which he calls, 'A Trialogue Between Orpheus, Alecto and Euridice'.

Judging by their frequent publication, both in John Playford's and in Henry Lawes' collections, and by their appearance in several manuscripts of the period, Lawes' dialogues were the most popular of the century. Of his twelve extant compositions in the form, mention must be made here of 'The Dialogue Between Thyrsis and Dorinda' by Andrew Marvell, the anonymous 'Nimph and Shepherd', Ben Jonson's 'Dialogue Between Joy and Delight', and Robert Herrick's 'Dialogue Between Charon and Philomel'. The latter was perhaps the best known of all and is especially interesting for its dramatic recitative, as in the following illustration:

Ex. 24.

A Dialogue Between Charon and Philomel (excerpt)

Charon: What's thy re-quest?   Philomel: That since she's __ now be-neath that

Thorow Bass

The passage is noteworthy also for its accentuation, speech rhythms and voice inflections. It is characteristic, however, that the dramatic tension is not sustained, for in the closing duet the mood of the lyrics takes on an even more flippant turn, bringing about a frivolous *dénouement* which can hardly be termed satisfying. The music follows suit.

While it is not within the scope or purpose of this chapter to engage in comparative analysis between Lawes' songs and those of his contemporaries, a brief discussion of William's work in relation to that of his brother is perhaps in order. Henry Lawes' accepted position as dean of seventeenth-century English declamatory song-writers may give the impression that William merely imitated his style. There is no basis for such a claim. Henry Lawes' early declamatory songs, e.g. those of *Comus*, are stylistically not more developed then those of his brother. The former's later songs do show a refinement and perfection of technique, but these were developments which occurred after William's death.[1] Indeed, the songs of both William and Henry follow identical principles of declamation, although they differ in the degree of emphasis upon certain techniques. William, for example, was given more to the use of word-painting, which Henry employed but sparingly. William also liked affective intervals and unusual turns of melody which were more emotional than his brother's. His harmonies were also more daring and changeable. William sometimes indulged in a limited amount of ornamental display while Henry avoided this almost entirely. As a melodist, William Lawes was by far the more original and inspired of the two, and in terms of productivity his total output in the combined instrumental and vocal fields, in spite of his short life span, greatly exceeds that of his brother.

There are extant but three texts to which both William and Henry Lawes set music. Unfortunately, two of William's pieces are only fragments, but these are sufficiently complete to warrant a comparison. William has set all three of the songs in through-composed declamatory style: the first is for solo voice and *continuo*, Thomas Cary's 'On His Mistress Crossing the Sea' ('Farewell Faire Sainct'); the second is for four voices with

---

[1] For a discussion of Henry Lawes' development in his declamatory songs see Hart, op. cit., passim.

an instrumental introduction or 'simphony',[1] William Herbert's sonnet 'Deere Leave Thy Home'; and the third is for five voices, Thomas Carew's 'Secresie Protested' ('Fear Not Dear Love'). Only the first is complete. Henry also set the latter in through-composed declamatory style, but of the second and third he made strophic 'ballads'. The elder Lawes has indeed been criticised for his handling of Carew's poem, which should never have been set in strophic 'ballad' form at all.[2] The content of the text is much too continuous in its thought to allow for this. William did not make the same mistake. The final fragment of his five-voiced setting suggests a masterpiece written in the style of the late English madrigal, charged with emotional expression, characterized by excellent part-writing and containing all of the pungent contrapuntal and harmonic techniques of the composer's large instrumental fantasias. Following is Carew's complete text, William's final fragment, and Henry's three-part 'ballad' setting with *continuo*:

Secresie Protested
by Thomas Carew

> Feare not deere love that Ile reveale
>   those howers of pleasure wee two steale
> Nor eye shall see nor yet the sun
>   descry what thou and I have done.
> Noe eare shall heare but wee
>   silent as the night will bee
> The God of Love him selfe whose dart
>   did first wound myne and then thy hart
> Shall never know, that we can tell
>   what Joyes in stolne embraces dwell.
> Only this meanes may find it out
>   that when I dye Phisitians doubt
> What causd my death. And then to view
>   of all their Judgements wch was true
> Ripp up my hart, O then I feare
>   the World will fynde thy Picture there.[3]

---

[1] This 'simphony' is No. 136 in Playford's *Court-Ayres* (1655), where it appears as an 'Ayre'.

[2] By Rhodes Dunlap in *The Poems of Thomas Carew* (Oxford: 1949), p. lvi. See also Hart, op. cit., No. 4 (October 1951), p. 335.

[3] This version of Carew's poem is that which is to be found in William Lawes' autograph in the Bodleian, Mus. Sch. B.2, p. 37.

Ex. 25a

Secresie Protested (final fragment)

THOS. CAREW   a 5 voc.   WILLIAM LAWES

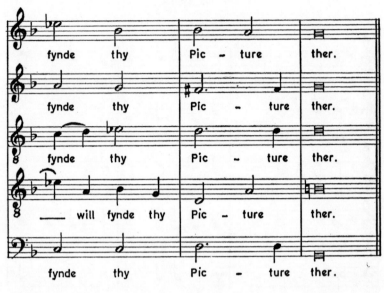

Ex. 25b

Secresie Protested

THOS. CAREW

HENRY LAWES

The content of William Herbert, Lord Pembroke's sonnet, 'Deere Leave Thy Home', lies somewhere between that of logical continuity and stanzaic self-sufficiency. Henry Lawes chose to set this poem as a single-voiced strophic ballad. William made of it a four-voiced madrigal with *continuo*. Each felt a different mood for the lyrics. While Henry's is light and gay, William's is serious, tender and emotional. The opening melodic lines are contrasted below:

Ex. 26a

Sonnet - Love's Content

William Herbert, Lord Pembroke

Beginning melody - Henry Lawes (Treasury of Musick, 1669)

Dear leave thy home and come with mee,

that scorn the world for love of thee Here we will live with-

-in this Park, a court of joy and pleas-ures Ark.

Ex. 26b Beginning melody - William Lawes (Bodl. Ms. Mus. Sch. B.2)

Dear leave thy home and come with mee that

scorn the world for love of thee Here we will live with-

-in this Park, a court of joy and pleas-ures Ark.

The declamatory settings of Thomas Cary's 'On His Mistress Crossing The Sea' (also known as 'Far(e)well Faire Sainct') vary in the texts. Indeed, William seems to have set an earlier version of the poem which is considerably shorter than that set by Henry Lawes.[1] Neither song is very successful, reflecting the complete mediocrity of the lyrics. They warrant no further discussion.

In the opinion of the present writer, the fragments referred to above are representative of what appears to be a missing collection of songs and madrigals in three, four and five parts by William Lawes. As pointed out in Chapter I, many of these part-songs must have originally been included in the large autograph volume in the Bodleian Library, Mus. Sch. B.2, from which they were torn out, probably for separate binding together with other vocal and dramatic music.[2] In examining the contents of the Lawes autograph the author has discovered that at least forty-two folios have been carefully removed close to the binding. All of these mutilations occur immediately preceding, immediately following, or in the midst of vocal music only. In some cases, as in the above fragments, the songs have not been torn out but scratched out with pen and ink so that instrumental music on the same page or on the reverse side of the folio might be preserved. The manner in which these pieces are crossed out is the same as that used by the composer when he made errors in copying. Fortunately, all of the pieces and fragments in the mutilated form are decipherable, and these agree identically with versions found in other manuscripts and in publications. They were definitely not scratched out because of mistakes in composition or in copying. There is, therefore, little doubt that Lawes himself was responsible for removing the vocal and dramatic music from this volume, leaving only the instrumental and masque music intact.

It has already been said that several autograph volumes belonging to William Lawes' original set are either missing or no longer extant.[3] One of these must certainly have been a very valuable collection of the composer's vocal music. In it were probably included the complete settings of the two fragments of Carew's and Pembroke's poems as well as that of another fine

[1] Crum, op. cit., pp. 124–5, points out that both William and Henry used the early version of the poem and that William omitted lines 7–12. Miss Crum compares this setting of the poem with the later versions found in *Parnassus Biceps* (London: 1656) and in Richard Fanshawe's *Il Pastor Fido* (London: 1647).

[2] See the discussion of the autographs in Chapter I, pp. 29–33.

[3] Loc. cit.

three-part fragment in the Bodleian autograph, 'Goe Bleeding Hart'. In it also may have been the music to Richard Lovelace's two songs mentioned earlier in the chapter. Finally, the missing autograph volume may well have contained those songs by William Lawes for which autographs have not been found but which do exist in Playford's publications and in commonplace manuscripts of the period.

There are, however, two excellent part-songs which were scratched out in the autograph but which are complete. One of these is a three-part setting of James Shirley's 'Cease Warring Thoughts' from the *Triumph of Beautie*, which will be discussed in Chapter IX. The other is an elegy 'On The Memory of My Friend: John Tomkins'.[1] This is the same piece which is in the Lawes brothers' *Choice Psalmes* of 1648. It is particularly interesting in its vivid portrayal of wailing and anguish, especially in the following excerpt:

Ex. 27 **On The Memory of My Friend : John Tomkins(excerpt)**

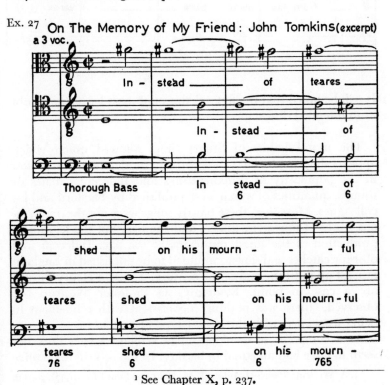

---

[1] See Chapter X, p. 237.

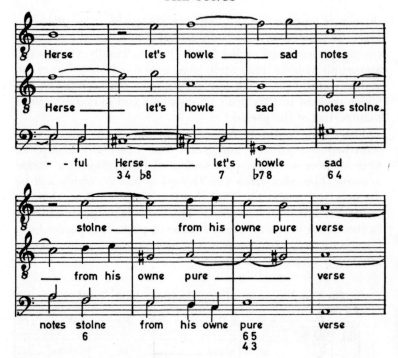

It will be noted that the figured thorough-bass leaves no doubt as to intended dissonances.

The moral habits of Stuart times allowed much which appears shocking by later standards. In music, this was manifest in the popularity of drinking-songs and indecent catches or rounds, quantities of which were published by Playford and his colleagues. Moreover, these bawdy songs were not the anonymous works of minstrels, tinkers and the like, but the legitimate production of the finest musicians of the age. Indecent and obscene catches and songs continued to be published in England at least up until the end of the century. Those of Henry Purcell are a case in point. Evidently, as Professor Westrup has observed, 'there was nothing inconsistent with refinement in being associated with the lowest type of verse'.[1]

As a composer of drinking-songs William Lawes does not seem to have had an equal in his day. In the taverns and coffee

[1] J. A. Westrup, *Purcell* (London: J. M. Dent and Sons Ltd., 1937), p. 162.

houses of seventeenth-century England his catches and bac-
chanalian part-songs were a familiar and popular entertainment. It is perhaps a bit ironical that a composer of Lawes'
stature should have been honoured in his own time for these
trivial pieces. But Lawes himself seems to have spent a good
many hours at the tavern with his friends and fellow musicians.[1]
Moreover, the tone of his tavern music betrays the composer's
enjoyment of it. He most certainly had a flare for that sort of
thing and probably dashed much of it off on the spot. To him
it probably afforded a means of relaxation and *camaraderie,* in
addition to winning him a wider following for his more serious
music.

Lawes' drinking-songs, as distinct from his catches, are all in
three parts. The style of these contains many diversified elements, including beginning passages in the declamatory vein,
semi-homophonic sections, solos, duets and trios, note-against-
note writing and sections in triple metre. The dramatic
quality of much of the composer's other work is absent here.
The pieces express a 'devil-may-care' attitude, with 'good sack
and brisk claret and sherry' as their basic theme. Some of these
songs are quite humorous and have real programmatic appeal,
as for example, 'The Catts', which is notable for its striking
conclusion:

Ex. 28   **The Catts**   (final excerpt)

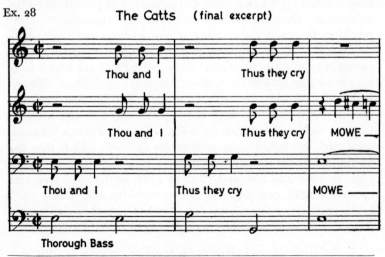

---

[1] See the anecdote given in Chapter **I,** p. 15.

In no country has the catch or round attained the popularity which it has held in England for over half a millennium. The famous *sumer-canon* stands as a monument to the degree of excellence which this form achieved in England as early as medieval times. It continued in favour during the Renaissance and was frequently alluded to and made use of in Elizabethan drama. The first printed collection of rounds and catches was the *Pammelia* of 1609 issued by Thomas Ravenscroft. This was closely followed by two more of the latter's publications in the same vein, *Deuteromelia* and *Melismata*. In the course of the seventeenth century the catch in particular came even more into vogue with the publication of John Hilton's *Catch that Catch Can* in 1652 and the later editions by John Playford, which were known as *The Musical Companion* (1667), (1673).[1] These editions included works by the foremost musicians of the age and gave rise to 'catch clubs' such as the still existing Hibernian Catch Club, which was founded in 1680. The movement continued unabated throughout the eighteenth century, which saw the formation of the famed Noblemen's and Gentlemen's Catch Club in 1761 and the Glee Club in 1787. Both lasted well into the nineteenth century. The early clubs usually made their headquarters in some tavern or coffee house, and in this respect it is interesting to note that the opening of the first coffee house

[1] Lawes' contributions to these publications are discussed in Chapter I, pp. 33–7.

in London coincides with the date of the first publication of Hilton's *Catch that Catch Can*. In the preface to the latter, Hilton expressly states that the rounds and catches in the volume are designed 'for the Mutuall *Society* of Friends in a Modest *Recreation*'. And in his 1667 edition of *The Musical Companion*, John Playford dedicates the music 'To His endeared Friends of the late Musick-Society and Meeting, in the Old-Jury, London'. He also gives a list of several 'citizens' and 'gentlemen' of the group. In the introduction to his 1673 edition Playford goes on to say that:

'This kind of Musick hath for many years past been had in much estimation by the most Judicious and Skilful Professors of Musick, for the Excellency of the Composition and Pleasant Harmony; and no late *Musick* that I have met with affords so much Delightful Recreation.'

There seems to be some question as to the exact nature of the seventeenth-century catch. Publications of the period refer to it as a catch, canon or round without making any clear distinction between the three. The term canon was apparently reserved for compositions employing strict imitation at various intervals and set to religious texts of a more serious nature. The round is a type of canon using a secular text. It is imitated at the unison only and the imitations enter at the same point in all parts. With respect to their musical form, there is no difference between the round and the catch. Rimbault claimed that the identifying element of the catch is a type of *hocketus* technique which produced new meanings, (usually obscene), as the parts interlaced while catching up to each other. His definition is as follows:

'The *Catch* is a humorous vocal composition of three or more harmonic parts in which the melodies are so opposed and interrupted by the contrivance of the composer, that in the performance the singers *catch up* each other's sentences, and give to the words a sense different from that of the original reading.'[1]

However, this attractive explanation is not entirely borne out by the facts. It is only occasionally that Rimbault's 'catching-up' formula applies in catches of the seventeenth century. Indeed, only one of Lawes' many examples in the form is a catch *a*

[1] Rimbault, op. cit., p. xii.

double entente. This is the three-part 'See How In Gathering Of Their May', which, unfortunately, may not be quoted from here because of the obscenity of the text as the words and phrases interlace with the addition of the parts. Playford himself defines the catch in his introduction to *The Musical Companion* (1673 ed.). He makes no mention of the hidden meanings:

'. . . a Catch is a Song for three Voyces, wherein the several Parts are included in one; or, as it is usually tearmed, Three Parts in One. Secondly, the mannore of Singing them is thus, The First begins and Sings the Catch forward, and when he is at that Note over which his (:S:) Mark or Signature is placed, the Second begins and Sings forward in like manner, and when he is Singing that Note over which the said Signature is, the Third begins and Sings, following the other, each singing it round two or three times over, and so conclude.'

The real distinction between the round and catch seems to be between the content of their respective verse. That of the catch is more humorous and less refined than the text of the round.

An adverse criticism which has been extended to rounds and catches of the seventeenth and eighteenth centuries is that they lack originality, the melodies being artificial and the harmonies static and uninteresting. This criticism is justified, although there are some fine examples of rounds and catches from the period. The composition of a round or catch was indeed a simple matter. One had but to compose a short tune, to harmonize it in as many parts as he wished, and then to string these out in succession in order to have completed a catch. This procedure accounts for the fact that many catches begin with a good tune but shortly take on the character of a harmonic filler or a bass line rather than a pleasing melody. It is only the exceptional round or catch which succeeds in presenting one continuous and attractive tune.

In bringing out *Catch that Catch Can* Hilton established for himself a reputation as the catch composer *par excellence*. But the 1652 edition was by no means entirely Hilton's work. In fact, he was the composer of only 48 of 133 pieces. William Lawes was second with eighteen works and eighteen additional composers were represented. Henry Lawes had five contributions; Simon Ives, four; and John Jenkins, two. In the 1667 edition, which almost doubled in size under Playford's editorship, Hilton's selections dropped to thirty-six, while Lawes' increased to twenty-nine. Finally, in the third revised edition, William Lawes' works outstripped those of Hilton, which had by now fallen to twenty-one. In popularity too, Hilton's catches were far behind such household favourites as 'The Wisemen Were But Seven', 'Come Let Us Cast The Dice', 'Drink Tonight of the Moonshine Bright', 'Let's Cast Away Care', and many others. This is proven by the greater number of extant manuscripts and publications in which the Lawes catches appear.

A discussion of these pieces would not be complete without the inclusion of what was perhaps the most famous of all seventeenth-century catches, the composer's 'Three Merry Boys', also known as 'The Wisemen Were But Seven'. Musically, this piece is inferior to many of the others, but evidently the tune was easily caught by all and well liked in its day:

Ex. 29   The Wise Men Were But Seven
Catch a 3 voc.

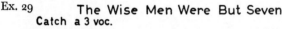

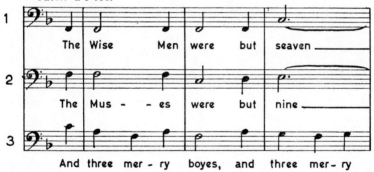

Many of Lawes' catches were also used in stage plays of the period. Some were even composed especially for certain productions. Among these are 'Some Drink Boy' from John Suckling's *The Goblins* (*c.* 1638); 'A Round, A Round, A Round Boys' from Richard Brome's *A Joviall Crew* (1641); and 'A Pox On Our Gaoler' from Richard Cartwright's *The Royal Slave* (1636).

VIII

MUSIC FOR THE THEATRE

Bᴿɪᴛɪꜱʜ drama of the sixteenth and seventeenth centuries abounds in dramatic lyrics, in stage directions for instrumental and vocal music and in references to music, musicians, musical instruments, dances and dance music of many kinds. But, although several attempts have been made to describe the use of this music in the early theatre, comparatively little of it has as yet been identified.[1] This is especially true of the period preceding the Commonwealth. Nevertheless, there is good reason to hope that a limited quantity of this music is still extant in early manuscripts and publications.[2] An examination of sources containing the works of William Lawes, for example, has uncovered music for sixteen stage plays, three Court masques, one school masque, and one royal entertainment.

By the time of the Stuarts, the various theatrical enterprises begun by ambitious actors and playwrights during the reign of Elizabeth had increased considerably. These 'actors' companies'

[1] The most recent study is that of Wm. R. Bowden, *The English Dramatic Lyric*, 1603–42 (Oxford University Press, 1951). Others are: John Manifold, 'Theatre Music in the Sixteenth and Seventeenth Centuries', *Music and Letters*, XXIX, No. 4 (October 1948), pp. 366–97; W. J. Lawrence, 'Music in the Elizabethan Theatre', *The Musical Quarterly*, VI (1920); E. B. Reed, *Songs from the British Drama*, (New Haven: Yale University Press; London: Oxford University Press, 1925); E. W. Naylor, *Shakespeare and Music* (London: 1931). See also bibliography.

[2] See, e.g., the statement by Manifold, op. cit., p. 390, to this effect, also the recent work of J. P. Cutts in identifying works in manuscripts of the period with stage plays and poems of the English dramatists.

maintained their own establishments under the licence of the Crown and enjoyed a monopoly on their own plays. Often they incorporated playwrights and musicians or else hired their services outright. Another feature of the make-up of an actors' group was the employment of young boys for female parts and for singing and dancing.

Two types of early theatre are commonly distinguished: the inexpensive, public open-air playhouses on the Bankside which shared their audiences with the nearby bull- and bear-baiting arenas, and the more expensive and closed-in private theatres, on the fashionable side of the Thames, which catered to a more exclusive clientele. By far the most famous and prosperous of the actors' companies was The King's Men, whose permanent home was the private Blackfriars Theatre in the winter and the renowned Globe on the Bankside during summer. This was the company of Richard Burbage, William Shakespeare, Ben Jonson, Beaumont and Fletcher, William Davenant and many others.[1] The musicians who wrote for The King's Men included Ferrabosco II, Thomas Morley, Giovanni Coperario, Campion and Rosseter, Nicholas Lanier, Robert Johnson and William Lawes. It was The King's Men who were at the beck-and-call of the Sovereign for performances at Court both in and out of the city.

In 1632-3 a special theatre was built at Whitehall by the noted architect and stage designer, Inigo Jones. Known as the Little Cockpit-at-Court, it is not to be confused with the more popular Cockpit or Phoenix Theatre in Drury Lane. It was in the former that most of the plays at Court were given. Charles I and his Queen, however, often hired the Blackfriars Theatre and the Cockpit in Dury Lane for performances as well. These stage presentations were held in the evening and attendance was by invitation only. The King's Men were paid ten pounds per performance in the city and twenty pounds when they accompanied the Sovereign on one of his progresses into the country, or when they played at Hampton Court.[2]

[1] For more detailed information regarding The King's Men, other actors' companies and their playhouses, see J. T. Murray, *English Dramatic Companies* (London: 1910), 2 vols. Also E. K. Chambers, *The Elizabethan Stage* (London: 1923), 4 vols., and J. Q. Adams, *Shakespearian Playhouses* (Boston: Houghton Mifflin Co., 1917). See also bibliography.

[2] J. Q. Adams, *The Dramatic Records of Sir Henry Herbert, Master of the Revels, 1623-1673* (New Haven: Yale University Press, 1917), passim.

Other actors' companies also performed before the Court, the most notable of these being Queen Henrietta's Men, which was owned and operated by Christopher Beeston, one of the original members of Shakespeare's troupe. The Queen's Men acted at the Cockpit in Drury Lane from 1625 until 1636. When the theatres were temporarily closed in 1636 due to the plague, Beeston disbanded the group and formed the King and Queen's Young Company, more popularly known as 'Beeston's Boys'. The latter proved quite successful and when Beeston died, in 1639, William Davenant was placed in charge of the boys, from 1640 until the closing of the theatres in 1642. Court performances were also recorded for Prince Charles' Men, who from the year 1631 acted successively at the Salisbury Court Theatre, The Red Bull and The Fortune, and for a visiting French company of actors under Josias Floridor, who came to England in 1635 and found favour at Court as a protégé of the Queen.

The tradition of music in the early drama owes much to the 'children's companies' which were increasingly active at the turn of the century. These groups were formed variously from the children of the Chapel Royal, Windsor and St. Paul's, ostensibly to present plays before the Queen, which they did. The true reason for their establishment, however, was to act in the private theatres. The two outstanding companies of child actors were, one known successively as the Children of the Chapel, of the Queen's Revels, and of Blackfriars, and the other made up of the Children of St. Paul's. The home of the former was in the old Blackfriars Theatre, while the latter gave their performances in the singing-school just behind the great cathedral. In the year 1600 the control of the first group—then the Children of the Chapel—was turned over to Henry Evans and Nathaniel Giles, two unscrupulous masters who obtained a patent from Queen Elizabeth to forcibly seize the most talented children 'within this our realm of England' for service in the Chapel Royal, and therefore, in the children's company as well.[1] With such power at their command Evans and Giles soon established a magnificent group of child actors and musicians, and all London was set agog by their splendid performances. The sudden popularity of the children's companies adversely

[1] C. W. Wallace, *The Children of the Chapel at Blackfriars* (London: 1906), p. 61, gives the full account of this patent.

affected the future King's Men whose permanent home at this time was at the Globe, and so Shakespeare's troupe was forced to travel in the country to secure large audiences. The fame of these children has been immortalized by Shakespeare himself (in *Hamlet*, Act II, sc. ii), who has characterized his own company as 'the tragedians of the city' and the Chapel children as the 'little eyases, that cry out on the top of question, and are most tyrannically clapped for't'.

One of the major attractions at the private theatres was the music, which not only fulfilled important functions within the plays themselves but also provided additional entertainment before the commencement of performances and in between the acts.[1] Indeed, the Children of the Chapel and of St. Paul's were chosen first and foremost for their musical ability, both vocal and instrumental, and received intensive daily instruction in their art. Since the children could not compete with the professional adult companies in the performance of serious tragedy, their music was an added attraction to draw an élite public to the private theatres, where comedies were more frequently performed. How highly the music of the Children of the Chapel was esteemed is indicated by a contemporary account of the Duke of Stettin-Pomerania, who stopped in England in 1602 on his grand tour of Europe and attended a play at Blackfriars:

'For a whole hour before the play begins, one listens to charming instrumental music played on organs, lutes, pandorins, mandolins, violins, and flutes; as, indeed, on this occasion, a boy sang *cum voce tremula* to the accompaniment of a bass viol, so delightfully that, if the Nuns at Milan did not excel him, we had not heard his equal in our travels.'[2]

The success of the musical children seems to have had an effect upon the use of music by the adult companies as well. This is not to say that the early public theatres did not employ music. Indeed, the musical tradition in the British theatre was begun long before the organization of children's companies and

[1] Further to this see W. W. Greg, 'Act-Divisions in Shakespeare', *Review of English Studies*, IV (1928); also, T. S. Graves, 'The "Act Time" in Elizabethan Theatres', *Studies in Philology*, XII (1915), pp. 103–34.

[2] Quoted by Adams, *Shakespearian Playhouses*, op. cit., pp. 207–8, from *The Diary of the Duke of Stettin-Pomerania*, printed in *Transactions of the Royal Historical Society* (1890).

the development of the private theatre. Shakespeare's early utilization of music is well known and, of course, the Elizabethan 'jig-time' was a favourite attraction after a dramatic performance at the Bankside.[1] The plays at the public theatres, however, were apparently begun with three loud blasts of the trumpets rather than with a lengthy musical concert. The performances at the Bankside were also more continuous, affording less opportunity for the playing of music in between the acts. It has been shown, moreover, that the incidence of song in the plays presented by the children of Blackfriars and St. Paul's during the period 1600–13, is practically double that of the number of songs used in the productions of The King's Men for those years.[2] The latter group, on the other hand, employed more music than did any of the other adult companies during the same period. When, in 1608, Burbage, Shakespeare and company took over the lease of the Blackfriars and received their Royal commission, the number of songs in their plays immediately began to rise. And indeed, between the years 1615–25 the plays of The King's Men actually show a higher incidence of song than did those of the children's companies during the peak of their popularity.[3]

By at least the third decade of the century, the theatre orchestra had become a standard feature of the English playhouse.[4] Professional musicians were employed not only to perform the incidental music and songs called for in the plays, but, following the example of the earlier private theatres, to entertain the audience before the start of the play itself and in between the acts. The great Puritan parliamentarian, Bulstrode Whitelocke, tells us that he himself composed an 'aier' (with the assistance of Simon Ives), and called it *Whitelocke's Coranto*:

'. . . which being cried up, was first played publiquely by the

[1] See C. R. Baskervill, *The Elizabethan Jig and Related Song Drama* (1929); also, W. J. Lawrence, *Pre-Restoration Stage Studies* (Cambridge: Harvard University Press, 1927), pp. 79–101.

[2] Bowden, op. cit., pp. 126–7.

[3] Ibid., p. 127.

[4] See, e.g., W. J. Lawrence, 'The English Theatre Orchestra, Its Rise and Early Characteristics', *The Musical Quarterly*, III, No. 1 (January 1917), pp. 9–27; also, Manifold, op. cit., and H. M. Fitzgibbon, 'Instruments and their Music in the Elizabethan Drama', *The Musical Quarterly*, XVII, No. 3 (July 1931), pp. 319–29.

Blackfryar's musicke, who were then esteemed the best of common musitians in London. Whenever I came to that house (as I did sometimes in those days), though not often to see a play, the musitians would presently play *Whitelocke's Coranto*, and it was so often called for that they would have it played twice or thrice in an afternoon. . . .'[1]

Later, when the theatres were closed during the Commonwealth, the musicians of the theatre orchestras were reduced to penury. In January 1644, less than two years after the playhouses were shut, an anonymous actor bitterly lamented:

'Our music that was held so delectable and precious that they scorned to come to a tavern under twenty shillings salary for two hours, now wander with their instruments under their cloaks—I mean, such as have any—into all houses of good fellowship, saluting every room where there is company with, *"Will you have any music, gentlemen?"* '[2]

Music in the early theatre was assigned varied functions which have led scholars to distinguish between a number of kinds of music employed in the plays.[3] While some differences of opinion exist regarding the various categories of this stage music, it is clear that there are at least four major divisions which are readily discernible. The first of these is the music of the introductory and inter-act concerts, which probably consisted of instrumental dance suites and songs. Apparently, this music formed a good share of an afternoon or evening's entertainment. The second consists of the songs called for in the plays themselves. These are designed for a number of purposes and may be classified into several types.[4] They are the same vocal forms discussed in Chapter VII: declamatory songs,

[1] Percy Scholes, *The Puritans and Music* (Oxford University Press, 1934), p. 164, prints the complete extract from an unpublished manuscript by Whitelocke entitled, *Whitelocke's Labours remembered in the Annales of his Life, written for the Use of his Children.*

[2] H. B. Baker, *The London Stage* (London: 1889), 2 vols., Vol. I, p. 38.

[3] See, e.g., Manifold, op. cit., Bowden, op. cit.; also, J. Isaacs, *Production and Stage-Management at the Blackfriars Theatre* (Oxford University Press, 1933), pp. 12–13.

[4] Bowden, op. cit., has made an elaborate breakdown of the functions of song in the early theatre derived from the 'psychology of music' which is perhaps a bit too elaborate.

'ballads', dialogues, part-songs, catches, etc. Indeed, there is no difference between the songs used in the drama and the settings which have already been discussed. Sometimes the texts of the songs were written by the dramatist expressly for a play. At others well-known folk tunes are specified, and often just 'A Song' is requested, without any indication as to its title. The latter has conveniently been termed 'blank-song'. The third type of theatre music may be called 'functional', i.e. music of a practical kind such as marches and various 'flourishes' designed to introduce or identify certain characters or scenes. Finally, there is that large body of music—of which scarcely a trace remains except in the stage directions of the plays themselves—which was designed to prepare or to intensify certain dramatic atmospheres, and which might be called 'atmospheric' music. Elizabethan and Stuart dramatists had a fairly uniform and consistent terminology for this type of music. Some of the more frequent cues one finds in drama of the period are 'loud music', 'soft music', 'still music', 'solemn music', 'martiall music', 'underground music', etc. Quite often these terms are identified with the instruments for which they were intended, but any indication of specific music or even of the composer of music for a stage play is practically never given. While the identification of individual songs may well reveal the composer's identity, it is extremely doubtful that much of the 'atmospheric' music will ever be recovered.

The location and dispersal of the musicians in the early theatre orchestra was closely bound up with the physical characteristics of the Elizabethan and Stuart stage and added a dimensional effect to the drama itself. Needless to say, this theatre orchestra was no orchestra if judged by later standards. It has been suggested that the typical playhouse employed a group of from nine to twelve musicians who could perform on various instruments within the respective instrumental families.[1] Moreover, no evidence has as yet been forwarded to prove that these musicians ever played together as a complete unit. They appear to have been dispersed in smaller groups about the stage and in the various levels of the 'tiring-house'—that maze of rooms behind the almost stereotyped façade of the early stage which housed the inner stage and served for dressing-rooms,

[1] Manifold, op. cit., pp. 388–9.

storage rooms, music rooms, and chambers for special effects.[1] The main '(at)tiring' or dressing-rooms were behind the proscenium doors on either side of the curtained inner stage. Stage directions sometimes call for music emanating from these rooms. But directly above the main 'tiring' rooms were the traditional 'musick rooms' whose large balconied windows were curtained by a thin cloth of sarsnet or silk so that the musicians could be shielded from sight and yet heard with good volume. Doubtless there were variations of this plan, but in general it would seem that the musicians might be heard from any of the areas behind the 'tiring-house' façade, especially at the direction 'music from within' which is so frequently encountered in early plays.

The playhouse orchestra included a full complement of strings, woodwinds, brass and percussion. Apparently, each group had its own particular functions, which had become somewhat standardized in the musical cues of the dramatists. The strings were the backbone of theatre music and included viols, violins, rebecs, lutes, cittern, pandora and harp. They were used to accompany singing and dancing, usually for the stage direction calling for 'soft music'. Among the woodwinds could be found wooden cornets, hautboys (oboes), and recorders. The first two appear to have been used together for the 'loud music' so often indicated in plays of this period and associated with festive occasions. They were also used as a substitute for the brass. The recorders, on the other hand, fulfilled the function of 'still music' as a background to religious, supernatural or mourning scenes.[2]

The brass instruments were represented only by the trumpets and the horns (at least the sackbuts (trombones) are not called for by name). As a matter of fact, the brass instruments in general are divorced from the larger body of theatre music, in the sense that they are used almost exclusively for functional purposes. The horns are employed in the traditional hunting symbolism, where 'horns winded off stage', or 'peal from afar', serve to represent an entire hunting scene. The long brass

[1] John Cranford Adams, *The Globe Playhouse* (Cambridge: Harvard University Press, 1942), Chapters V–X. Chapter IX deals with the music gallery and serves as the basis for the present discussion.

[2] For a detailed discussion of the instruments and their function in the early plays see Manifold, op. cit., passim.

trumpets were reserved to herald the entry or exit of persons of the highest rank, usually Kings, Queens and Emperors. The trumpets had a repertory of several calls, including 'tuckets', 'sennets', 'flourishes', 'alarums', etc. The instruments used for military music included the pipe and tabor, the drum, the fife and the bagpipes; not the brass as one might suspect.

Often the instrumental musicians, especially the lutenists, were vocalists as well. Sometimes the actors themselves were competent musicians who could sing and accompany themselves on the theorbo-lute or bass viol. Many plays of the period, especially those of The King's Men, require the actors to do their own singing. But when the actors were not musical their songs were usually heard from off stage, i.e. 'from within', performed by the professional musicians of the playhouse orchestra. So much then for the musical tradition of the early English theatres, of which William Lawes was a part. We turn now to the composer's specific works for the stage.

Practically the only clues which exist for an attempted chronology of any of Lawes' compositions are the dates of the performances of stage plays, entertainments and masques for which songs and instrumental music have been identified. Even this chronology is based upon the assumption that the songs associated with certain dramatic productions were written expressly for plays and revivals presented before the Court, for there is always the remote possibility that the composer may have set the texts of these songs from the Caroline drama as lyrics *per se*, quite apart from any specific performances. The present writer, however, is of the opinion that William Lawes did indeed write his songs for the presentation of stage plays at Court. Those texts set by Lawes, which can be identified with dramatic productions, are all from plays performed before the King and Queen while Lawes was in the Royal service or shortly before. All of these performances were presented by The King's Men or by 'Beeston's Boys', the players for whom Lawes would naturally write. In some instances more than one song from a given production has been identified with Lawes' music. None of the lyrics set by the composer appear to be from earlier Elizabethan and Jacobean dramatic productions, unless the plays were revived for the Court of Charles I. It was, in fact, the practice in the early theatre for music to be composed anew for each successive production and especially for revivals. It is, moreover, reasonable to suppose that Lawes' popularity as a composer of masques caused many literary men to seek his services.

The earliest record of Lawes' dramatic writing is entitled 'A Dialogue Between the Passions, Doubt and Love' from Ben Jonson's *Entertainment at Welbeck*. This Royal entertainment was produced by William Cavendish, Earl of Newcastle, on the occasion of the King's progress to Scotland in 1633. The dialogue was sung while the Royal party was at dinner and served to welcome the King and introduce the entertainment. Since William Lawes was not at this time one of the private musicians to the King, his presence at Welbeck may be explained by his being in the employ of the Earl, one of the musicians of The King's Men, or in some other way unofficially attached to the Court.[1]

Early in 1634 Lawes collaborated with Simon Ives, a vicar-choral of St. Paul's, in composing the music to James Shirley's masque, *The Triumph of Peace*. Lawes' reputation as a composer of dramatic music must already have been great, since he was chosen for the task by Whitelocke, himself an amateur composer who knew well the music and musicians of his age. It was probably Lawes' work on this masque which helped to earn him his position at Court in the following year.[2]

A new play by William Davenant, entitled *Love and Honour*, was performed for the Court by The King's Men at Blackfriars on December 12, 1634, and again on New Year's Day, 1637, at Hampton Court. One song, 'O Drawe Your Curtaynes and Apeere', is extant from the play in Lawes' autograph,[3] but because of the two performances it is not possible to date the music with certainty. This is true of several of Lawes' songs from plays. When the performances were close together it is possible to assume a fairly accurate date, but when older plays were revived we find the task of dating the songs more difficult, since it was sometimes the practice to compose new music for

[1] The music is in William Lawes' vocal autograph in the British Museum, Add. 31432, under the title 'A Dialogue Between Joy and Delight'. See also Chapter I, p. 16.

[2] The complete discussion of this masque, as well as the others, is reserved for Chapter IX.

[3] Br. Mus., Add. 31432, f. 39.

these revivals. The evidence upon which the present chronology is based is the fact that all of Lawes' songs that have been identified with plays, are from productions which were presented at Court by The King's Men between the years 1634 and 1642.

A case of an older revival is that of Ben Jonson's *Epicoene*, or *The Silent Woman*, which was first published in 1610 and had several performances before William Lawes could have set the beautiful lyric, 'Still to bee Neate, Still to bee Dresst'.[1] The play was revived twice in the year 1636, once at the Court of St. James and again at the Cockpit-in-Court. It was probably for one or both of these performances that Lawes' setting was used. The song itself is a composed 'ballad' or dance-song. It is double-barred in the manuscript and employs the *hemiola* pattern characteristic of Lawes' work in this form:

Ex. 30   **Still to Bee Neate, Still to Bee Drestt**

---

[1] The song is attributed to William Lawes in John Gamble's Commonplace Book in the New York Public Library, where it is No. 179.

197

la - die tis to bee pre - sum'd;
such sweett ne - glectt more tak - eth mee

though artts hidd caus - ses are not found;
then all the a- dult - erate ways off artt

all is nott sweett, all is nott sound.
those pleas mine eyes; butt thatt my hartt.

Lawes' next large dramatic work was Davenant's *The Triumphs of the Prince d'Amour*, in February of 1636. In this masque, as in William Cartwright's musical play, *The Royal Slave*, which was produced later in the same year by the students of Christ Church in Oxford, William collaborated with his brother, Henry. During the summer of 1636 the Lawes brothers were part of the household of the King and Queen as they travelled about the countryside visiting various estates of the nobility in an effort to escape the ravages of the plague which had flared up again in London. The Royal pair, together with Prince Charles and the King's nephews, the Elector Palatine and Prince Rupert, and many additional members of the Court, were to be guests of Archbishop William Laud, Chancellor of the University of Oxford, towards the end of August. Four plays were planned at Oxford to entertain King Charles and his party during their short stay.[1] These were William Strode's *Floating*

---

[1] M. S. Steele, *Plays and Masques at Court During the Reigns of Elizabeth, James I, and Charles I, 1558–1642* (Oxford University Press, 1926), p. 259.

Island, Cartwright's *The Royal Slave*, Wilde's *Love's Hospital* and Jasper Mayne's *The City Match*. The latter play, for which William set the song 'We Show No Monstrous Crocodile', was not presented at Oxford due to lack of sufficient time.[1] *The City Match* was performed for the Sovereign later, in 1637, at the Royal retreat in Hampton Court. It must have met with good success for it was acted several times afterwards for the King and Queen at Blackfriars. Of the other three plays, only one catch, 'A Pox On Our Gaoler', from *The Royal Slave*, can be attributed to William Lawes.[2] It is possible, however, as Evans points out, that William wrote music for all of these plays.[3] Songs by Henry Lawes are extant for the *Floating Island* and *The Royal Slave*, but no instrumental music. Because of William's greater activity in the instrumental field it is likely that he was entrusted with the instrumental part of all of the performances. Indeed, the brothers Lawes may have collaborated to a far greater extent than our present knowledge indicates.

So great was the number of deaths from the horrifying plague as it spread to every quarter of London in the early days of the year 1636 that all of the theatres were closed on May 12. For almost a year and a half following, the playhouses remained shut as the disease claimed thousands upon thousands of lives and a large part of the population fled the city. For only one week did the plague subside enough to allow the theatres to reopen, from February 23 to March 2, 1637, after which they remained closed again until the following October.[4] Apparently the closing of the theatres did not curtail Court performances completely. Christopher Beeston's newly organized King and Queen's Young Company gave their first performance before the Court at St. James's on February 7, 1637. The play was a revival of Beaumont and Fletcher's *Cupid's Revenge*, which had originally been produced by the King's Revels Company in 1611. It was probably for the 1637 performance that Lawes composed the music for the song 'Lovers, rejoice! your pains

[1] This song is attributed to Lawes in the Drexel manuscript 4041 in the New York Public Library, pp. 8–10.

[2] This catch is in John Playford's *Musical Companion* (London: 1667 and 1673). Playford states that it definitely was sung in the play.

[3] Willa McClung Evans, *Henry Lawes* (Oxford University Press, 1941), pp. 123–4, n. 3; p. 127, n. 7.

[4] J. Q. Adams, *Shakespearian Playhouses*, op. cit., pp. 356–7.

shall be rewarded', which is sung in the temple scene in Act II.[1] Interestingly enough, this is Lawes' only dramatic setting for this year.

When the plague finally subsided and the Court returned to London from its retreat at Hampton Court, the theatres were once again reopened. The new year, 1638, was apparently William Lawes' most active one in the dramatic field, for in this year he composed music for at least seven new productions which were presented before the Court. The first presentation of the year was the masque, *Britannia Triumphans*, in which Davenant, Inigo Jones, the great architect and stage designer, and William Lawes collaborated. This was followed in about a month by Sir John Suckling's *Aglaura*, which was acted before the Court twice in 1638, once at the Cockpit at Whitehall, on February 7, and again at the Blackfriars, on April 3. Both performances were by The King's Men. Like the production of *The Royal Slave* in Oxford two years before, *Aglaura* made use of stage scenery and elaborate and costly costumes. Moreover, Suckling paid for all of this himself, as Aubrey testifies:

'When his [Suckling's] Aglaura was [acted], he bought all the cloathes himselfe, which were very rich; no tinsill, all the lace pure gold and silver, which cost him . . . I have now forgott. He had some scaenes to it, which in those dayes were only used at masques.'[2]

William and Henry both wrote music for this play and at least one song of each of the brothers is extant. Henry's setting of the song 'Noe, noe faire Herritick' is well known, but William's charming music to Orsames' song in Act IV, 'Why Soe Pall and Wan Fond Lover', has received less attention than it merits.[3] The song is cleverly constructed of rising scale lines which portray the questioning of the text and of charming melodic

---

[1] John P. Cutts, 'British Museum Additional MS. 31432 . . .', *The Library*, Vol. VII, No. 4 (December 1952), p. 233, mentions a revival of the play in 1639. Mr. Cutts has probably confused that date with the patent of monopoly which was granted Beeston's Boys for *Cupid's Revenge* in 1639.

[2] John Aubrey, *Brief Lives* (London: Longman *et al.*, 1813), 2 vols., ii, p. 244.

[3] Henry's song may be seen in Playford's *Ayres and Dialogues*, 1652 and later editions. William's song is in the New York Public Library, Drexel manuscript 4041, pp. 10–12, where it is attributed to him.

Ex. 31

Why Soe Pall and Wan Fond Lover

from John Suckling's "Aglaura"

Thorough Bass

Why soe pall and wan fond lov-er pre-thee why soe pall

will when lookinge well can't move her look-ing ill pre-vaile

pri-thee why soe pall why soe dull and mutt young sin-ner

pri-thee why soe mutt will when speaking well can't win her

say-inge noth-inge doott pre-thee why soe mutt

quitt quitt for shame this will nott move this

turns for the after-questions. All of these build towards the final and flippant afterthought. Here there is good declamation, fine melody and a preconceived formal plan which adds much to the success of the music.

Lawes also composed the music for Suckling's next play, *The Goblins*, which was acted before the Court by The King's Men sometime during the spring of the same year. Two songs are extant: a three-part drinking-song, 'A Health to the No(r)therne Lass', and the catch, 'Some Drink, Boy'.[1] The remaining dramatic productions of 1638 for which the composer wrote music include *The Lost Lady* by Sir William Berkeley, *The Unfortunate Lovers* by William Davenant and John Ford's *The Lady's Trial*. All were presented before the Court by either The King's Men or Beeston's Boys. The last-named play was performed at the Cockpit Theatre in Drury Lane and included at least two songs by Lawes: the three-part 'What Hoe, Wee Come to be Merry', and a popular 'ballad', 'Pleasure's Bewty Youth Attend Yee'.[2]

Lawes' dramatic activity almost comes to a halt in 1639, with only one three-part drinking-song from Suckling's *The Tragedy of Brennoralt* which was performed by The King's Men at Black-friars.[3] This and the following year witness a general lull in

[1] The first song is in Lawes' autograph, Add. 31432; the catch may be seen in the 1667 edition of *The Musical Companion*.

[2] Both pieces are in the vocal autograph, Add. 31432. The ballad may also be seen in Playford's *Treasury of Musick* (1669), where it appears erroneously under Henry Lawes' name.

[3] The song is 'A Hall, A Hall' and is also to be found in the autograph, Add. 31432.

Court entertainment as the political horizon darkens and the Bishops' Wars break out with Scotland. It is possible that during this time Lawes was occupied in writing religious music and his larger chamber works for strings. At any rate, he probably did not join the army until after 1641, since in that year he wrote music for three more plays: James Shirley's *The Cardinal*, Richard Brome's *A Joviall Crew* and Sir John Denham's *The Sophy*.[1] After King Charles retired to Oxford in 1642 and Parliament closed the theatres, Lawes probably took up his new duties at the University Court Headquarters as a commissary. None of his music has as yet been identified as having been written during the Court's residence at Oxford. Indeed, his musical activities may well have been cut short during these troubled years which preceded his death at the Siege of Chester in 1645.

There are three works, in addition to the above, for which the dates of performance have evidently not been recorded. The most important of these is James Shirley's school masque, *The Triumph of Beautie*, which was published in 1646 together with his *Poems*. The present writer has identified the music by William Lawes to the song 'Cease Warring Thoughts' which is from this masque.[2] The two remaining plays are by Thomas Middleton, *The Widow* and *The Phoenix*.[3] There is also a good possibility that further investigation, especially of the texts of unpublished drama of the period, will reveal that more of Lawes' vocal music has its source in the Cavalier theatre. Several of the texts of the composer's songs show every indication of being connected with stage plays of the period.

The record, as sketched above, presents William Lawes in a new light. It establishes him as one of the leading composers in the field of English dramatic music prior to the advent of Henry Purcell to the musical stage. It also proves him a logical successor of such early dramatic composers as Ferrabosco II,

---

[1] These songs are, 'Come My Daphne', from *The Cardinal*, V, iii; 'A Round, A Round, A Round Boys' from *A Joviall Crew*, and 'Somnus the 'Umble God' from *The Sophy*, V.

[2] For an account of this song and the masque see Chapter IX, pp. 230-4.

[3] The song from *The Widow* is 'I Keep My Horse, I Keep My Whore', which is attributed to Lawes in Br. Mus., Add. 29396, where the play is erroneously stated to be by Ben Jonson. This song was also used for a production of *Master Turbulent* in 1682. One instrumental piece only is extant from *The Phoenix*, which was originally produced in 1607.

Coperario, Daniel, Campion, Nicholas Lanier and Robert Johnson. Interestingly enough, Lawes' dramatic activity dates from the very year that Johnson died. Johnson, too, wrote predominantly for The King's Men and for the Court. Considered as a group, William Lawes' collection of songs for the British drama is perhaps the largest body of songs for the theatre by a single composer which is extant from pre-Commonwealth times. When the music of the masques is added to this, Lawes' stature as a dramatic composer increases even more.

IX

THE MASQUES

JACOBEAN and Caroline extravagance is nowhere more in evidence than in the lavish Court spectacles, masques and entertainments that were produced at Whitehall and at the great estates and castles of the nobility. The aristocracy took particular delight in participating personally in these sophisticated *divertissements* which were designed to offer them the opportunity to display their individual talents in music, poetry and dancing, to show off their fine clothes and jewellery, to demonstrate their high station in Court favour, and to receive the flattery of the artists whom they patronized. The cost of these spectacles was positively staggering, and at a time when the Royal treasury could little afford it. No wonder then that the Puritans could point to these wasteful expenditures as one excuse to demand the closing of the playhouses, and that they could use these excesses as a political weapon against the King. Charles I, in his turn, attempted to use the masque as an instrument for his own political propaganda. But, inasmuch as only the aristocracy was permitted to attend the performances, he succeeded only in bolstering the ego of the Court itself, and further antagonizing the masses of his subjects.

As one of Charles' favoured musicians, William Lawes was frequently called upon to write music for these shows. In collaboration with Simon Ives, Henry Lawes and others, he supplied the major portions of the music to Shirley's *Triumph of Peace* (1634) and the latter's *Triumph of Beautie*, and to Davenant's *Triumphs of the Prince D'Amour* (1636) and *Britannia*

Triumphans (1638). Fortunately, a quantity of Lawes' music for each of these masques has been preserved in one of the autograph volumes in the Bodleian Library in Oxford, Mus. Sch. B.2. Although the scores to none of these are complete, yet together they make up the largest collection of music which is extant for the Caroline Court masque. Indeed, aside from a few pieces by Henry Lawes, they are the only music extant from these masques.

For more than two centuries masques in one form or other had been the chief entertainment at the English Court. They were usually presented to celebrate the festival seasons. In Caroline times it became traditional to perform one masque on Twelfth Night in honour of the King and one on Shrove Tuesday for the Queen. But masques were also produced for special occasions, such as the entertainment of foreign dignitaries, the marriage of persons of high rank and to celebrate the granting of high titles of nobility by the King.

The *raison d'être* of the masque and climax of the evening's entertainment was the formal dance presented by the King and Queen and other members of the nobility. In its earliest history this was all there was to a masque, but in the course of time other entertainment was added. The Caroline masque usually began with a grand procession in which everyone connected with the production took part. Sometimes, as in the case of Shirley's *Triumph of Peace*, this was a lavish affair which paraded through the streets of London for hours before the actual performance. Here one clearly sees the influence of Renaissance festivals and carnivals, especially the masquerade and the Florentine *trionfo* which was so popular with Lorenzo dei Medici. After the procession had entered the hall and everyone had taken his appointed place the curtain flew up and the spectator was presented with some form of allegorical plot by a group of professional actors. Often this was preceded by a speech of welcome to the King and Queen.

Allegory was a permanent feature of the masque, descending from the early English morality plays. It was revitalized by the spread of the Humanistic movement. Influenced by the *ballet de cour*, the plot of the masque attained a degree of dramatic unity, and by the efforts of one man, Ben Jonson, a degree of literary excellence which was even superior to its continental counterpart. Accredited to Jonson as well was the introduction of the humorous and farcical element. According to the poet himself, it was James I's Queen, Anne of Denmark, who had requested some sort of 'shew' which might lend variety and contrast and precede her own, i.e. the main masquing dance, and thus act as a foil or 'false masque'. To accomplish this Jonson turned to a contemporary French source for inspiration, the more informal *ballet-masquerade*. The resulting 'antimasques' consisted of grotesque dances or pantomimes which were performed by professional actors representing either the 'meaner sort' (housewives, fishmongers, blacksmiths, tradesmen, etc.), lesser mythological beings (nymphs, sprites, satyrs, etc.), or birds and animals. These often served as vehicles for biting satire and ridicule. The number of antimasques within the masque gradually increased until in the last of the Court masques, Davenant's *Salmacida Spolia* (1640), no less than twenty antimasques were included. This tendency proved a cancerous growth which, together with the increasing complexities and extravagance of the stage machinery, designs and costuming, contributed not only to the literary decline of the masque, but to the break-up of the form itself.

Songs and choruses formed another part of the masque and were usually interspersed between the figured dances of the masquers and the revels, which constituted the closing portion of the work. These were serious songs performed by the allegorical characters or the deities themselves, extolling the virtues and deeds of the Royal pair through the use of allegory. The vocal forms were largely the same as the secular forms employed in setting Cavalier poetry or lyrics from the drama. They included declamatory songs, composed 'ballads', dialogues, and 'trialogues'. The choruses varied between part-songs of three, four and five voices in familiar 'ballad' style (note-against-note), to others in the style of the late English madrigal, or more frequently, a blend of both styles. The music of the antimasques probably consisted of humorous and lively dance tunes, catches, drinking-songs and traditional folk music.

The figured dances of the *Grand Masquers*, i.e. the King and Queen and the nobility, were, as stated above, the high point of the evening's entertainment. These were presented in the sequence of an 'entry', a 'main dance', and a 'going-off'. The masquers, who numbered either eight, twelve or sixteen, usually made a surprise appearance from some place of concealment on the stage and then descended to a lower stage or 'apron' for the masquing dances. The latter consisted of stately pavans, almans, corants, galliards and sarabands, or in other words the same instrumental dance forms which formed the basis for so much of the serious instrumental music of the period.[1] The 'main dance' of the *Grand Masquers* was a lengthy and majestic pavan, which was often referred to as the 'measures', a term which had become traditional for the pavan at the English Court.[2] As has been pointed out in previous chapters, the pavan was the most serious of the dance forms and often served as the first movement of a suite. After the 'main dance' there occurred the famous 'revels', in which the masquers descended from the stage on specially provided staircases or ramps and chose partners from the audience for informal dancing. After this the masquers returned to the upper stage instead of remaining in the hall with the guests, as was the practice in similar continental entertainments such as the Italian *veglia* and *masquerie*, or the French *ballet de cour*. At this point the final dance or 'going-off' was presented by the masquers, followed by an epilogue addressed to the King and Queen. In the later Caroline masques the last dance was often discarded in favour of a 'Grand Chorus'. The latter is true of all of Lawes' masques.

As in the theatre orchestra, the location of the musicians during the masque performances was one of dispersal into several small groups about the stage and behind the scenes. There was no main orchestra. Unfortunately, accounts of the exact numbers, types and placement of these groups are exceedingly rare, the best being that of Thomas Campion for the *Masque in Honour of Lord Hay* (1607), for which he wrote some music. Campion places his musicians in three groups: ten, including two violins, lutes, harpsichord and trombone, to the right of the stage near to the audience; twelve, made up entirely of bowed strings, to the left of the stage; and twelve, six voices and six

[1] For a discussion of all these dances and their steps see Chapter III, pp. 81–4.

[2] Further to this see Otto Gombosi, 'Some Musical Aspects of the English Court Masque', *Journal of the American Musicological Society*, Vol. I (Fall 1948), No. 3, p. 12 and passim.

cornets, again to the right but upon a higher platform and further back. In addition to these there seems to have been a group of 'hautboys' in the gallery.[1] It was also the practice for singers on the stage to accompany themselves with lutes, and 'music from within' is used effectively in the masque as it is in the drama of the period. By the placement of these groups it is noted that the orchestration of the masque is primarily concerned with dimensional effects. Presumably, each group, or any combination of groups, could support the actions taking place on any of the stage levels. They could also combine all of their resources with full dimensional effect, for the grand finale.

The only reference which we have to William Lawes' orchestra is that given by Whitelocke for the *Triumph of Peace*. According to this parliamentarian there were 'Fourty Lutes at one time, besides other instruments and voices of the most excellent musicians in Consort'.[2] We learn even more of the groups that participated in the *Triumph of Peace* from Whitelocke's account of the procession which preceded the masque proper. 'A dozen of the best Trumpeters' provided an escort for the one hundred Gentlemen of the Inns of Court. This was contrasted with 'Musick of Keys and Tongues and the like, snapping and yet playing in a Consort' by the cripples and beggars of the first antimasque. And after this 'came other Musicians on Horseback playing upon Bag-pipes, Horn-pipes, and such kind of Northern Musick' which introduced the antimasque of the Projectors. At several additional points throughout the long procession Whitelocke states that there were groups of six renowned musicians mounted on horseback and attended by laquies and footmen who carried torches. In one of the Roman chariots, which immediately preceded those of the *Grand Masquers*, there were again 'about a dozen Musicians'. These 'play'd upon excellent and loud musick all the way as they went', and before each of the chariots bearing members of the nobility 'came six more Musicians on Footclothes'. According to the complete report the total number of instrumental musicians alone for this masque must have been well over one hundred. This is more than twice the number used by Campion.

---

[1] E. J. Dent, *Foundations of English Opera* (Cambridge: 1928), p. 22.

[2] For this and the following quotations see Bulstrode Whitelocke, *Memorials of the English Affairs* (London: Nathaniel Ponder, 1682), pp. 19–20.

The staging of Jacobean and Caroline masques included highly ornate prosceniums, complex stage machinery, magnificent costumes, elaborate scenery, revolving stage sets or *periaktoi* and numerous special effects. All of these were the province of the ingenious Inigo Jones. The Stuarts spared no expense in their efforts to exceed the spectacles of foreign courts and gave Jones a free hand to design and construct the most lavish sets and costumes. The latter had studied his craft in Italy and closely copied Italian as well as French models for his productions, especially the sets of Giulio Parigi. The Court masques were usually presented at the great Banqueting House at Whitehall, which Jones specially adorned for the occasion. The audience was seated upon scaffolding or 'degrees' expressly built for the performance. The King and Queen were seated on the 'State' which was covered by a canopy at the head of the audience. Immediately in front of the Royal pair was the dancing place and beyond that rose the stage, consisting of two or more levels which carried the eye up to the gallery when the entire scene was disclosed. Workmen were stationed on the roof, at the stage windows and beneath the stage itself to manage the complicated machinery and special effects for situations involving *deus ex machina* and scenery changes.

Ben Jonson and Inigo Jones dominated the development of the Court masque in England. Together, during the reign of James I, they brought the form to the peak of its popularity. But after the accession of Charles I a jealous rivalry developed between the two men which finally ended in the retirement of the poet. Jonson was intent on making of the masque a lasting literary art form. Jones, as chief surveyor of His Majesty's works, would not allow anything or anyone to interfere with his grandiose staging and insisted that he be given 'top billing' on all masque publications. Because he refused to submit to Jones' demands, Ben Jonson received no commissions to write for the Court masques after 1631. Thereafter they were turned over to James Shirley and William Davenant, both of whom agreed to meet the demands of Inigo Jones. Thus, by drastically reducing the importance of the plot, by greatly increasing the farcical element, and by subordinating the action of both to the demands of Jones' spectacular stage techniques, Shirley and Davenant loosened the cords which unified the work as a whole and they thereby contributed to the deterioration of the masque itself.

Shirley's *Triumph of Peace* was the most elaborate and costly of all Court masques. According to Whitelocke, who was in charge of the music, the total outlay exceeded twenty-one thousand pounds. Today this would be roughly equivalent to some 420,000 pounds or equal to the cost of some of the most expensive Hollywood extravaganzas. For their parts in composing the music, William Lawes and Simon Ives received one hundred pounds apiece and the entire cost of the music alone was one thousand pounds. The circumstances surrounding the masque were political, which accounts in part for the excessive expenditure. The Puritan opposition was becoming increasingly vehement in their denunciation of stage plays and entertainments. In 1633, William Prynne, a barrister of Lincoln's Inn and a Puritan pamphleteer, published his famous *Histrio-Mastix*, in which he claimed that kings and emperors who were enthusiasts of drama had always met with violent deaths, and in which he also included a phrase in the table of contents to the effect that '*Women actors*' were '*Notorious Whores*'. In this publication Archbishop William Laud saw his opportunity to be rid of Prynne, who was a formidable opponent of Arminianism and Ceremonialism. Laud waited until a certain pastoral, in which Henrietta Maria was taking part, was presented and the next day he showed the book and the questionable passages to the King and Queen. The Sovereigns, though greatly annoyed, chose to ignore the book until Laud and others, taking other writings of Prynne out of context, built up a strong enough case. Prynne was then sent to the Tower to await trial by the Star Chamber.

In the meantime the King let it be known to some of his servants who were members of the four great societies of the legal profession that he would look favourably upon the presentation of a masque some time during the season of the Christmas festivities as a testimony of their loyalty and affection for the Crown. By this it was hoped that the honourable societies of the Inns of Court would demonstrate their unanimous difference of opinion with Prynne, who was of course himself a member of Lincoln's Inn, and thus refute the *Histrio-Mastix*. The Royal suggestion was seized upon and the Inns of Court decided to present the masque 'in the noblest and most stately manner, that could be invented'.[1] Two members were chosen by each of the societies, the Middle Temple, the Inner Temple, Lincoln's Inn, and Gray's Inn, to form a committee to plan and carry out the details. Whitelocke himself was one of the members for the Middle Temple and was chosen by the committee to supervise the entire production. This parliamentarian, as it has already been noted, was an accomplished musician who was well acquainted with the best composers in London through the weekly chamber music concerts which were held at his father's house. It was Whitelocke who chose William Lawes and Simon Ives to write the music, and to supervise the entire musical part of the masque, for in addition to Lawes and Ives 'Four of the most excellent Musicians of the Queen's Chappel, *Monsieur la Mare, Monsieur du Vall, Monsieur Robert*, and *Monsieur Mari*, and divers others of foreign Nations, who were most eminent in their Art', and other English musicians were 'to bear their parts in the Musick; and for the better preparation and practice of the Musick, they had meetings together of English, French, Italians, Germans, and other Masters of Musick'. Whitelocke also tells us that 'the Dancers, Masquers, Anti-Masquers and Musicians, did before-hand practice in the place where they were to present the Masque'.

Four 'Gentlemen' from each of the Inns of Court were chosen as the Grand Masquers on the basis of their 'Persons, Dancing and Garb'. They were to be drawn in 'Roman Triumphant Chariots' which 'being of an Oval Form, in the Seats there would be no difference of place in them'. On Candelmas Day, February 2, 1634, all of 'the Masquers, Horsemen, Musicians, Dancers, and all that were Actors in this business, according to order met at Ely-house in Holborn, there the grand Committee sate all day to Order all Affairs; and when the Evening was come, all things being in full readiness, they began to set forth in this order down *Chancery Lane* to *Whitehall*'.

Whitelocke's vivid account of the procession that followed has already been referred to in relation to the musicians taking part in the masque. But the music was only one feature of a much more luxurious display. The entire procession, consisting

[1] Ibid., pp. 18–19.

of hundreds of men, was dressed in the most expensive and colourful costumes, trimmed with solid silver and with gold. Even the horses were outfitted and plumed in the colours of their riders and each group had its colour scheme, 'The Torches and flaming huge Flamboys born at the sides of each Chariot, made it seem lightsom as at Noon-day'. We can well imagine the effect this created on all London as the giant procession of Gentlemen, guards, dancers, actors, musicians, masquers, horses, chariots, laquies, footmen, antimasquers and others, all in their dazzling finery and lighted by torchlight, slowly marched down Chancery Lane to the rhythm of various music and the cheers of 'the multitude of Spectators in the Streets [and] besides the windows' who 'seemed loth to part with so glorious a Spectacle'. Charles I and his Queen were so impressed with the procession that they ordered 'that the whole show might fetch a turn about the Tilt-yard, that their Majesties might have a double view of them'.

Arriving at Whitehall-Gate the entire pageant alighted and dispersed to the Banqueting Hall 'and several Rooms and places prepared for them'. 'In the meantime the Banquetting-house at *White-hall* was so crowded with fair Ladies, glittering with their rich cloths and richer Jewels, and with Lords and gentlemen of great quality that there was scarce room for the King and Queen to enter in.' 'The *King* and Queen, and all Their Noble Train being come in, the Masque began, and was incomparably performed in the Dancing, Speeches, Musick, and Scenes; the Dances, Figures, Properties, the Voices, Instruments, Songs, Airs, Composures, the Words and Actions, were all of them exact and none failed in their Parts of them, and the scenes were most curious and costly.'[1]

Shirley's text demonstrates how completely the Jonsonian ideals were abandoned to bare exteriors.[2] There is no dramatic unity or continuity in the *Triumph of Peace*. Instead, there is a regression to sheer pageantry: some inconsequential dialogue, antimasques in the guise of dance pantomimes, songs, choruses, dances, and allegory, with little connection between them. The

[1] Ibid., pp. 20-1.
[2] The entire masque is printed in The Mermaid Series edition, *James Shirley*, with an introduction by Edmund Gosse (London: Vizetelly & Co., 1888), pp. 437-66.

opening scene was the favourite early Baroque perspective of palaces, porticoes, 'and other noble pieces of architecture', forming two oblique rows on either side of the stage and leading the eye to the central *Piazza of Peace*, which was seen in the distance. A number of characters enter at spaced intervals, representing Opinion, Confidence, Fancy, Jollity, Laughter, Novelty and Admiration. The playful dialogue that follows reveals that they have come to Court to help in the presentation of the masque. It also indicates how important the antimasque had become in the Caroline masque, as evidence the following conversation:

> *Fancy:* How many antimasques have they? of what nature?
> For these are fancies that take most; your dull
> And phlegmatic inventions are exploded.
> Give me a nimble antimasque.
> *Opinion:* They have none, sir.
> *Laughter:* No antimasque! I'd laugh at that, i'faith.
> *Jollity:* What make we here? No jollity!
> *Fancy:* No antimasque!
> Bid 'em down with the scene, and sell the timber,
> Send Jupiter to grass, and bid Apollo
> Keep cows again . . .[1]

The characters decide to present the first antimasque themselves and they dance, 'expressing the natures of the presenters'. After this Opinion calls for something in a different vein and Fancy obliges with a scene change to 'A spick and span new tavern'. Here the second antimasque is presented, consisting of a series of dance pantomimes; first, by the master of the tavern, his wife and servants; after these, '*a* Maquerelle, *two* Wenches, *two wanton* Gamesters'; and third, a Gentleman and four beggars:

'*The* Gentleman *first danceth alone*; *to him the* Beggars; *he bestows his charity*; *the* Cripples, *upon his going off*, *throw away their legs, and dance*.'

After another bit of dialogue in which Opinion is still not satisfied, Fancy brings on the third antimasque of six 'Projectors', who come on individually and perform dances as Fancy describes each one. Whitelocke tells us that Attorney Noy had a great hand in this antimasque 'because by it an information

[1] Ibid., p. 448.

was covertly given to the King, of the unfitness and ridiculousness of these Projects against the Law'.[1] Whitelocke is referring to the practice of the Crown in granting patents of monopoly to individuals or 'projectors' for all kinds of nonsensical purposes. The fifth 'projector', for example, demands a patent of monopoly 'to fatten poultry with scrapings of a carrot'. The fourth 'projector' claims the invention of an utterly 'fantastic' device, no less than a diving bell or suit with which the occupant could 'fetch up gold or whatever jewels have been lost, in any river o'the world'. When all have been presented, the 'projectors' are joined by the characters of the preceding anti-masque and they dance.

Opinion now asks for 'some other than human shapes', and Fancy obliges with another scene change to a woody landscape and another dance pantomime:

'An Owl, a Crow, a Kite, a Jay, a Magpie. The birds dance and wonder at the Owl. When these are gone, enter a Merchant, a'Horseback with his portmanteau; two Thieves, set upon him and rob him: these by a Constable and Officers are apprehended and carried off. Then four Nymphs enter dancing, with their javelins; three Satyrs spy them and attempt their persons; one of the Nymphs escapeth; a noise of hunters and their horns within, as at the fall of a deer; then enter four Huntsmen and one Nymph; these drive away the Satyrs, and having rescued the Nymphs, dance with them.'

Opinion is still not content and asks 'This all you will present?' Fancy claims that his invention cannot be exhausted and he changes the scene once more to another landscape. Again there is a sequence of dances and pantomimes; first, between three dotterels and three dotterel-catchers, and next, this scene borrowed from Cervantes:

'. . . enter a Windmill, a fantastic Knight, and his Squire armed. The fantastic adventurer with his lance makes many attempts upon the Windmill, which his Squire imitates: to them enter a Country-gentleman and his Servant. These are assaulted by the Knight and his Squire, but are sent off lame for their folly.'

[1] Whitelocke, op. cit., p. 20.

After the antimasques are concluded, some solemn music introduces the serious part of the masque, which takes the form of an allegory between Irene (Peace), Eunomia (Law) and Diche (Justice). Each descends from the heavens, *deus ex machina*, on differently coloured clouds, and sings: first, a declamatory song with chorus by Irene, then a dialogue between Irene and Eunomia which is also concluded by a chorus, and finally, a trio or 'trialogue' between Irene, Eunomia, and Diche with a short interlude again for the chorus. William Lawes' music to most of this part of the masque is extant.[1] After another song by 'the whole train of Musicians' the scene is changed 'and the Masquers appear sitting on the ascent of a hill, cut out like the degrees of a theatre'. The masquers are then presented in a speech by 'a Genius or angelical person'. 'Here, with loud music, the Masquers descend and dance their entry to the violins'; which ended, they retire to the scene. At this point Shirley unexpectedly introduces a hoax. 'A crack is heard in the works, as if there were some danger by some piece of the machines falling' and some workmen and their wives force their way onto the stage claiming that they have a right to see the masque. Suddenly, realizing where they are, they decide to 'dance a figary' themselves so that 'somebody will think this was meant for an antimasque'. When the commoners are gone 'the Masquers are encouraged by a song, to their revels with the ladies'. This dancing ended, the scene again changes and it is dawn. Amphiluche, forerunner of the morning, appears on a cloud of vapour and sings what is probably the finest song in the masque, 'In Envye of the Night'. Fortunately, Lawes' music for this piece has been preserved in his autograph volume of songs in the British Museum. It is given on page 218.

The masque closes as Amphiluche ascends upon her cloud and the masquers are called from their revels by other voices in a final song. The music to the latter was also written by Lawes. The final fragment of this is in the autograph in the Bodleian Library, Mus. Sch. B.2 and appears to have been overlooked by Professor Dent, in his account of the music.[2]

---

[1] Most of Lawes' score for the *Triumph of Peace* is printed by E. J. Dent, *Foundations of English Opera* (Cambridge: 1928), pp. 30–7. This does not, however, include the song 'In Envye of the Night', which is in the British Museum autograph, Add. 31432, and a final fragment in Bodleian, Mus.

Sch. B.2. A few corrections must also be noted in Dent's transcription. On p. 36, at the words 'Although I am but wild about thee', Dent prints the music with Lawes' own bar-lines and states that the second phrase is a minim short. Lawes, however, has crossed out the stem of the last minim and made it a semibreve. Also, on p. 34 (top of page), Dent has wrongly transcribed the middle part at the words 'to show the evening's glory', and wrongly set the words. The correction is as follows:

Triumph of Peace, masque by James Shirley
(excerpt Song II)   a 3 voc.

[2] Loc. cit.

Song VIII: In Envye of The Night (sung by Amphiluca)
from the masque "The Triumph of Peace" by James Shirley

From Lawes' music it is possible to form a good picture of the general musical plan of the *Triumph of Peace*. Each song is introduced by a short instrumental 'simphony.' Of these we have only a treble and an unfigured bass part. These 'simphonies' are no different than the usual 'lessons', 'almans', 'aires' or other dance tunes in two parts which were published by Playford in such profusion. Indeed, many of Lawes' 'simphonies' from his masques are actually included under their regular dance titles in Playford's collections.[1] This music is rather stately in character and the bass parts maintain some freedom of motion. Its purpose was undoubtedly to bring the more serious characters of the masque onto the stage, usually via *deus ex machina*, serving at the same time to introduce their songs. There was, however, no thematic relationship between the 'simphonies' and the songs that followed them. The songs themselves, as stated previously, do not differ from Lawes' other vocal work. The choruses are in four real parts, except where a single voice or a few voices are used independently. The part of Irene was written for a male tenor and may well have been designed especially for John Lanier, who apparently sang the part at the performances.[2] Henry Lawes, it appears, also took part in the masque, if only to sing the part of one of the five 'constellacions' who made up the chorus.[3] The alto parts also seem intended for male voices. Another peculiarity of the vocal writing is the close position of the lower voices, with the treble separated from them at some distance. As Professor Dent has observed, this is one of the technical habits of the day. The same characteristic has already been noted in Lawes' instrumental music.

Just what part of the music Simon Ives composed it is impossible to know. No music by him for the *Triumph of Peace* has as yet been indentified. Of the nine vocal numbers in the serious part of the masque Lawes is definitely known to have composed the first, second, third, eighth and ninth. Moreover, in the autograph in the Bodleian Library, Mus. Sch. B.2, at least three folios have been removed from the binding between the ending of the third song and the last fragment of the ninth. The latter

[1] Further to this on pp. 228-9.
[2] *Historical Manuscripts Commission Reports*, Vol. I, p. 355, cited by Willa McClung Evans, *Henry Lawes* (Oxford University Press: 1941), p. 83.
[3] Loc. cit.

has been scratched out but is still decipherable. It is possible that all of the remaining songs to the *Triumph of Peace* were contained on the missing folios. If Lawes did write the music to all of the songs, as it seems likely he did, then Ives must have been occupied with some of the instrumental music for the antimasques, revels and masquing dances. As regards the latter it would be interesting indeed to know just how much such collections as Lawes' *Royall Consort* figured in the dances of the evening. We can have a good idea, from Matthew Locke's *Masque of Cupid and Death* (1653), of the instrumental dances of the antimasques.[1] These again are the same short dances of the type found in Playford's *Court-Ayres* (1655) and *Courtly Masquing Ayres* (1662), of which the largest single contribution is by Lawes. From the directions given in the masques themselves it is certain that violins were the main instruments used for these dance tunes and that they were accompanied by bass viols and perhaps lutes. Thus, in the *Triumph of Peace*, after the masquers are discovered, the following direction is given in the printed text: 'Here, with loud music, the Masquers descend and dance their entry to the violins'.

The *Triumph of Peace* so pleased the Queen, who incidentally took part in the revels 'until it was almost morning', that she desired to see the entire production acted over again. Consequently, the King and Queen were invited by the Lord Mayor of London, some ten days later, to the Merchant-Taylor's Hall in the city for a second performance. This time the complete procession marched through the streets of the city as before, to the delight of the populace. The description and text of the masque was immediately published and went through three editions in its first year. As for William Lawes' part, there is little doubt that his popularity was greatly enhanced for his being chosen to write the music for this, the most spectacular masque ever presented in England. Moreover, in the several editions of the masque, both Lawes and Ives were praised for their work to the detriment of the dramatist himself. The final appended footnote reads as follows:

'The composition of the music, was performed by Mr.

---

[1] This masque, which is also by Shirley, is published in its entirety as edited by E. J. Dent in *Musica Britannica*, Vol. II.

William Lawes, and Mr. Simon Ives, whose art gave an harmonious soul to the otherwise languishing numbers.'

No doubt Lawes' successful and important work for the *Triumph of Peace* earned him the recognition at Court which led to his appointment as 'musician in ordinary for yᵉ lutes and voices' in the following year.

Politically, the *Triumph of Peace* seems to have been successful in rallying the followers of the King and renewing their faith in the magnificence and power of the Crown. But how much this spirit carried over into the Puritan camp it is difficult to say. For his part, Archbishop Laud vigorously prosecuted Prynne for his writings and in the following year the latter was sentenced to life imprisonment, fined five thousand pounds, expelled from Lincoln's Inn, disbarred from the practice of the legal profession, his book, the *Histrio-mastix*, was to be burned, his degree from the university was rescinded, and he suffered in addition the painful and humiliating experience of being set upon the pillory and having his ears cut off. During the Interregnum, however, Prynne was released, and in a thoroughly vindictive mood he aided in the prosecution of the Archbishop, who was convicted by the Parliament of high treason and sentenced to the axe.

The next Court masque for which Lawes' music is extant in part is Davenant's *The Triumphs of the Prince D'Amour* (1636). In this William collaborated with his brother, Henry Lawes. The masque was conceived and produced by the members of the Middle Temple of the Inns of Court in honour of the arrival in England of Charles I's nephews, Charles and Rupert, the Palatine Princes. The King's sister, Elizabeth, Queen of Frederick V, the Elector Palatine of Bohemia, had sent her sons for an extended visit to Charles' Court during the fall of 1635 in the hope that the King might thereby be moved to support her claims and those of her sons for regaining control of the Palatinate.[1] Since the late arrival of Prince Rupert coincided with the oncoming Christmas festivities, Davenant was given but three days in which to write the libretto. The title of the masque was derived from the long-established tradition of the

[1] For a more detailed account of the visit of the Palatine Princes see Arthur H. Nethercot, *Sir William D'Avenant* (University of Chicago Press, 1938), pp. 132–7.

four societies of the Inns of Court, each of which appointed a Lord of Misrule to preside over the Christmas revels at their respective palaces. At the Middle Temple this Christmas Prince was known as the Prince d'Amour. It was his function 'to preside over the festivities of the season by setting up his court of misrule and governing in precedence of other constituted authority'.[1] The performance of the masque, so hastily prepared, was delayed for several days, but Davenant was not permitted to revise the libretto as he so ardently wished.[2]

Even more so than in the *Triumph of Peace*, *The Triumphs of the Prince D'Amour* is lacking in dramatic continuity. This absence of any serious plot is of course intentional. Davenant, like Shirley, devised the masque as a series of ballets and interludes, similar in design to the *ballet de cour*. The masque opens with a speech by the Master of Ceremonies to the Prince Elector, Charles Louis, who was seated in the 'State', and to whom the masque was dedicated. This is immediately followed by the first antimasque, a tavern dumb-show performed by drunken soldiers, etc. The scene then changes to a camp of war tents, in the midst of which stands the Temple of Mars. The Priests of Mars come out of the temple playing on instruments (probably lutes), and sing about a battle lately fought. A chorus sings a refrain between each stanza. They retire and the masquers appear from several of the tents dressed as 'heroique Knights Templars', disguised by the bevirs of their helmets. They dance their entry, but upon leaving discover Cupid 'descending in a bright cloud'. The latter sings his charming song, 'Whither so gladly, and so fast', and shoots his arrows among all present, dispelling all 'warlike hearts' to love.

The scene then changes to a 'square Piazza' and the second antimasque is presented by five lovers, 'a grave formal Spanish lover, a jealous Italian lover, a giddy fantastic French lover, a dull Dutch lover, and a furious debauch'd English lover', each of whom demonstrates his technique in wooing his mistress beneath her balcony window. Once more the scene is changed,

[1] Ibid., p. 134.
[2] Davenant explains this in his preface 'To Every Reader', in the printed edition of the masque. James Maidment and W. H. Logan, *The Dramatic Works of Sir William D'Avenant* (Edinburgh: William Paterson, 1872), Vol. I, pp. 317-40.

and this time to a grove of trees, in the middle of which is a clearing for the Temple of Venus. The priests of Venus emerge from the temple, also playing on instruments, and sing their song, which calls for an end to all strife. Now the masquers re-appear and dance a second entry. After this, another scene change and the Temple of Apollo is discovered in a grove of laurel trees. The priests of Apollo approach from various parts of the temple and sing 'Make room for our God too' who unites all in war and love. From behind the trees appear twelve slaves bearing sections of a banquet table laden with precious fruits and disguised with green boughs. The priests of Apollo, in another song, call to these 'industrious slaves of plenty' to bring in their 'Indian fruits'. This the slaves do, joining their several sections into one long banquet table in front of the 'State'. As the princes taste the fruits, all of the priests join in the 'Song of Valediction', in which each of the priestly orders wishes their particular attributes upon the two Royal Princes. In the final *Grand Chorus*, all join in tribute to Charles Louis.

Like Ben Jonson's *Lovers Made Men* (1617), *The Triumphs of the Prince D'Amour* was entirely set to music, except for a short pro-logue to the Prince Elector, but not entirely in *stylo recitativo*. The only extant music for the masque by Henry Lawes is Cupid's solo, which is in the key of G and in declamatory style. The rest of the music which has survived is by William Lawes and begins with the 'simphony' which precedes the second song of the priests of Apollo, in which the latter command the slaves to bring in the banquet. From this point on William's music continues uninterrupted to the end of the masque. This music is more interesting than that of the *Triumph of Peace*, although Davenant's masque is dramatically less appealing. And since Davenant had only three days to prepare the text, Lawes had even less time to write the score. The separate entrances of the priests in particular offered the composer an opportunity to display his ingenuity in varying the textures of the choruses. Lawes has made the most of this, using solo declamatory song, dialogues, three-part songs and full choruses interspersed. There is also added contrast at several points where the songs vary from duple to triple metre, interrupting the musical declama-tion with the more tuneful settings of composed 'ballads'. More interesting is the fact that the entire 'Song of Valediction' is knitted together by the last half of the 'simphony' which precedes it, and which Lawes uses as a *ritornelle* between each of the songs of the priests as they descend from the stage to a position in front of the 'State.' Finally, before the *Grand Chorus*, the complete 'simphony' is repeated once more. Lawes has thus introduced a unifying element to balance the variety of song forms, textures and rhythms. The *ritornelle* itself is a dignified tune in the triple rhythm of the corant and is well suited for its purpose. The key is Lawes' favoured tonality, C minor.

In his analysis of Lawes' music to the *Triumph of Peace*, Edward Dent has called attention to the composer's strong sense of balanced tonality.[1] This is true of all of Lawes' masque music. It may be seen even more clearly in the *ritornelle* from the *Prince d'Amour* described above. The song and 'simphony' preceding this are in C major, and we recall that Henry Lawes' 'Song of Cupid', which occurs earlier, is in the key of G. Lawes' modulations are almost always to the dominant, relative minor, tonic minor or subdominant keys and he uses these to suit the mood of the action or text. Thus, when the priests of Apollo happily call for the banquet to be brought in, the key is major, as it is also for the song of the priests of Mars, but when the priests of Venus sing of passion and love, the minor tonality is maintained throughout. It is clear that Lawes did conceive of his score as one large musical design unified by a balanced tonality. It is in this anticipation of one continuous and organized piece of music from beginning to end, having a broad sense of tonality, according to Dent, 'that we can see the masques to be real forerunners of opera'.[2]

In the same autograph which contains Lawes' music to the *Triumph of Peace* and *The Triumphs of the Prince d'Amour*, there is music to yet another masque, which the composer simply entitled *The King's Masque*. The present writer has been able to identify this music as belonging to William Davenant's *Britannia Triumphans* which was presented before the King and Queen on the Sunday after Twelfth Night, 1638.[3] This was one

---

[1] Dent, op. cit., p. 39.   [2] Loc. cit.

[3] The second performance of *Britannia Triumphans*, in a shortened form, was given at the Juilliard School of Music on December 11, 1953, as the climax and finale of *A Festival of British Music* in honour of Coronation Year. The score for this production was prepared by the author from the original music and other of Lawes' vocal and instrumental works.

of the last three masques presented at the Court of Charles I. It is the last Court masque to which music is extant. Whether or not William Lawes collaborated with another musician in the composition of the music it is not yet possible to determine. In the author's opinion it is probable that he did, not only because such collaboration was traditional but because, as in the case of the other masques, the musical score for *Britannia Triumphans* is not complete. The 'remarkable' Inigo Jones did the scenery and designs for this production, as he did for the others, and more than fifty sketches of the costumes and scenery are still extant.[1] In a short introduction to the printed edition of the work Davenant informs us that a new masquing hall was especially built for this masque because the ceiling of the old hall had been richly adorned with paintings, and lest these should be ruined by the smoke of many torchlights and candles, King Charles ordered Inigo Jones to construct the new and temporary hall of timber. A letter from George Garrard to the Earl of Strafford places the site of the new hall, which took two months to build, between the Guard-Chamber and the Banqueting House. Garrard adds that the new masquing place 'will cost too much Money to be pulled down, and yet down it must when the Masks are over'.[2]

Britannia Triumphans was the first masque to be presented at Court in two years. This time the subject was both political and religious. Indeed, the last Court masques almost seem to have their sole justification as political or religious instruments of propaganda. The King, aided by the sterling loyalty of the poets, musicians and artists of his household, was attempting to use the masque for his own aggrandizement in a desperate attempt to bolster his already diminishing power and prestige. Charles I was currently embroiled with the Commons over the question of 'ship-money'. In the previous year the King had proclaimed himself 'Sovereign of the Seas', claiming the Channel

---

[1] Some of these are in Percy Simpson and C. F. Bell, *Designs by Inigo Jones for Masques and Plays at Court* (London: 1924). Others are in Allardyce Nicoll, *Stuart Masques and the Renaissance Stage* (New York: Harcourt Brace., Co., 1938). The complete collection is in the library of the Duke of Devonshire at Chatsworth.

[2] *Strafford's Letters*, ii, p. 130, cited by M. S. Steele, *Plays and Masques at Court During the Reigns of Elizabeth, James I and Charles I, 1558–1642* (Oxford University Press, 1926), p. 269.

and the North Sea for his own and forbidding anyone to navigate or fish in those waters without his consent. But Charles was faced with a powerful Dutch fleet, as well as an expanding French navy under Cardinal Richelieu, and he desperately needed funds to build the naval power necessary to back up his pretentious claims. To obtain these funds he decided, without the consent of Parliament, to resort to the unpopular 'ship-money' tax. This aroused a general resentment throughout the country and added substantially to the already widespread discontent. *Britannia Triumphans* sought to vindicate the King's actions and to assure Charles' loyal subjects that, despite the rebellious mood of the times, the King 'in his Secret Wisdome' would triumph over the forces of evil, restore order and bring lasting peace to the western world. Charles himself appeared in the masque as 'Britanocles, the glory of the western world' who 'hath by his wisdom, valour and piety, not only vindicated his own, but far distant seas, infested with pirates, and reduc'd the land, by his example, to a real knowledge of all good acts and sciences'.[1]

At the same time that the King was having his troubles over the 'ship-money' tax, Archbishop Laud and the episcopate were growing ever more unpopular with the citizenry. The masque, when it was performed, created a *furor* in powerful Puritan religious circles for the fact that it was acted on a Sunday immediately following Twelfth Night. And to compound this 'blasphemy' the masque heaped much ridicule upon the Puritans directly, inasmuch as one of the chief characters of the allegory—indeed, the villain of the masque—was habited as a Puritan and given the name 'Imposture'. The storm of protest which this created was still very much remembered as late as 1698, when a follower of Jeremy Collier devoted nineteen pages of bitter invective against this same production in an anonymous pamphlet entitled *The Stage Condemn'd*.

The opening allegory of the masque itself is a verbal contest between Action and Imposture. The former may be termed the spirit of the King's loyal followers, while the latter, in puritan garb, is ridiculed as an apostle of fraudulence and detraction. After some rather lengthy dialogue in which each contests the

---

[1] Quoted from the introduction to the first printed edition of the masque in 1638.

other's philosophy, Imposture calls upon the magician, Merlin, to raise the spirits of the 'mean and low', the multitude, who take no stock in the cultivation of learning or in the arts and sciences. These invoked spirits, cavorting in the setting of a 'horrid hell', form the entries of the antimasques, which are six in number. Included in these interludes is an antimasque of 'mock music' made up of a consort of pipe and tabor, knackers and bells, tongs and key, and gridiron and shoeing horn. Davenant probably modelled this scene after the first antimasque of cripples and beggars who played similar instruments in Shirley's *Triumph of Peace*. Other entries consisted of 'four old-fashioned Parasitical Courtiers' and one of 'rebellious Leaders in war', which included Cade, Kett, Jack Straw and their soldiers. In these short pantomimes the poet was unsparing in his satire of the 'graver sort of people' as contrasted with the 'noble personages' of the masque proper. Thus, 'Imposture governs all' in the vulgar antimasques and Action 'fancies nobler hopes . . . , the arts and sciences' in the serious portion of the performance.

The antimasques being ended, the mythological hero, Bellerophon, enters astride his famous winged steed, Pegasus. For him, Merlin conjures up a 'Mock Romanza' which is a fine piece of true burlesque on the vulnerable subject of chivalry. The characters are a giant, a knight, a damsel, a squire and a dwarf. Here the dramatist has borrowed freely from Italian 'shews and intermedii' as he himself boasts in the introduction to the printed edition. But Bellerophon is unimpressed with the efforts of Imposture and Merlin and he orders them from the scene, calling instead to Fame to appear and help celebrate Britanocles' happy hour. The scene is then changed as the earth opens up and the palace of Fame, fashioned of gold, silver and precious jewels, rises onto the stage. Fame is seen standing atop a high tower, her attendants leaning against the rail of the balustrade below. She calls, by way of a song, for Britannocles to show himself: 'Breake forth: thou treasure of our sight.' The masquers make their surprise entry from behind the columns of the *peristilium* and at that instant the gate of the palace opens and Britanocles (Charles I) appears. The palace sinks into the ground while Fame flies upward to remain hidden in the clouds. There follows a series of choruses and songs and it is from this point onward that William Lawes' music is extant. After this the masquers descend into the room and dance their entry, while the scene on the stage changes back to Britain. A chorus of poets makes an address to the Queen and the scene is changed again, this time to a nautical background from whence the sea-nymph, Galatea, emerges astride a Dolphin. She sings a song with choruses, acknowledging in behalf of the sea-world the King's sovereignty over the seas, and exits 'floating on the waves as she came in'. While the masquing dances continued, ships were seen sailing on the sea and a large fleet, 'with a prosperous gale, entered into the haven'. After the dancing the Valediction was sung, concluding in a *Grand Chorus* beginning 'To Bed, to bed'. Besides the King, the list of Grand Masquers, which occurs at the end of Davenant's printed libretto, included such notables as Lord Philip Herbert, Lord Lodowick Stuart, Lord Russel, the Duke of Lennox and the Earls of Devonshire, Newport and Andevor.

Lawes' music to *Britannia Triumphans*, like that of the other Court masques, comprises the latter and serious part of the work, including the 'simphonies', 'declamatory songs', 'ballads', choruses, Valediction and Grand Chorus. This fact is significant in that it indicates the dominating position William Lawes was accorded when collaborating with other composers. It should be noted that this is also true of the *Triumphs of the Prince d'Amour*, in which William worked together with Henry Lawes. Just how much more of the music to *Britannia Triumphans* was Lawes' work it is difficult to say. Certainly, many of the dances must have been by him. This may be deduced from the large number of dance tunes written by the composer which were included in Playford's *Court-Ayres* of 1655 and the later enlarged edition, the *Courtly Masquing Ayres* of 1662. The titles of these collections do, in fact, betray the origins of their contents in the masques and revels of the Court. Definite proof of this is furnished by the fact that two of the 'simphonies' which introduce the Songs in *Britannia Triumphans* are printed in the *Court-Ayres*. The first of these was played for the scene change and entrance of Galatea, but in Playford's publication it bears the title, 'Almaine', and contains an added section in triple rhythm.[1] This may be

---

[1] The piece is No. 135 in Playford's *Court-Ayres* (1655). The added section in triple metre is in reality an instrumental arrangement of the third verse of Galatea's song, 'On Ever Moving Waves They Dance', from *Britannia*

accepted as a tacit acknowledgement that the 'simphonies' of the masques were in reality the ordinary dance tunes which were so common during the period, a fact that is also borne out by musical analysis. Indeed, it is another early example of the developmental thread which leads from the simple dance tune to the early masque and opera 'simphonies' and thence to the opera overture itself.

The next 'simphony' in the music to *Britannia Triumphans* serves as the introduction to the Valediction. In Playford's *Court-Ayres* this is entitled 'Ayre', a term which Lawes himself uses for many of his dance tunes.[1] Like the previous 'simphony', this one is also in three parts in Lawes' autograph but the inner part has been left out of the printed version by Playford. Like the first piece also, this one has a section in triple metre appended to it. The added section, which appears to be a saraband, is, however, not extant in Lawes' autograph score of the masque. Indeed, it is probably the music of another song or dance tune from *Britannia Triumphans*. In fact, several 'ayres' or almans in the *Court-Ayres* and *Courtly Masquing Ayres* have sarabands or corants added to them. It is probable that these too are from some of the masques or plays of the period. Still another 'simphony' by Lawes is in the *Court-Ayres* as No. 12, but it has not been possible to place it in its proper masque. Another piece by Lawes, entitled the 'Temple Mask', may have been a 'simphony' or dance tune in the *Triumphs of the Prince d'Amour*, which was presented at the Middle Temple. Other of Lawes' 'simphonies' are found as dance tunes in manuscripts of the period, especially in the Bodleian, Mus. Sch. D.220.

The *Court-Ayres* and *Courtly Masquing Ayres* are publications which have been largely ignored by historians. But their value as sources for the original dances, 'simphonies' and songs of the Jacobean and Caroline masque, and possibly for stage plays as well, is paramount. No doubt, further study of these books will disclose still more valuable information about the dances, songs, masques and plays of the period. It is also possible that the entire suites in these publications, of which the identified pieces are a part, are from the same masques. Thus, what at first glance

Triumphans. This is further evidence that 'ballads' were danced to as well as sung.

[1] This 'Ayre' is No. 143 in the *Court-Ayres.*

appear to be two rather large and inconsequential collections of simple two-part dance tunes may be the most complete extant record of dramatic music from the reign of Charles I.

After Davenant's *Salmacida Spolia*, which was performed at Court in 1640, masques were no longer produced at Whitehall because of the ominous events leading up to the Great Rebellion and because popular resentment against these lavish spectacles could no longer be ignored. But masques continued to be endorsed in private schools for young gentlemen of the upper classes. The form of these sometimes differs considerably from that of the Court masque, especially in the antimasques and in the masquing dances. The plot becomes once more a unified and important component of the whole. In the school masque there was also less emphasis placed upon the staging, designs and costumes because of the large expenses involved. The music too is curtailed to some extent. Therefore, they are in many instances closer to the literary drama than they are to the traditional masque form.

In 1646 Shirley published his *Poems*, including in the volume a play entitled *Narcissus, or, The Self-Lover*, and a school masque, *The Triumph of Beautie*. The latter is faintly linked to the *Triumph of Peace*, in that the legal nymphs, Irene, Eunomia and Diche, are mentioned in the last lines of the text, but there is no other direct connection between the two masques, either in the plot or otherwise. The subject of the *Triumph of Beautie* is the judgement of Paris and the libretto calls for a fair amount of singing, much of which occurs off stage. The composer of the music to this masque as well as the music itself has hitherto been unknown.[1] The present writer, however, has identified the music to the song 'Cease Warring Thoughts', which occurs immediately following the shepherd scene. The discovery is important, not only because it reveals the name of the composer, William Lawes, and some of the original music for the masque, but because it places Shirley's composition of the text prior to 1645, the year of Lawes' death. The latter's music is also in the Bodleian, Mus. Sch. B.2. In the autograph, 'Cease Warring Thoughts' has been scratched out, but it is complete and clearly decipherable. As in similar cases, three folios have been

[1] See, e.g., the statement by E. J. Dent in the introduction to his edition of Shirley's *Cupid and Death*, op. cit., p. xi.

Ex. 33

Cease Warring Thoughts (excerpt)

from "The Triumph of Beautie" by James Shirley   a 3 voc.

Thorough Bass

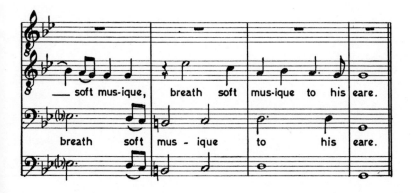

removed from the autograph immediately following this song. Once again, it is possible that other music to the *Triumph of Beautie* may have made up the contents of the missing pages.

X

RELIGIOUS MUSIC

Lawes' sacred compositions, like his songs and dramatic works, have been overshadowed by his chamber music. In the religious field he is chiefly remembered for his posthumous contribution to the *Choice Psalmes*, which was published by his brother in 1648. A single verse anthem, 'The Lord is My Light', had the good fortune to be included in Boyce's *Cathedral Music* in the latter half of the eighteenth century, and we recall in the writings of Samuel Pepys, the diarist's particular fondness for singing 'some psalmes of Will Lawes' before retiring for the night. But the full extent and importance of Lawes' religious music has until now remained obscure. Besides the works mentioned above, there are extant in manuscript at least a dozen anthems of considerable length, several religious canons and some additional freely composed psalms. Moreover, this music is of considerable merit and includes at least one collection which is of unique historical interest.

It is the psalms which form the bulk of Lawes' sacred texts, not only for his freely composed psalms, but for his anthems and religious canons as well. The various psalm settings in England during the sixteenth and seventeenth centuries may be classified into six types. They are: (1) the unharmonized versions of the proper or 'common' church tunes, such as appeared in the numerous editions of the English psalters of Sternhold and Hopkins and which were chanted or sung by the congregation after morning or evening prayer; (2) these same traditional proper tunes regulated by an unfigured bass line for the organ;

(3) settings in three, four or more parts employing the church tunes as *canti fermi*, like those in Thomas Ravenscroft's psalter of 1621; (4) newly composed tunes, (as distinct from the traditional church tunes), with an unfigured bass line for the organ such as those by Henry Lawes for George Sandys' *A Paraphrase Upon The Divine Poems* (1638), and Orlando Gibbons' little known tunes for George Wither's admirable metrical translations, *Hymns and Songs of the Church* (1623); (5) religious songs, anthems, and verse-anthems set in the secular declamatory style, and (6) freely composed settings (i.e. not employing *canti fermi*), in three or more parts, with or without instrumental accompaniment, such as William Child's *First Set of Psalms* (1639). The latter are frequently indistinguishable from the full anthems of the period. It is to this category that the *Choice Psalmes* of the Lawes brothers belongs.

The metrical paraphrases of George Sandys, traveller, American colonist and religious poet, first appeared in print in 1636, although licensed the year before. A second edition, with an appendix containing the psalm tunes of Henry Lawes set to an unfigured bass line, was published in 1638. Sandy's psalms, however, never attained great popularity, even though they were dedicated to King Charles and were approved by the Sovereign. The poet was a member of the King's Privy Council, which probably explains his access to the services of the Lawes brothers for musical settings of his psalms. But dominant conservative forces in the Anglican Church, at odds with the King and his Archbishop, ignored Sandys' paraphrases and they gained no foothold in the singing of the congregation during services. In the private devotions of the King, however, they no doubt had an important place. This may be surmised from the fact that both William and Henry Lawes chose to set Sandys' paraphrases for their own freely composed settings of the psalms, sixty of which appeared in the *Choice Psalmes* of 1648. Henry Lawes' dedication of the latter work to Charles I, when the King was already confined in Carisbrooke Castle, suggests that Sandys' versions were used at the Court and also gives a clue to an approximate composition date. In the opening statements of his dedicatory remarks, Henry says:

'I could not answer mine owne Conscience (most Gracious

Soveraigne) should I dedicate these Compositions to any but Your Majestie; they were born and nourish'd in Your Majesties service, and long since design'd (such as they are) an Offering to Your Royall hand.'

In the same paragraph Henry Lawes also refers to the King's 'known particular affection to *David's* Psalmes', which may well have inspired William and Henry's interest in psalm composition. The *Choice Psalmes* were in all probability favourites of the Chapel Royal and possibly of other private chapels of the aristocracy.

From Henry Lawes' opening statement it is evident that some years had passed between the actual composition of the psalms and their publication. But it is unlikely that they were set to music before their first appearance in print. Sandys himself had only returned from the crown colony of Virginia, where he was a member of the council, in 1631. William Lawes, as we know, did not become one of the King's private musicians until the year 1635, the very year that the poet's psalms were licensed for publication. Sandys' own work on the psalms was probably done between these years. Included in the 1648 publication also is at least one work by William Lawes which offers an additional clue. This is his beautiful elegy 'On The Memory of My Friend; John Tomkins'. The latter, a younger brother of the more famous Thomas Tomkins, was organist of the Chapel Royal. He died on September 27, 1638. This piece is written in the same general style of the psalms themselves and, from internal evidence, may be attributed to the same period of composition. And further, in his valuable epistle *To The Reader*, Henry Lawes states that both his and his brother's psalms were composed 'at the same time' and were 'of the same kinde'. But earlier he says that the compositions were 'set at several times, and upon severall Occasions'. What appears to be a contradiction is merely a reference to the fact that both William and Henry worked together in supplying music for the King's Chapel when the occasion demanded. Considering the evidence it is reasonably safe to conclude that the *Choice Psalmes* were composed some time between the years 1636–9. The author believes them to have been written mainly during the period 1637–8, when the playhouses were closed because of the plague and King

Charles is known to have sought solace as well as entertainment in his Chapel.

Although Henry Lawes refers to the contents of the *Choice Psalmes* as the work of George Sandys, a closer examination shows that this is not entirely so. Only forty-three of the seventy compositions in the volume (seventy-eight, including the elegies 'set in Musick by sev'rall Friends, upon the death of William Lawes') are paraphrases by this poet. Moreover, even these are not all from the Book of Psalms. Nos. 5, 6, and 7 of William's collection are Sandys' paraphrases of three eight-line segments from *The Lamentations of Jeremiah*. No. 16 is the beginning of Sandys' paraphrase of *Isaiah*, xxxviii. In reality, therefore, only 18 of Sandys' psalm paraphrases set by William Lawes were included in the *Choice Psalmes*. These, added to the four works just mentioned, bring the total of Sandys' paraphrases used by William to twenty-two. Of the remaining eight pieces by the younger Lawes (excluding the canons and the elegy for John Tomkins), four are to Latin texts, including a *Gloria Patri*, and four are Old Translations.[1] None of William Lawes' pieces in the *Choice Psalmes* are King James' authorized versions or metrical paraphrases from the psalters of Sternhold and Hopkins.

Henry Lawes' dedication and introduction to the *Choice Psalmes* have already been quoted extensively in Chapter I.[2] It is important, however, to restate the fact that the publication was conceived primarily as a memorial to his brother. It was with this thought in mind that Henry Lawes included in the publication several of William's religious canons in three and four parts and eight elegies mourning the young composer's death written by many of the foremost English musicians of the age, including John Jenkins, John Wilson, Simon Ives, John Hilton, and others. Indeed, the *Choice Psalmes* remain, as Henry intended that they should, 'but a small testimony of his [William's] greater Compositions, (too voluminous for the Presse)'. The publication is also a lasting tribute of the older man's undying love, devotion, and admiration for his brother.

The style of William Lawes' pieces in the *Choice Psalmes* in

[1] The pieces employing Old Translations are No. 13 (Psalm CXXXIII); No. 14 (Psalm CXLIX); No. 15 (Psalm VI); and No. 17 (Psalm XIII).
[2] For the complete dedication and introduction see Chapter I, pp. 27-9.

many ways resembles that of the late English madrigal. There is the same emphasis on horizontal and vertical 'word-painting', the same preoccupation with affective melody and the employment of the dissonant, chromatic style of the late Renaissance. One still finds, in Lawes' psalms, the employment of *fugato* imitations. It is evident too that the composer deliberately chose those psalm texts which offered the best opportunity to exploit these techniques to the fullest possible extent, especially psalms portraying grief, mourning, lamentation and such like. But Lawes has also set a number of psalms in which the theme is rejoicing and praise. These are in a pure, solid block style. The setting of Psalm CL, e.g., is jubilant in its praise and exaltation and has an almost heroic quality. The text is Sandys':

Ex. 34 **Psalm CL: Praise The Lord Enthron'd on High**
(opening section)   a 3 voc.

But this exalted style is in contrast to the composer's writing
in a less joyful vein. Thus, when Lawes sets music to one of his
favourite religious texts, *The Lamentations of Jeremiah*, the tears
flow in endless descending chromatic streamlets until finally
absorbed by one of the composer's characteristically dissonant
cadences, as in this striking illustration from the second part of
Chapter I of Sandys' text.

Ex. 35   Lamentations of
Jeremiah Chapt. 1. (second part): Judah in Exile Wanders
from Choice Psalms 1648 (concluding section)   a 3 voc.

Four of Lawes' psalm settings in the *Choice Psalmes* are important historically as some of the earliest examples of a practice usually associated with Restoration times, a practice which eventually led, through Henry Purcell among others, to one of our great musical treasures, George Frederic Handel's immortal 'Hallelujah Chorus'. The practice of extending the Hallelujah to a florid chorus in the Hallelujah Psalms, especially when these were used as texts for anthems, is a fairly commonplace of the period following the Commonwealth, but its employment in Caroline times is less known. Lawes' examples are therefore especially interesting in tracing the development of this form. The four psalms which have hallelujah choruses appended are No. 9 (Psalm CL), No. 14 (Psalm CXLIX), No. 25 (Psalm CXVII) and No. 29 ('In Resurectione tua Domine'). A fine illustration is the hallelujah chorus from Psalm CXLIX, 'O Sing Unto The Lord a New Song':

Ex. 36

242

Another interesting feature of the psalms is their setting, for
two trebles, bass, and thorough-bass.[1] Here again is the familiar
arrangement of the Baroque trio sonata employed for voices.
We learn more about the setting of these psalms from the title
page of the second edition of William Child's similar collection,
The First Set of Psalmes of III Voyces (1650), in which Child's
psalms are described as 'Fitt for private Chappels or other
private meetings with a continuall *Base* either for the *Organ* or
Theorbo newly compsed after the Italian way'. From this we
conclude that the Lawes brothers' psalms, which are of the same
kind, were written for private devotional singing, that the
indicated thorough-bass was meant for either an organ or a
theorbo, and that the voicing imitated the new Italian trio
settings which were more harmonically conceived. Both collections are strongly secular in character and demonstrate the
influence of instrumental music on the sacred vocal works of
the day. This secular influence is felt not only from instrumental
music but from the madrigal and secular song as well. Hence the

[1] Only the four pieces in Latin are for alto, tenor and bass voices.

employment of word-painting, declamation, and dissonant chromaticism. These are the same influences which one still finds, for example, in the religious music of Henry Purcell.

Fortunately, Henry Lawes has included in the thorough-bass part-book of the *Choice Psalmes* the figures for the realization of the thorough-bass of William's pieces as well as his own.[1]

The thorough-bass parts provide a key to the thorough-bass realizations of pre-Commonwealth times. The figuring is rudimentary and sparse. By a few simple rules the largest part of the realization was accounted for. These rules specified the type of intervals which might be set above a given bass note or progression. When notes appeared unfigured they usually signified root position chords within the key, with certain exceptions for the chords of the leading note, mediant and submediant. Special rules existed also for cadences. The choice of intervals to be set above a given bass note was largely dependent upon the movement of the bass line to and from that note. This gave rise to certain stock progressions which the player immediately recognized by the motion of the bass and which therefore need not be figured. Thus, the common progression of chords frequently employed by Lawes, moving by alternate root position and first inversion, was known as progressing from 'fifts to sixts' and occurred in passages of ascending or descending scale lines. Following is an example of this practice from a chorus in one of Lawes' verse-anthems 'to the cõmon tunes':

Ex. 37

Example of "fifts to sixts" from the Verse Anthem "Cast Mee Not Lord, Out from Thy Face", (Psalm LI, part 2) by William Lawes.

a 3 voc.

Build up Thy walls, build up Thy

Thorough Bass

Build up Thy walls, build up

---

[1] The *Choice Psalmes* were printed in parts only. Seven of the psalms, in full score, are evidently in Charles Burney's handwriting in the British Museum, Add. 11587. A marginal note at the head of one of these states 'the best died first'.

Recognized dissonant combinations received similar treatment. All of these rules for setting intervals, or chords, to an unfigured bass line were learned by the thorough-bass player as part and parcel of his musical education. Consequently, few figures were necessary, and these only at points where unusual combinations, dissonances or arbitrary choices were desired or possible.

The earliest extant English treatise upon the art of playing from a figured thorough-bass was written in 1673 by Matthew Locke. It is entitled *Melothesia Or Certain General Rules for Playing upon a Continued-Bass*.[1] Locke's rules are virtually the same as those used by Henry Lawes in the *Choice Psalmes*, but the latter in some cases uses figures which would have been omitted by Locke, and in others he is not at all consistent in his numbers. Tonic six-four cadences, for example, are sometimes entirely without figures, sometimes they are indicated by 643, and at others by 65. It is typical of the figures of this period that only one horizontal set of numbering was used. None of the figuring in the *Choice Psalmes* employs a double row of numbers. In all cases the thorough-bass doubles the lowest bass voice and fills in the true bass when the latter has pauses. In this respect it is a *continuo* rather than a *basso seguente*, in the sense that the *seguente* type always extracted the lowest bass from the other voices only, whereas the *continuo* would supply the missing bass notes during the pauses.[2] Realizations of the thorough-bass on the organ were kept fairly simple with usually one or two harmonies to the bar. When performed by the theorbo they were even more sparse because of the increased difficulty of performing chords on that instrument.

[1] Locke's treatise may be seen in F. T. Arnold, *The Art of Accompaniment from a Thorough-Bass* (Oxford University Press, 1931), pp. 154–63.

[2] Arnold, op. cit., p. 899.

The religious canons and rounds which are appended to the thorough-bass part of the *Choice Psalmes* are fine works and pleasant to sing. The title-page of the publication states that there are nine of these, but there are in reality ten. Henry Lawes may simply have counted the two short canons entitled 'Regi, Regis, Regum' as one piece. In his religious canons William once again proves himself an inspired melodist. This is evident, for example, in the beautiful *'Gloria in Excelsis Deo*. A Canon of 3 Voc. in the 5th above and 4th below', which John Hilton used to introduce the second part of *Catch that Catch Can* (1652):

Ex. 38

Two of the canons in the *Choice Psalmes* fit into the category of religious rounds. These are both exquisite pieces. The first, 'Jesus is Harmonius', is for three voices and is characterized by profound emotional power and depth. The second canon, 'She Weepeth Sore in the Night', is for four voices and employs selected verses from the second paragraph of one of Lawes' favourite texts, *The Lamentations of Jeremiah*. This canon was extremely popular in its day and has indeed weathered the test of three centuries, for it is still sung today. The melody is among Lawes' finest and has a continuous flow seldom found in the rounds, canons and catches of the period. The harmonies produce a long line of contrary motion between the upper three and the lowest parts. The mood of the text finds realistic expression in the opening descending chromatic line, a technique which is characteristic of Lawes at the mere mention of tears, weeping, lamentation, etc.:

Ex. 39

She Weepeth Sore a 4 voc.

It is difficult to single out a few of these canons without mentioning them all. Suffice it to draw attention to 'These Salt Rivers', 'Lord, Thou Hast Been Favourable', and 'Why Weep'st Thou,

Mary?' All are to be found in the *Choice Psalmes* or in Lawes' autograph in the Bodleian Library, Mus. Sch. B.2.

In the Christ Church Library at Oxford is yet another of those unexplored manuscripts which are of unique significance to this study. This is MS. Ch. Ch. 768–70, which for some reason has never received any notice except for a few scant references in catalogues and dictionaries of music. The manuscript consists of three small part-books: a countertenor, a tenor and a bass, loosely bound together in a cardboard cover. The title reads *3 Bookes—Mr. Will Lawes his Psalmes —for 1, 2 & 3 partes, to the comon tunes. E. L.* The initials E. L. are those of Edward Lowe and the manuscript is apparently in his handwriting. Lowe, who became organist at Christ Church in 1630 and was later one of the organists of the Chapel Royal, as well as Professor of Music at Oxford, is credited with copying much pre-Restoration music and with preserving the manuscripts at Christ Church. He died in 1682. From evidence provided by the watermarks, this particular manuscript would seem to have been copied *c.* 1670.

The title of the manuscript is misleading since one might easily conclude from it that the contents consisted of part settings of the psalms in which the common tunes serve as *canti fermi*, such as those of the Ravenscroft psalter of 1621. The manuscript, however, contains twelve large verse anthems which are singular in the literature of music for religious devotion, and are important stepping-stones in the development of the English anthem. The most original feature of these anthems is the fact that the proper tunes are sung either by the congregation or the choir or both (it has not been determined which), accompanied by a thorough-bass for the organ, and in between the composed, declamatory verses of the soloists. Perhaps the best description of the plan of one of these verse anthems can be shown by taking an actual case in point. By way of illustration, therefore, the formal scheme of Lawes' setting of the whole of Psalm XXII is listed overleaf (Ex. 40).

A comparison of this plan with those of the other verse anthems of the set reveals that each work is constructed individually, there being no recurring pattern for the common tune or the various solos, duets and trios. Certain principles, however,

Ex. 40

PART 1

Verses 1 and 2:	*common tune* (sung by congregation and/or choir).
Verse 1:	countertenor solo.
Verse 2:	a 2 voc., countertenor and tenor.
Verses 3 and 4:	*common tune.*
Verse 5:	countertenor solo.
Verse 6:	tenor solo.
Verses 7 and 8:	a 2 voc., countertenor and tenor.
Verses 9 and 10:	*common tune.*

PART 2

Verses 11 and 12:	countertenor solo.
Verse 13:	bass solo.
Verse 14:	a 3 voc., countertenor, tenor and bass.
Verse 15:	tenor solo.
Verse 16:	countertenor solo.
Verses 17 and 18:	a 2 voc., tenor and bass.
Verses 19 and 20:	*common tune.*
Verses 21 and 22:	(These are not included in the manuscript. They may also have been sung to the common tune by the congregation or choir.)

PART 3

Verse 23:	bass solo.
Verse 24:	countertenor solo.
Verses 25 and 26:	a 2 voc., countertenor and bass.
Verses 27 and 28:	*common tune.*
Verses 29 and 30:	a 3 voc., countertenor, tenor and bass.
Verse 31:	*common tune.*

FINIS

are apparent. The foremost of these is the principle of variety. Each verse, or pair of verses, is varied in the texture by the ordering of the solos, duets and trios, interspersed here and there with the entrance of the congregation or choir which sings the simple church tunes. Moreover, the latter are concentrated at the beginning and the end of the work for added strength at these points. The common tune, for instance, is left out of the second part of the anthem until the final verses and then returns twice more in the third part for an effective conclusion. Each of the anthems closes in this manner, with the final verse or two sung by the choir or congregation.

The possibility of these common tunes having been meant for the congregation itself is indeed exciting. The practice of a responsorial between soloists and the congregation is, to the best of the present writer's knowledge, unknown in the history of the English anthem. However, a precedent is established in an account of a similar practice by Thomas Mace. Reporting of his presence in a Cathedral during the Siege of York in 1644, he speaks of a Cathedral Service:

'. . . where was heard (I believe) the most *remarkable*, and most *excellent singing of Psalms*, that has been *known* or *remembered* any where in These our *latter* Ages . . . they had then a *Custom in that Church*, (which I hear not of in any other *Cathedral*, which was) that always before the *Sermon*, the *whole Congregation sang a Psalm*, together with the *Quire and the Organ*. . . . This *Organ* . . . being let out, into all its *Fulness of Stops*, together with the *Quire*, began the Psalm.

'But when *that Vast-Conchording-Unity* of the whole *Congregational-Chorus*, came (as I may say) *Thundering in*, . . . it made the very *Ground shake* under us.' [1]

Granted that Mace's account does not include soloists, yet the idea of a responsorial involving the congregation is worth noting.

In the Christ Church manuscript all of the parts to the verse anthems have the thorough-bass written out with the music. It is unfigured. The common tunes, with what is apparently William Lawes' own unfigured bass line for organ, are written out in the bass part-book only, and before each work. The verses to be sung by the choir or congregation are indicated in all three parts by the words 'coṁon tune' and the incipits to the desired verses. The soloists were thereby advised which verses were to be sung to the common tunes by the choir or congregation. The indication 'Cho:', signifying 'chorus' or 'choir', precedes the incipits of the common tunes.

The texts of the psalms used in these verse anthems are from the old version found in the Sternhold and Hopkins psalters. But not all of the anthems employ the texts of psalms. Three are

---

[1] Thomas Mace, *Musick's Monument* (London: 1676), pp. 18–19.

spiritual songs from the psalter. They are 'The Lamentation of A Sinner', 'The Humble Suite of A Sinner', and the *Lamentation* ('O Lord in Yee Is All My Trust'). As for the common tunes themselves, they vary a bit from those in the psalters of the period. Two are tunes not even associated with the psalms to which Lawes has set them. They are the 'Windsor Tune' which is usually employed for Psalm CXVI and which Lawes uses for Psalm VI; and the 'second tune' of Psalm XIV which Lawes has fitted to Psalm XXII.[1] Lawes' settings of the common tunes are interesting in themselves, since his thorough-bass lines are sometimes a bit daring for ordinary church use. Indeed, they would have been acceptable only in places of private devotion—the chapels of the nobility or the King's own Chapel Royal.

But it is the musical style of the verses for the soloists which are of the greatest interest. If secular influence has been detected in Lawes' religious music up to this point, then the present collection is the capstone of the practice. The verses for solo voice, duets or trios follow the same general style as Lawes' secular declamatory songs, dialogues and songs for three voices. Only the ballad style is conspicuous by its absence. In the verses, therefore, we find the same slavish representation of words in music as we did in the declamatory songs. In fact, its employment in the verse anthems appears more rudimentary, even crude, so much so that one cannot help but feel a touch of humour in some passages, a humour which was not at all intended. A good illustration of this occurs in the verse anthem based upon the text of the eighteenth psalm at the bass solo for verses nine and ten. It is printed opposite with its chorus for three voices.

But this, after all, is the same practice which runs on through all of the later music of the Restoration and is nowhere more evident than, for example, in the church music of Henry Purcell.

These verse anthems 'to the com̃on tunes' were probably early works, written during Lawes' employment at the estate of the Earl of Hertford, or in the service of some other patron before he received his appointment at Court. There is, however,

[1] Both of these tunes may be seen under their respective psalms in Maurice Frost, *English and Scottish Psalm and Hymn Tunes* (Oxford University Press, 1953).

Ex. 41

Psalm XVIII (part 1) "O God My Strength"
Bass Solo: Verses 9 and 10 "The Lord descended"

255

no positive proof of this. The rudimentary character of the declamation has already been singled out, and indeed it may be used as one argument. The present writer, therefore, tried to get some further indication of the date of the collection by comparing Lawes' variants of the common tunes with the many editions of old version psalters of the period. Exact variants were not found, but the closest similarity seems to be with those in psalters dating from before 1631. This brings up another argument which may be advanced towards an early composition date. It was in 1631 that the first edition of Sir William Alexander's version of James I's own translation of the psalms was published. Charles I ardently strove to have his father's psalms supplant all others, both the old and the authorized versions, in private as well as public worship. In 1634 he enjoined the Privy Council of Scotland 'that no other Psalmes of any edition whatsoever be either printed heirefter within that our Kingdome or imported thither'.[1] As Charles' efforts were of no avail, he had Alexander revise the first edition and a new one was issued in 1636 and bound into Archbishop Laud's Service Book as the official psalter of England as well as Scotland. The people, however, seizing the opportunity to show the King their displeasure of him and his demands, avoided the use of the edition; and although Charles insisted on their use until his dying day the psalm paraphrases of King James I were destined for obscurity. It would seem that one who was as ardent a supporter of the King as William Lawes would not have set the Sternhold and Hopkins versions of the psalms in defiance of his Sovereign's wishes to the contrary. Taking these several factors into consideration, the date advanced for the collection by the present writer is before 1631. It is the largest single collection of verse anthems dating from before the Restoration and may well have influenced the later development of the form.

The collection in Christ Church apparently did not contain all of the verse anthems composed by William Lawes. The words of two others, unfortunately without the music, are extant in a manuscript in the British Museum, Harleian 6346. This volume is from the reign of Charles II and bears the inscription, 'The

[1] Philip Von Rohr-Sauer, *English Metrical Psalms from 1600–1660* (Inaugural Dissertation at Freiburg: 1938), pp. 44–6.

Anthems Used in the King's Chapel'. The first of Lawes' anthems in this manuscript is set to Psalm XC and is entitled 'An Antheme with verses for Cornetts & Sagbutts'. It is the only indication we have that William Lawes ever composed music for wind instruments. It is unfortunate indeed that the music has not survived. The second anthem in the Harleian manuscript utilizes the texts of selected paragraphs from chapters three and four of *The Song of Solomon* and begins, 'Who is this that Cometh out of the Wildernesse'. Still another anthem, this one for a solo bass voice with thorough-bass in the style of the Christ Church anthems, but without the common tunes, is extant in both the British Museum and in the library at Christ Church. It is set to Psalm LXVIII, 'Let God Arise'.

The last of the extant verse anthems and certainly the best known is that which Lawes set to Psalm XXVII, 'The Lord Is My Light'. It is mentioned in Walker-Westrup's *History of Music in England* as the best example of Anglican service music produced during the reign of Charles I.[1] William Boyce included this one in his collection, *Cathedral Music*, which was compiled between 1760–78, and it is chiefly due to his efforts that this anthem too was not relegated to gather dust in the archives of some library. Boyce, however, in his zeal to make the anthem conform to eighteenth-century standards, edited out of the work much of the dissonant harmonies and even altered the melody and rhythm wherever he thought necessary.

If we judge by the arrangement of the text and the entrance of the choruses, 'The Lord Is My Light' is the same type of verse anthem intended for the two pieces without music in Harleian 6346. This suggests that Lawes may have composed other anthems of this kind, and it supports my claim that an autograph volume of the composer's religious music did exist, or is still missing. The style of 'The Lord Is My Light' is not the same as in the verse anthems 'to the com̃on tunes'. It is less secular in its techniques and seems to have been designed for public worship rather than for private devotion. It is not written in the massive style of the earlier generation but it nevertheless follows the imitative style, which is more closely allied to the *Choice Psalmes* than to the 'com̃on tune' collection.

[1] Ernest Walker, *A History of Music in England*, 3rd ed., revised and enlarged by J. A. Westrup (Oxford University Press, 1952), p. 156.

Considering William Lawes' religious music as a whole, we have one of the most valuable collections of seventeenth-century English church music and certainly one of the earliest to be written under the strong secular influences of the times. Although, in the present chapter, attention has been focused primarily upon the purely 'interesting' features of this music from a historian's viewpoint, the author wishes to recommend it, or at least a good share of it, as music worthy of performance. No doubt church musicians will soon discover this for themselves.

CONCLUSION

WILLIAM LAWES was a true representative of the seventeenth-century Baroque. His music establishes him as a leading figure in the acceptance and development of new styles and techniques in England. He was an artist who worked in advance of his times. Versatile, prolific and highly original, he must be considered a major composer of the first half of the seventeenth century—one of the great figures of English music.

Many of the forms and techniques which Lawes used can be traced to his teacher, Giovanni Coperario, and to Alfonso Ferrabosco II. These, in turn, may be seen in their final development in the works of Henry Purcell. Lawes, in fact, stands midway between the earlier generation of Byrd, Morley, Ferrabosco, and Coperario, and that of Purcell. The latter knew of Lawes' work and could not have escaped his influence. In this respect, there is the 'possibility' that much of Purcell's work may actually show 'traces' of English influence. It has become only too common, of late, to attribute, indiscriminantly, all English musical forms, styles and techniques of the late seventeenth century to foreign influence. An examination of Lawes' music alone proves that it was the era preceding the Commonwealth which experimented with, and founded, the forms and techniques which Restoration composers later developed and extended. Indeed, much of that which has so eagerly been labelled Italian or French in England during the latter half of the century can be found in its embryonic and adolescent stages in the neglected manuscripts of Jacobean and Caroline times. If extensive foreign influence is to be found it must certainly be sought after at an earlier date. This is not to say that Italian and French influence had no effect in England during the seventeenth century, for they most certainly did. A reciprocal stream of influences continually crossed and re-crossed the Channel throughout the century. And yet, one should not overlook the dominant position of a strong English musical tradition, an aspect which has, unfortunately, been all too trodden under in the quest for spectacular outside influences. The subject is still an open one and only further research can hope to complete the picture.

It was not my aim to go into extended and detailed comparisons between Lawes' music and that of his contemporaries. I wanted to focus attention upon Lawes' works only. It is to be hoped that more of these individual and detailed studies will be undertaken in the future. Only after these have been completed, upon such men as Ferrabosco, Coperario, Jenkins, Locke, Simpson, and others, will it be possible to arrive at accurate conclusions, and to assign to each composer of the period his proper due.

APPENDIX A

Extracts Concerning Rules for Division Playing from Christopher Simpson's *The Division-Viol* (London: 1667 ed.).

12. *Concerning ordering of Division:*

When you are to Play *Division* to a *Ground*, I would have you, in the first place, to Play over the *Ground* it Self, plainly and distinctly; for these reasons: 1. That others may hear what Notes you divide upon. 2. That your self may be better possessed of the *Ayre* of the *Ground*, in case you know it not before. 3. That he who Plays the *Ground* unto you may better perceive the *Measure* of *Time*.

The Ground being Played over, you may then break it into *Crotchets* and *Quavers*; or Play some neat peece of slow Descant to it, which you please. If your *Ground* consist of two or three *Strains*, you may do by the second or third, as you did by the first.

This done, and your *Ground* beginning over again, you may then break it into *Division* of a quicker motion, driving on some *Point* or *Points* as hath been shewed.

When you have prosecuted that manner of Play so long as you think fitting, and shewed some command of Hand; you may then fall off to slower *Descant* or *Binding-Notes*, as you see cause; Playing also sometimes loud or soft, to express Humour and draw on Attention.

After this you may begin to Play some *Skipping Division*; or *Points*, or *Tripla's*, or what your present fancy or invention shall prompt you to, changing still from one variety to another; for variety it is which chiefly pleaseth: The best *Division* in the world, still continued, would become tedious to the Hearer; and therefore you must so place and dispose your *Division*, that the change of it from one kind to another may still beget a new attention: And this is generally to be observed, whether your *Ground* consist of one or more *Strains*, or to be a *Continued Ground*; . . .

13. *Of a Continued Ground:*

A *Continued Ground* used for Playing or Making *Division* upon, is (commonly) the *Through-Bass* of some *Motet or Madrigal*, proposed or selected for that purpose. This, after you have played two or three *Semibreves* of it plain, to let the Organist know your measure; you may begin to divide, according to your fancy or the former Instructions, until you come near some *Cadence* or *Close*, where I would have you shew some Agility of Hand. There, if you please, you may rest a *Minim*, two or three, letting him that Plays the *Ground* go on: and then come in with some *Point*: after which you may fall to *Descant*, *Mixt Division*, *Tripla's*, or what you please. In this manner, Playing sometimes swift Notes, sometimes slow; changing from This or that sort of *Division*, as may best produce Variety you may carry on the rest of the *Ground*; and if you have anything more excellent than other, reserve it for the Conclusion.

14. *Of Composing Division for one Viol to a Ground:*

When you compose *Division* to a *Ground*, endeavour to make it easie for the Hand: for, of things equally excellent as to Musick, That is always to be preferred, which is more easie to be performed. Hence we may conclude, that no man is fit to Compose *Division* to a *Ground* (how great a Master in Musick soever he be) unless he know the neck of the Instrument, and the Method of Fingering belonging unto it.

This is all I have to say concerning *Division* for one *Viol*; more than that I would have you peruse the *Divisions* which other men have made upon *Grounds*; as those of Mr. *Henry Butler*, Mr. *Daniel Norcome*, and divers other excellent men of this our Nation, who (hitherto) have had the preheminence for this particular Instrument; observing and noting in their *Divisions*, what you find best worthy to be imitated.

15. *Of two Viols Playing together ex tempore to a Ground:*

After this Discourse of *Division* for One *Viol*, I suppose it will not be unseasonable to speak something of Two *Viols* Playing together upon a *Ground*; in which kind of Musick, I have had some experimental knowledg; and therefore will deliver it in such order and manner as I have known the practice of it; referring the Improvement thereof to further experience.

First, let the *Ground* be prick'd down in three severall Papers; One for him who Plays upon the *Organ* or *Harpsechord*: the other two for them that Play upon the two *Viols*: which, for order and brevity, we will distinguish by three Letters; *viz. A.* for *Organist*, *B.* for the *First Bass*, and *C.* for the second.

Each of these having the same *Ground* before him, they may all three begin together; *A.* and *B.* Playing the *Ground*, and *C.* Descanting to it, in slow Notes, or such as may sute the beginning of the

Musick: This done, let *C*. Play the *Ground* and *B*. Descant to it, as the other had done before, but with some little variation. If the *Ground* consist of two Strains, the like may be done in the second: One *Violl* still Playing the *Ground* whilest the other Descants or Divides upon it.

The *Ground* thus Play'd over, *C*. may begin again, and Play a Strain of quicker *Division*; which ended, let *B*. answer the same with another something like it, but of a little more lofty Ayre: for the better performance whereof, if there be any difference in the Hands or Inventions, I would have the better Invention *lead*, but the more Able Hand still *follow*, that the Musick may not seem to flaccess or lessen, but rather increase in the performance.

When the *Viols* have thus (as it were) Vied and Revied one to the other, *A*. if he have ability of Hand, may, upon a sign given him, put in his Strain of *Division*; the two *Viols* Playing one of them the *Ground*, and the other *slow* Descant to it. *A*. having finished his Strain, a reply thereto may be made, first by one *Viol*, and then by the other.

Having answered one another in that same manner so long as they think fit, the two *Viols* may divide a Strain Both together. In which doing, let *B*. break the *Ground*, by moving into the *Octave* upward or downward, and returning from thence either to his own Note, or to meet the next Note in the *Unison* or *Octave*. By this means, *C*. knowing *B*'s motion, he knows also how to avoyd running into the same, and therefore will move into the Third or Fifth (or Sixth where it is required) meeting each succeeding Note in some one of the said Concords, until he come to the Close; where he may (after he has divided the Binding) meet the Close Note in the *Octave*; which Directions well observed, two *Violls* may move in *Extemporary* Division a whole Strain together, without any remarkable clashing in the Consecution of *Fifths* or *Eighths*.

When they have proceeded thus far; *C*. may begin some Point of *Division*, of the length of a *Breve* or *Semibreve*, naming the said word, that *B*. may know his intentions: which ended, let *B*. answer the same upon the succeeding Note or Notes to the like quantity of Time; taking it in that manner, one after another, so long as they please. This done, they may betake themselves to some other Point of a different length, which will produce a new variety.

This contest in *Breves*, *Semibreves*, or *Minims* being ended, they may give the Signe to *A*. if (as I said) he have the ability of Hand, that he may begin his Point, as they had done one to another; which Point may be answered by the *Viols*, either singly or joyntly; if joyntly, it must be done according to the former instructions of Dividing together; Playing still *slow* Notes and *soft*, whilest the

Organist Divides; for that Part which Divides should always be heard lowdest.

When this is done, both *Viols* may Play another Strain together, either in quick or slow Notes, which they please; and if the Musick be not yet spun out to a sufficient length, they may begin to Play *Tripla's* and Proportions, answering each other in whole Strains or parcels; and after that, joyn together in a Thundering Strain of *Quick* Division; with which they may conclude; or else with a Strain of slow and sweet Notes, according as may best sute the circumstance of time and place.

I have known this kind of *Extemporary* Musick, sometimes (When it was performed by Hands accustomed to Play together) pass off with greater applause, than those Divisions which had been most studiously composed.

16. *Of Composing Divisions of Two or Three Parts:*

In Composing Division for two *Bass Viols*, you may follow the forementioned method, making sometimes This, sometimes That *Part* move above or below: Sometimes answering one the other in Points joyned together in Division; sometimes in *slow*, sometimes in *quick* Motions, such as may best produce Variety: but after their answering one another in Points, I would always have them joyn together in some lofty Strain of *Division*, with which, or with some slow and pleasing Descant you may Conclude your Composition.

If you make *Division* for *two Trebles*, both must be in the way of *Descant* to the *Ground*: So, that (the *Ground* considered) the Composition is Three distinct Parts. When the *Trebles* move together, their most natural passage is in *Thirds* one to the other; sometimes in *Sixths* or a mixture with other *Concords*, but still such as have relation to the *Ground*. As for their answering one another in *Points*; their several Motions or Changes, in order to Variety; the same is understood as of the former.

In Composing for a *Treble* and *Bass*, you are to consider the nature and compass of either Part, framing your *Division* according thereunto; which, in the higher Part will be *Descant*; in the lower, a more frequent *Breaking* of the *Ground*.

The same regard, to the nature of the Parts, must be had in Composing for *two Trebles* and a *Bass*, or for *two Basses* and *one Treble*.

In *Divisions* made for *three Basses*, every *Viol acts* the *Treble, Bass* or *Inward* Part by turns. But here you are to take notice, that *Divisons* of Three Parts, are not usually made upon *Grounds*; but rather Compose in the manner of *Fancies*; beginning commonly with some *Fuge*, and then falling into Points of *Division*; answering one another; sometimes two against one, and sometimes all engaged at once in a contest of *Division*; but (after all) ending commonly in grave and harmonious Musick.

Howbeit, if, after each *Fancie* there follow an *Ayre* (which will produce a pleasant Variety) the *Basses* of these consisting of two short Strains, differ not much from the nature of *Grounds*. These *Ayres* or *Almains* begin like other *Consort Ayres*; after which the Strains are repeated in divers Variations, one Part answering another, and sometimes joyning together in *Division*, as formerly mention'd.

APPENDIX B

Catalogue of Instrumental Works

In the following lists, only the major manuscript sources for William Lawes' instrumental music have been included. In all cases, autographs or the most important manuscripts are listed first. See also the discussion and description of the autographs in Chapter I, pp. 29–33.

The abbreviations used are as follows:

(a) Manuscript References.

Add.	— Additional manuscripts in the British Museum, London.
Ch. Ch.	— Manuscripts in the library of Christ Church, Oxford.
Mus. Sch.	— Manuscripts originally belonging to the Oxford Music School and now in the Bodleian Library, Oxford.
Res.	— Manuscript in the Paris Conservatory of Music.
Ten.	— Manuscript in the library of St. Michael's College, Tenbury.

(b) Printed Publications, edited by John Playford.

CA	— *Court-Ayres* (London: 1655).
CMA	— *Courtly Masquing Ayres* (London: 1662).
MB	— *A Musicall Banquet* (London: 1651), part 2, *Musica Harmonia*.
MDC	— *Musick's Delight on the Cithren* (London: 1666).
MH	— *Musick's Hand-maide* (London: 1663).
MRLV	— *Musick's Recreation on the Lyra Violl* (London: 1652 and 1661 editions only).

(c) Instrumental Abbreviations.

A.	— Alto Viol.
B.C.	— *Basso continuo.*
B.V.	— Bass Viol.
Org.	— Organ.

T.V. — Tenor Viol.
Tr. V. — Treble Viol.
Vln. — Violin.

THE 'CONSORT SUITES' ('FOR Yᵉ VIOLLS')

In Four Parts:

No. *1* in C Minor: Fantazy, Aire, Aire	2 Tr.V., 2 B.V.	Mus. Sch. B.2.
No. *2* in C Major: Aire [Fantazy], Aire, Aire		

In Five Parts:

No. *1* in G Minor: Fantazy, 'On The Playnesong', Aire	2 Tr.V., 2 T.V. (or A. & T.), B.V. with Org.	Mus. Sch. B.2; Mus. Sch. D.229; Add. 29410–15.
No. *2* in A Minor: Fantazy, Fantazy, Aire		
No. *3* in C Minor: Fantazy, Aire, Paven, Aire		
No. *4* in F Major: Fantazy, Paven, Aire		
No. *5* in C Major: Fantazy, Paven, Aire		

In Six Parts:

No. *1* in C Minor: Fantazy, Fantazy, Inominy, Aire	2 Tr.V., 2 T.V. (or A. & T.), 2 B.V., with Org.	Mus. Sch. B.2; Mus. Sch. D.229; Add. 29410–15.
No. *2* in C Major: Fantazy, Fantazy, Aire		Mus. Sch. B.3, *et al.*
No. *3* in B♭ Major: Fantazy, Inominy, Aire		Mus. Sch. B.2, *et al.*
No. *4* in G Minor: Fantazy, Paven, Aire		Mus. Sch. B.3, *et al.*
No. *5* in F Major: Fantazy, Aire, Fantazy, Aire		

THE 'ROYALL' CONSORT SUITES

In Four Parts for Six Instruments:

No. *1* in D Minor: Fantazy, Aire, Alman, Corant, Eccho, Corant, Saraband	2 Vlns., 2 B.V., with *B.C.* for 2 Theorboes	Mus. Sch. B.3; Ch. Ch. 754–9; Ch. Ch. 391–6; Ch. Ch. 479–83; Add. 31431; Add. 31433.

No. 2 in D Minor: Pavan,
Aire, Aire, Aire [Galliard],
Corant, Saraband, Saraband

No. 3 in D Minor: Aire, Aire,
Corant, Corant, Alman,
Corant, Saraband

No. 4 in D Major: Pavan, Aire,
Aire, Aire [Corant], Corant,
Saraband

No. 5 in D Major: Aire, Aire,
Alman, Aire [Corant],
Corant, Aire [Corant],
Saraband

No. 6 in D Major: Fantazy,
Aire, Alman, Corant, Eccho,
Aire [Morris Dance]

No. 7 in A Minor: Pavan, Aire,
Alman, Alman, Aire
[Corant], Corant, Saraband

No. 8 in C Major: Pavan, Aire,
Alman, Aire [Corant],
Corant, Saraband

No. 9 in F Major: Pavan, Aire,
Alman, Corant, Alman,
Corant, Saraband

No. 10 in B♭ Major: Pavan,
Alman, Corant, Alman,
Corant, Saraband

(This and the follow-
ing suites are not in
Mus. Sch. B.3.)

THE 'HARPE' CONSORTS

In Three Parts with basso continuo:

No. 1 in G Minor: Almane,
Corant, Corant, Saraband

Vln., B.V. & Harp,
with *B.C.* for a
Theorbo

Mus. Sch. D.238–40;
Mus. Sch. D.229;
Ch. Ch. 5.

No. 2 in G Minor: Aire, Corant,
Corant, Saraband

No. 3 in G Major: Almane,
Corant, Corant, Saraband

No. 4 in D Minor: Aire, Aire,
Corant, Saraband

No. 5 in D Major: Almane,
Corant, Corant, Saraband

No. 6 in D Major: Almane,
Almane, Corant, Corant,
Saraband

No. 7 in G Major: Aire

(This and the follow-
ing consorts are also
in Mus. Sch. B.3.)

No. *8* in G Major: Paven
No. *9* in D Major: Paven (upon
a Bass Theme by Cormacke)
No. *10* in G Minor: Paven
(upon a Bass Theme by
'Coprario')
No. *11* in D Minor: Fantazia

THE VIOLIN SONATAS

In Three Parts:

No. *1* in G Minor: Fantazia; Aire [Alman], Aire [Galliard]	Vln., B.V. & Org.	Mus. Sch. D. 238–40; Mus. Sch. D. 229; Mus. Sch. C. 90; Ch. Ch. 430; Add. 29290.
No. *2* in G Major: Fantazia, Aire [Alman], Aire [Galliard]		
No. *3* in A Minor: Fantazia, Aire [Alman], Aire [Galliard]		
No. *4* in C Major: Fantazia, Aire [Alman], Aire [Galliard]		
No. *5* in D Minor: Fantazia, Aire [Alman], Aire [Galliard]		
No. *6* in D Major: Fantazia, Aire [Alman], Aire [Galliard]		
No. *7* in D Minor: Fantazia, Aire [Alman], Aire [Galliard]		
No. *8* in D Major: Fantazia, Aire [Alman], Aire [Galliard]		Also in Mus. Sch. B.2.

In Four Parts:

No. *1* in G Minor: Fantazia, Aire [Alman], Aire [Galliard]	2 Vlns., B.V., & Org.	Mus. Sch. D.238–40; Mus. Sch. D.229; Mus. Sch. C.89; Ch. Ch. 430; Add. 29290. Res. 770 (inc.)
No. *2* in G Major: Fantazia, Aire [Alman], Aire [Galliard]		
No. *3* in A Minor: Fantazia, Aire [Alman], Aire [Galliard]		
No. *4* in C Major: Fantazia, Aire [Alman], Aire [Galliard]		
No. *5* in D Minor: Fantazia, Aire [Alman], Aire [Galliard]		
No. *6* in D Major: Fantazia, Aire [Alman], Aire [Galliard]		

No. 7 in D Minor: Fantazia,
  Aire [Alman], Aire [Galliard]
No. 8 in D Major: Fantazia,
  Aire [Alman], Aire [Galliard]

SUITES FOR TWO BASS VIOLS AND ORGAN

In Three Parts:

No. 1 in G Minor: Paven,	2 B.V. & Org.	Mus. Sch. B.2;
Aire, Aire		Mus. Sch. D.238–40;
		Mus. Sch. D.229.

No. 2 in C Major: Paven, Alman
  (on bass theme by 'Alfonso'
  Ferrabosco)
No. 3 in C Major: Aire, Aire

LYRA VIOL SUITES

In Three Parts:

No. 1 in D Major: Fantazia,	3 Lyra Viols	Ch. Ch. 725–7
'Serabrand'		(in Tablature).
No. 2 in D Minor: 'ffantasie',		
Alman		
No. 3 in D Minor: 'Pavin',		
'Almaine'		

DANCES IN TWO PARTS

Sixty-seven pieces	Tr.V. & B.V. or	CA; CMA; MB;
(Almans, Aires, Corants,	Vln. & B.V.	Mus. Sch. D.233–6.
Sarabands, etc.)		
Eighteen pieces		Mus. Sch. D.233–6.
(Almans, Aires, Corants,		
Sarabands, etc.)		

DANCES IN THREE PARTS

Twenty-four pieces	2 Tr.V. & B.V. or	Add. 31429;
(Almans, Aires, Corants,	2 Vlns. & B.V.	Add. 18940–44;
Sarabands, etc.)		Add. 31423;
		Ten. 302.

DANCES IN FOUR PARTS

Seven pieces	2 Vlns. (or Tr.V.),	Mus. Sch. D.233–6;
(Alman, Aire, 4 Corants,	T.V., B.V. with	Mus. Sch. E.431–6;
Saraband)	*B.C.*	Mus. Sch. F.568–9.

APPENDIX B

Suite in G Minor (An arrangement of the Suite No. 1 in G Minor for Two Bass Viols and Organ) Paven, Aire, Aire	2 Vlns. (or Tr. V.), T.V., B.V. with B.C.	Mus. Sch. E.431–6 Ch. Ch. 367–70; Add. 18940–44.

MISCELLANEOUS PIECES IN TABLATURE

Suite for Two Lutes Alman, Corant, Corant	2 Theorbo-lutes	Mus. Sch. B.2.
Three Pieces for One Lyra Viol Saraband, Corant, Saraband	Lyra Viol	Add. 31432.
Four Pieces for One Lyra Viol (Saraband, Preludium, Coranto, Coranto)	Lyra Viol	Mus. Sch. D.245–6. Mus. Sch. F.575.
Ten Pieces for One Lyra Viol (Almans, Corants, Sarabands, Jigge)	Lyra Viol	MRLV.
Eight Pieces for the Cithren (*Golden Grove* Suite and Songs)	Cithren	MDC.

WORKS FOR THE KEYBOARD

Suite in A Minor Allmaine, Coranto, Sellabrand	Virginals or Harpsichord	Res. 1185; MH.
Eight Pieces (Aire, Corants, Sarabands, 'Symphony', *Golden Grove* Suite)	Virginals or Harpsichord	MH.

FRAGMENTS

Twenty-three Pieces (similar to the '*Royall*' Consort)	2nd Tr. and T. only	Mus. Sch. F.568–9.
Forty-six Pieces (Almans, Aires, Corants & Sarabands)	Bass part only, but a 2	Mus. Sch. D.220.
Twelve Pieces (Almans, Aires, Corants & Sarabands)	Bass part only	Mus. Sch. D.233–6. Mus. Sch. E.451.
Two unnamed pieces in three parts	Instrumental or Vocal	Mus. Sch. B.2.

271

APPENDIX C

Catalogue of Vocal and Dramatic Works

The following lists are for the most part alphabetically arranged according to first lines. In all cases the old English spellings are retained. Songs from dramatic productions, excluding those from masques, are included both in the lists of songs and in the list of plays for which Lawes composed music. The dates given for the dramatic works are for the performances for which the songs were written and not for the year of publication.

The manuscript references are as follows:

Add. — Additonal manuscripts in the British Museum, London.

EG. — Egerton manuscripts in the British Museum, London.

HARL. — Harleian manuscripts in the British Museum, London.

Ch. Ch. — Manuscripts in the Christ Church Library, Oxford.

Mus. — Music manuscripts in the Bodleian Library, Oxford.

Mus. Sch. — Manuscripts originally belonging to the Oxford Music School and now in the Bodleian Library, Oxford.

Don. — Manuscript in the Bodleian Library, Oxford.

DR. — Drexel manuscripts in the New York Public Library.

Gamble — John Gamble Commonplace Book in the New York Public Library.

RCM — Manuscript in the Royal College of Music, London.

Manuscript Code:

A — Add. 31432 (autogr.)   F — Don. C. 57
B — Gamble   G — Mus. E. 451
C — DR. 4041   H — Add. 29,396
D — EG. 2013   J — Add. 31,813
E — Mus. Sch. C.5.   K — Add. 29,291

L — Add. 11,608	X — Add. 31,460
M — Add. 29,397	Y — Add. 17,784
N — Add. 35,043	Z — Ch. Ch. 18
O — Ch. Ch. 17	AA — Add. 31,429
P — Mus. Sch. B.2. (autogr.)	BB — Ch. Ch. 768–70
Q — Add. 31,462	CC — Add. 17,840
R — Add. 31,463	DD — Add. 30,382
S — Add. 29,386	EE — Add. 30,478
T — RCM 1123	FF — HARL. 7337
U — Add. 30,273	GG — Ch. Ch. 12
V — Add. 11,587	HH — Ch. Ch. 1220–24
W — Add. 10,337	JJ — HARL. 6346

Key to Publications:

1 — *New Ayres and Dialogues* (1678).
2 — *The Musical Companion* (1673 ed.).
3 — *Select Ayres and Dialogues* (1652).
4 — *Select Ayres and Dialogues* (1653).
5 — *Treasury of Musick* (1669).
6 — *The Musical Companion* (1667).
7 — *Musick's Recreation on the Lyra Viol* (1652).
8 — *Musick's Delight on the Cithren* (1666).
9 — *Introduction to the Skill of Musick* (1662 ed.).
10 — *Choice Psalmes* (1648).
11 — *A Musicall Banquet*, part 1, *Musick and Mirth* (1651).
12 — *Catch that Catch Can* (1652). Ed. John Hilton.
13 — *The Rounds, Catches and Canons of England* (1865). Ed. E. F. Rimbault.
14 — *Cathedral Music*, Vol. II (1760–78). Ed. William Boyce.
15 — *The Divine Companion* (1709). Ed. Henry Playford.

SECULAR SONGS

SOLO SONGS WITH CONTINUO

In declamatory style:

Amarilis teare thy haire ('Love's Dying Passion').		A, 1.
Com, Shepherds, com, com away.		C.
Cupids wearie of the court.		A, 1, C.
Dos't see how unregarded now ('Sonnet').	John Suckling, *Fragmenta Aurea*, 1646.	A.
God of winds.		A.
Had you but herd her sing.		A, 1.
Harke, Harke, how in every grove ('Cupid's Call').	James Shirley, *Poems*, 1646.	C.

273

Hence flatt'ring hopes.		A.
I burne, and beg of you to quench or coole me ('To The Deeres').	Robert Herrick, *Hesperides*, 1648.	A.
If you a wrinkle on the sea have seen (frag.).		A.
I would the God of love would dye.	James Shirley, *Poems*, 1646.	A.
I'm sick of Love ('To The Sycamore').	Robert Herrick, *Hesperides*, 1648.	A, D.
Larke now leaves his wattry nest, The (with two-part chorus).	William Davenant, *Works*, 1673.	C.
Like Smoaky Flitches (Bass solo).		A.
Lovers rejoice.	Beaumont and Fletcher, *Cupid's Revenge*.	A.
O drawe your curtaynes and apeere.	William Davenant, *Love and Honour*, 1634.	A, C, 1.
O Love, are all those Arrowes gone.		A.
O thinke not Phoebe cause a cloud.	James Shirley, *Poems*, 1646.	A.
Perfect and endles circles are.		A.
Somnus, the 'umble God.	John Denham, *The Sophy*, 1642.	C.
Stay Phoebus stay ('Song').	Edmund Waller, *Poems*, 1645.	A.
Sullen Care.		C.
There can be noe glad man.		C.
Those Lovers only Hapye are.		A.
To whome shall I complaine.		A, 1, C.
Virgins as I advise forbeare.		A.
When I by thy faire shape ('Sonnet').	Richard Lovelace, *Lucasta*, 1649.	B.
Whieles I this standing Lake swathe up with ewe ('Sadness').	William Cartwright, *Comedies, Tragi-Comedies, with other Poems . . .*, 1651.	A.
White though yee bee ('On The Lillyes').	Robert Herrick, *Hesperides*, 1648.	A.
Why soe pall and wan fond lover.	John Suckling, *Aglaura*, 1646.	C.

Composed 'ballads':

Aske me noe more where Jove bestowes.	Thomas Carew, *Poems*, 1640.	A, 1.
Be not proud pretty one.		A, D, E.
Can Bewtyes spring Admitt.		A.
Come Lovely Cloris (a 3).		E. 2.
Deerest all faire.		A, B.
Erly in the morne.		A.
Faith be noe longer coy.		A, B, 3, 4, 5.

Gather Yᵉ Rosebuds while yᵉ may ('To The Virgins'), (also a 3).	Robert Herrick, *Hesperides*, 1648.	A, B, C, F, G, H, J, 1, 2, 3, 4, 5, 6, 7, 8.
Here's A Jolly couple.		C.
I can love for an hour ('Love's Flattery').		B, 4, 5.
I love thee for thy ficklenesse.		B.
Love I obey, shoot home thy dart.		A, 1.
O My Clarissa, thou cruel faire (also a 3).		B, C, K, L, 2,3,4,5,6,8.
Pleasures, Bewty, youth attend yee.	John Ford, *The Lady's Trial*, 1639.	A, B, C.
Still to bee Neate, still to bee Dresst.	Ben Jonson, *The Silent Woman*, 1609.	B.
Suppose (how faire), suppose I know itt.		B.
Tell me noe more her eyes.		A, B, C, 3, 4, 5.
That flame is borne of Earthly fire ('Love's Constancy').		A.
Thou that excellest.		A, B.
Upp Ladyes up ('Cupid's Progress').		A, B.
Why should great bewty vertuous fame desire.		A, B, C.

Bipartite songs beginning in declamatory style and ending as composed 'ballads':

Ah Cruell love ('To Pansies').	Robert Herrick, *Hesperides*, 1648.	A.
Beliza shade your shining eyes.		A, D.
Cloris I wish that Envye were as just.		A.
Come Adonis, come away ('Upon My Noble Friend, Richard Lovelace, esq. his being in Holland').	John Tatham, *Ostella*, 1650.	C, 1, 5.
Doris, see the Am'rous flame.		A.
Fair as unshaded light ('To the Queene, entertain'd at night by the Countesse of Anglesey').	William Davenant, *Madagascar*, 1638.	1.
Far well faire sainct ('On his Mistress crossing the sea').	Thomas Cary, in *Il Pastor Fido*, by R. Fanshawe, 1647.	A, 1.
He that will not love ('Not to Love').	Robert Herrick, *Hesperides*, 1648.	A, 5.
I keepe my horse ('The Cuttpurse Song').	Thomas Middleton, *The Widow*.	H.
It tis her voice.		A.

Loves a child and ought to be won with smyles.	Henry Glapthorne, *Argalus and Parthenia,* 1639.	A, 1.
Now in the sad declenshion of my time.		A.
O let mee still and silentt lye.		C.
O tell me Damon canst thou prove.		C.
Renounce this humour and attend.		B.
Wee show noe monstrous crockadell.	Jasper Mayne, *The City Match,* 1637.	C.
Wher did you borrow that last sigh.	William Berkeley, *The Lost Lady,* 1639.	A, C.
Yee Feinds and Furies.	William Davenant, *The Unfortunate Lovers,* 1638.	A, 1.

PART-SONGS WITH CONTINUO

Dialogues:

Charon, O Charon Hear a wretch opprest ('Charon and Amintor').		5.
Charon, O gentle Charon, let me wooe thee with teares.	Robert Herrick ('Charon and Phylomel').	A, F, M, N, 2, 3, 4, 5, 6.
Come heavy hart, whose sighs thy sorrowes shew.		A.
Come my Daphne, come away ('Strephon and Daphne').	James Shirley, *The Cardinal,* 1641.	A, L, 1, 2, 3, 4, 5, 6.
God Morrow, God morrow.		C.
Hast you Nimphs, make hast away ('Nimph and Shepherd').		5.
Orpheus O Orpheus gently touch thy Lesbyan Lyre ('A Trialogue between Orpheus, Alecto and Euridice').		A, 1.
Tis not Boy thy Amorous looke.		A.
Vulcan, Vulcan, O Vulcan, my Love! ('Vulcan and Venus').		4, 5.
What if I dye for love of thee.		H, L, O.
What Softer Sounds are these ('The Passions, Doubt and Love').	Ben Jonson, *Entertainment at Welbeck,* 1633.	A.
When death shall snatch us from these Kidds ('Thirsis and Dorinda').	Andrew Marvell.	A.

Madrigals:

Cease Warring Thoughts (a 3).	James Shirley, *Triumph of Beautie,* 1646.	P.

Deere Leave Thy Home (frag.) ('A Sonnet') (a 4).	William Herbert, *Poems* 1660.	P.
Feare Not Deere Love (frag.) ('Secresie Protested') (a 5)	Thomas Carew, *Poems*, 1640.	P.
Goe bleeding hart (frag.) (a 3).		P.
Musick, the Master of thy Art is dead ('On the Memory of My Friend: John Tomkins') (a 3).	William Lawes, *Choice Psalmes*, 1648.	P, 10.

Three-part drinking songs:

A hall, a hall: To welcome our freind.	John Suckling, *Tragedy of Brennoralt*, 1639.	A.
A health, . . . to the Notherne Lasse.	John Suckling, *The Goblins*, 1638.	A, C.
Catts as other creatures doe, The.		A, C.
Come take a carouse.		A.
On, on, compassion shall never enter heere.		A.
What Hoe, wee come to bee merry.	John Ford, *The Lady's Trial*, 1639.	A.
When each lynes a faithfull drinker.		A, C.

Two-part glees:

All these lye howling.		C.
Fill, fill ye bowele.		C.
Love is lost and gone astray.		9.
Now that the spring hath filled our veins.	William Browne.	2.
What should my mistresse doe.		C.

CATCHES AND ROUNDS

In three parts:

A knot of good fellows.		6.
A Round, a Round, a Round Boys.	Richard Brome, *A Joviall Crew*, 1652.	2, 6.
Bess black as a Charcole.		6.
Brisk Clarett and Sherry (*incipit* only).		P.
Come follow me brave Hearts.		2, 6.
Come let us cast the Dice.	James Shirley, *Poems*, 1646.	Q, R, S, 2, 6, 11, 12.
Come let us have a merry heart.		6.
Come quaffe apace this brisk Canary Wine.		12.
Dainty fine Aniseed water.		12.
Drink tonight of the Moonshine bright.		T, 2, 6, 12, 13.

Goose law'd with Goose.		2, 6, 12, 13.
Hang sorrow and cast away care.		Q, S, U, 2, 6, 12, 13.
Harke Jolly lads (*incipit* only).		P.
I doe Confesse (*incipit* only).		P.
If you will drink Canary.		L, 2, 6, 12, 13.
Ile tell you of a matter.		12.
It is folly to be jolly.		6.
Lets Cast away care.		P, 2, 6, 12, 13.
Listen near to the Ground.		6.
Never let a man.		P, 6, 12, 13.
Now my lads, . . . now let's be merry.		6.
See how Cawoods Dragon looks.		2, 6, 13.
See how in gath'ring of their May.		Q, R, S, 2, 6, 12.
Some drink, Boy some drink.	John Suckling, *The Goblins*, 1638.	K, P, 6.
Stand still and listen.		P, 12.
Though I am not Bachus Preist (*incipit* only).		P.
Tom, Ned and Jack (*incipit* only).		P.
Whither goe yee?		P.
Wise Men were but seven, The.		Q, R, S, U, 2, 6, 8, 12, 13.

In four parts:

A Pox on our Gaoler.	Richard Cartwright, *The Royal Slave*, 1636.	2, 6, 13.
Call for the Ale.		P, U, 6, 12, 13.
Come Amarillis, now let us be merry.		2, 6.
HA we to the other world.		2, 6, 12, 13.
Pot, The Pipe, the Quart, the Can, The.		Q, S, 2, 6, 13.

In six parts:

Come my lads (*incipit* only).		P.
Warrs ar our delight.		P, U, 6, 12.

WORDS ONLY, MUSIC NOT EXTANT

Heark faire one ('A Guiltlesse Lady Imprisoned').	Richard Lovelace, *Lucasta*, 1649.
Sing out pent soules ('The Vintage to the Dungeon').	Richard Lovelace, *Lucasta*, 1649.

APPENDIX C

DRAMATIC WORKS

Plays:

Aglaura. 1638. (John Suckling.)
 'Why soe pall and wan fond lover?'
Cardinal, The. 1641. (James Shirley.)
 'Come my Daphne, come away.'
City Match, The. 1637. (Jasper Mayne.)
 'Wee show noe monstrous crockadell.'
Cupid's Revenge. 1637. (Beaumont and Fletcher.)
 'Lovers rejoice.'
Goblins, The. 1638. (John Suckling.)
 'A health, . . . to the Notherne Lasse.'
 'Some drink, Boy some drink.'
Joviall Crew, A. 1641. (Richard Brome.)
 'A Round, a Round, a Round Boys.'
Lady's Trial, The. 1639. (John Ford.)
 'Pleasures, Bewty, youth attend yee.'
 'What Hoe, wee come to bee merry.'
Lost Lady, The. 1639. (William Berkeley.)
 'Wher did you borrow that last sigh.'
Love and Honour. 1634. (William Davenant.)
 'O drawe your curtaynes and apeere.'
Royal Slave, The. 1636. (Richard Cartwright.)
 'A Pox on our Gaoler.'
Silent Woman, The. 1636. (Ben Jonson.)
 'Still to bee Neate, still to bee Dresst.'
Sophy, The. 1642. (John Denham.)
 'Somnus the 'umble God.'
Tragedy of Brennoralt, The. 1639. (John Suckling.)
 'A hall, a hall! To welcome our freind.'
Unfortunate Lovers, The. 1638. (William Davenant.)
 'Yee Feinds and Furies.'
Widow, The. (Thomas Middleton.)
 'I keep my horse.'

Masques and Entertainments:

Entertainment at Welbeck. 1633. (Ben Jonson.) Add. 31432.
 'A Dialogue Between the Passions, Doubt and Love.'
Triumph of Peace, The. Court Masque. 1634. (James Shirley.) P.
 Symphony: Two parts. P.
 Song I: 'Hence, yᵉ profane.' (T. solo with S.A.T.B.
  chorus) P.
 Symphony: Two parts. P.
 Song II: 'Wherefore do my sisters stay?' (T. solo with P.
  A.A.B. chorus.)
 Symphony: Two parts. P.
 Song III: 'Thinke not I could absent myself.' P.

W.L.—T　　　　279

Song VIII: 'In Envye of the Night.' (Soprano solo.)   A. C.
(not in P.)

Song IX: 'Come away, away, away' (frag.). S.A.T.B. P.
chorus.

Triumphs of the Prince d'Amour. Court Masque. 1636. P.
(William Davenant.)
Symphony: Two parts.
Song VI: *Priests of Apollo.* (Duet for T. & B. with S.A.T.B.
chorus.) 'Behold how this conjunction thrives.'
Valediction: Songs and Choruses.
Symphony: Two parts.
Song: *Priests of Mars.* (T. solo with S.A.T.B. chorus.)
Symphony: (*ritornelle*).
Song: *Priests of Venus.* (Duet for S. & T. with S.A.T.B.
chorus.)
Symphony: (*ritornelle*).
Song: *Priests of Apollo.* (Trio for A.T. & B. with S.A.T.B.
chorus.)
Symphony: (*ritornelle*).
Grand Chorus: (S.A.T.B.) 'May our three Gods so long
conjoyne.'

Britannia Triumphans. Court Masque. 1638. (William P.
Davenant.)
Full Chorus: 'Britanocles, the great and good appears.'
(S. M-S. A.T.B.)
Song of Fame: 'Why move these Princes.' (S. solo with
choruses.)
Symphony: Three parts.
Song of Galatea: 'Soe well Britanocles o're seas doth
Raigne.' (S. solo with choruses.)
Symphony: Three parts.
Valediction: 'Wise Nature, that the Dew of sleepe pre-
pares.' (A. solo with A.T.B. chorus.)
Grand Chorus: (S. M-S. A.T.B.) 'To bed, to Bed.'

Triumph of Beautie, The. School Masque. Before 1645. (James P.
Shirley.) 'Cease Warring Thoughts.'

SACRED SONGS

PSALMS IN THREE PARTS WITH CONTINUO

Behold how good and joyful a thing it is (*Ps. cxxxiii*).	10.
Come sing the great Jehovah's praise (*Ps. xcv*).	10, G, V.
Gloria Patri et Filio.	10.
How hath Jehova's wrath (*Lamentations, ii*).	10, V.
How like a widow! (*Lamentations, i*).	10.
How long wilt thou forget me, O Lord (*Ps. xiii*).	10, G.
I am weary of my groaning (*Ps. vi*).	10, G.

I to thy Wing for refuge fly (frag. *Ps. lxxi*).	P.
In resurectione.	10.
In the substraction of my yeares (*Isaiah, xxxviii*).	10, G.
Judah in exile wanders (*Lamentations, i*).	10.
Let all in sweet accord clap hands (*Ps. xlvii*).	10, G, V.
Let God, the God of Battell rise (*Ps. lxviii*).	10, G, W.
Lord, as the Hart imbost with Heat (*Ps. xlii*).	10, G, V, W.
Lord, thy deserved wrath asswage (*Ps. vi*).	10, G, V.
Memento, Memento Domine.	10.
My God, my rock, regard my cry (*Ps. xxviii*).	10.
My God O why hast thou forsook? (*Ps. xxii*).	10, G.
Ne irascaris, Domine.	10.
O Sing unto the Lord a new song (*Ps. cxlix*).	10.
Oft from my early Youth (*Ps. cxxix*).	10, G.
Out of the horrour of the deep (*Ps. cxxx*).	10, G.
Praise the Lord enthron'd on high (*Ps. cl*).	10, G, V.
Sing to the King of Kings (*Ps. xcviii*).	10, G, V, W.
They who the Lord their fortresse make (*Ps. cxxv*).	10, G.
Thou mover of the rowling spheres (*Ps. cxxiii*).	10, G.
Thou that art inthron'd above (*Ps. xcii*).	10.
To thee I cry, Lord hear my cries (*Ps. cxli*).	10, G.
To thee O God my God (*Ps. lxiii*).	10, G.
To the God whom we adore (*Ps. cxlix*).	10, G.
Yee Nations of the earth (*Ps. cxvii*).	10, G.

VERSE ANTHEMS

For solo voice with continuo:

Let God Arise (bass solo) (*Ps. lxviii*).	X, Y, Z.
When man ffor sinne Thy Judgment feeles (*Ps. xxxix*).	W, AA.

For three voices (countertenor, tenor and bass), chorus and continuo, 'to the Comon Tunes':

All people that on earth doe dwell (*Ps. c*).	BB.
All yee yᵗ feare him prasie yᵉ Lord (*Ps. xxii*, pt. 3).	BB.
Cast mee not Lord out from Thy face (*Ps. li*, pt. 2).	BB.
Have mercye on us Lord (*Ps. lxvii*).	BB.
Humble Suite of A Sinner ('O Lord of whom I doe depend').	BB.
Lamentation, The ('O Lord in yᵉᵉ is all my trust').	BB.
Lamentation of a Sinner, The ('O Lord turne not away thy face').	BB.
Lord in Thy wrath reprove mee not (*Ps. vi*).	BB.
O God, my God wherefore doest thou forsake me utterly (*Ps. xxii*).	BB.
O God my strength and fortitude (*Ps. xviii*, pt. 1).	BB.
O Lord consider my distresse (*Ps. li*, pt. 1).	BB.
O Lord depart not now from mee (*Ps. xxii*, pt. 2).	BB.

APPENDIX C

For four voices, chorus and organ:
Lord is my light, The (*Ps. xxvii*).

Y, CC, DD, EE,
FF, GG, HH, 14.

Words only, music not extant:
Before the mountains were brought forth (*Ps. xc*). With
   chorus, 'cornetts' and 'sagbutts'.   JJ.
Who is this that Cometh out of the Wildernesse (*Song of* JJ.
   Solomon, selected verses).

RELIGIOUS CANONS

For three voices:

Gloria in Excelsis Deo.	10, 12.
Happy Sons of Israel.	G, K, P, 10.
Jesus is Harmonius.	10, Q.
Lord Thou hast been favourable.	G, K, P, 10.
Re, me, re, ut, sol.	P.
These Salt rivers of mine eyes.	10.
Tis Joy to see.	A, 10.
Why weepst thou Mary.	10.

For four voices:

Regi, Regis, Regum. (1)	P, 10.
Regi, Regis, Regum. (2)	P, 10.
She weepeth sore in the night.	G, K, P, S, FF, 10, 12, 15.

APPENDIX D

Selected Music

First Mov't., "Aire" from the "Royall
Consort" Suite No. 3 in D minor

Saraband from "Harpe" Consort No. 4 in D Minor ("O My Clarissa") with "divisions"

Sonata No. 8 in D Major
Fantazia

294

297

($\flat = \flat.$)

70

Aire

Aire

APPENDIX E

Selected Bibliography[1]

ADAMS, JOHN CRANFORD: *The Globe Playhouse* (Cambridge: Harvard University Press, 1942).

ARBEAU, THOINOT: *Orchésographie*, transl. by Mary Stewart Evans (New York: Kamin Dance Publishers, 1948).

ARNOLD, F. T.: *The Art of Accompaniment from a Thorough-Bass* (London: Oxford University Press, 1931).

AUBREY, JOHN: *Brief Lives*, ed. by Rev. Andrew Clark (Oxford: Clarendon Press, 1898).

—— *Lives of Eminent Men* (London: Longman *et al.*, 1813).

—— *The Natural History of Wiltshire*, ed. by John Britton (London: J. B. Nichols and Son Ltd., 1847).

—— *Wiltshire: the Topographical Collections of John Aubrey*, corrected and enlarged by John Edward Jackson (London: Longman and Co., 1862).

BANISTER, JOHN, and THOMAS LOW (editors): *New Ayres and Dialogues* (London: 1678.)

BOWDEN, WILLIAM R.: *The English Dramatic Lyric, 1603–1642* (New Haven: Yale University Press, 1951).

BOYCE, WILLIAM: *Cathedral Music*, 3 vols. compiled between 1760–1778 (London: Ashley, 2nd ed., 1788).

BURNEY, CHARLES: *A General History of Music* (London: 1789).

BUSH, DOUGLAS: *Mythology and the Renaissance Tradition in English Poetry* (University of Minnesota Press, 1932).

CAMPION, THOMAS: *Campion's Works*, ed. by Percival Vivian (Oxford: Clarendon Press, 1909).

COPERARIO, GIOVANNI (JOHN COOPER): *Rules How to Compose* (*c.* 1610), with an introduction by Manfred E. Bukofzer, facsimile edition (Los Angeles: Ernest E. Gottlieb, 1952).

CRUM, MARGARET C.: 'Notes on the Texts of William Lawes' Songs in B.M. MS. Add. 31432', *The Library*, Fifth Series, Vol. IX, No. 2 (June 1954).

CUNNINGHAM, P., and J. P. COLLIER: *Inigo Jones: a Life*, with five Court Masques (London: The Shakespeare Society, 1848).

CUTTS, JOHN P.: 'British Museum Additional MS. 31432, William Lawes' writing for Theatre and Court', *The Library*, Fifth Series, Vol. VII, No. 4 (December 1952).

---

[1] Additional bibliography will be found in the footnotes to the text.

DART, THURSTON, and WILLIAM COATES (editors): *Jacobean Consort Music*, Vol. IX of *Musica Britannica* (London: Stainer and Bell Ltd., 1955).

DENT, EDWARD J.: *Foundations of English Opera* (Cambridge, 1928).

DOLMETSCH, ARNOLD: *The Interpretation of the Music of the XVII and XVIII Centuries* (London: Novello & Co., Ltd., 1916).

DOLMETSCH, MABEL: *Dances of England and France from 1450–1600* (London: Routledge and Kegan Paul Ltd., 1949).

DUCKLES, VINCENT: 'The Gamble Manuscript as a Source of *Continuo* Song in England', *Journal of the American Musicological Society*, Vol. I, No. 2 (Summer 1948).

ERLEBACH, RUPERT: 'William Lawes and His String Music', *Proceedings of The Musical Association*, Fifty-ninth session, 1932–3.

EVANS, WILLA MCCLUNG: *Henry Lawes, Musician and Friend of Poets* (London: Oxford University Press, 1941).

FISCHER, WILHELM: 'Instrumentalmusik von 1600–1750', *Handbuch der Musikgeschichte*, 2 vols., 2nd ed., ed. by Guido Adler (Berlin, 1930).

FITZGIBBON, MACAULAY H.: 'Instruments and Their Music in the Elizabethan Drama', *Musical Quarterly*, Vol. XVII, No. 3 (1931).

FROST, MAURICE: *English and Scottish Psalm and Hymn Tunes, c. 1543–1677* (London: Oxford University Press, 1953).

FULLER, THOMAS: *The Histories of the Worthies of England* (London: 1662).

GALPIN, FRANCIS W.: *Old English Instruments of Music* (London: Methuen & Co., Ltd., 3rd ed., 1932).

GOMBOSI, OTTO: 'Some Musical Aspects of the English Court Masque', *Journal of the American Musicological Society*, Vol. I, No. 3 (Fall 1948).

HART, ERIC FORD: 'Introduction to Henry Lawes', *Music and Letters*, Vol. XXXII, No. 3 (July 1951), and No. 4 (October 1951).

HATCHER, HENRY: *Old and New Sarum*, Vol. VI of *The History of Modern Wiltshire*, ed. by Sir Richard Colt Hoare (London, 1843).

HAWKINS, JOHN: *A General History of the Science and Practice of Music* (1776), new ed. (London: Novello, Ewer & Co., Ltd., 1875).

HAYES, GERALD: *King's Music* (London: Oxford University Press, 1937).

HAYES, GERALD R.: *Musical Instruments and Their Music, 1500–1750* (London: Oxford University Press, 1930).

HILTON, JOHN (ed.): *Catch that Catch Can* (London: 1652).

HUGHES, CHARLES W.: 'John Gamble's Commonplace Book', *Music and Letters*, Vol. XXVI, No. 4 (October 1945).

KIDSON, FRANK: 'John Playford and Seventeenth-Century Music Publishing', *Musical Quarterly*, Vol. IV, No. 4 (October 1918).

LAFONTAINE, HENRY CART DE: *The King's Musick* (London: Novello and Co., Ltd., 1909).

LAWES, HENRY: *Select Ayres and Dialogues* (London, 1653).

LAWES, HENRY, and WILLIAM LAWES: *Choice Psalmes* (London: Printed by James Young for Humphrey Moseley, 1648).

LAWRENCE, W. J.: 'The English Theatre Orchestra, Its Rise and Early Characteristics', *Musical Quarterly*, Vol. III, No. 1 (January 1917).

MACE, THOMAS: *Musick's Monument* (London: P. Ratcliffe Thompson, 1676).

MANIFOLD, JOHN: 'Theatre Music in the Sixteenth and Seventeenth Centuries', *Music and Letters*, Vol. XXIX, No. 4 (October 1948).

MEYER, ERNST HERMANN: *English Chamber Music* (London: Lawrence and Wishart, 1946).

—— *Die Mehrstimmige Spielmusik des 17. Jahrhunderts in Nord- und Mitteleuropa* (Cassel: Bärenreiter Verlag, 1934).

MORLEY, THOMAS: *A Plain and Easy Introduction to Practical Music* (1597), ed. by R. Alec Harman (London: J. M. Dent and Sons Ltd., 1952).

MORRIS, REGINALD OWEN: *Contrapuntal Technique in the Sixteenth Century* (Oxford: The Clarendon Press, 1922).

NAGEL, WILIBALD: *Geschichte der Musik in England* (Strassburg: Karl J. Trubner Verlag, 1897), 2 vols.

NICOLL, ALLARDYCE: *Stuart Masques and the Renaissance Stage* (New York: Harcourt Brace and Co., 1938).

NORTH, ROGER: *Memoirs of Musicke* (1728), ed. by Edward F. Rimbault (London: G. Bell, 1846).

—— *The Musicall Gramarian*, ed. by Hilda Andrews (London: Oxford University Press, 1925).

PARRY, C. HUBERT: *The Music of the Seventeenth Century*, Vol. III of the *Oxford History of Music* (London, 1938).

PATTISON, BRUCE: *Music and Poetry of the English Renaissance* (London: Methuen and Co., Ltd., 1948).

PEPYS, SAMUEL: *The Diary of Samuel Pepys*, 10 vols. ed. by Henry B. Wheatley (New York: The Limited Editions Club, 1942).

PLAYFORD, JOHN: *A Musicall Banquet* (London, 1651).

—— *Catch that Catch Can*, ed. by John Hilton (London: 1652).

—— *Court-Ayres* (London, 1655).

—— *Courtly Masquing Ayres* (London, 1662).

—— *Introduction to the Skill of Musick* (London, 1672 ed.).

—— *Musick's Delight on the Cithren* (London, 1666).

—— *Musick's Hand-maide* (London, 1663).

—— *Musick's Recreation on the Lyra Violl* (London, 1652, 1661).

—— *Select Musicall Ayres and Dialogues* (London, 1652, 1653).

—— *The Musical Companion* (London, 1667, 1673).

—— *The Treasury of Musick* (London, 1669).

PRYNNE, WILLIAM: *Histrio-mastix. The player's scourge or, Actor's tragedie* (London: E. A. and W. I. for M. Sparke, 1633).

PULVER, JEFFREY: *A Biographical Dictionary of Old English Music* (London: Kegan Paul, Trench, Trubner & Co., Ltd., 1927).

—— *A Dictionary of Old English Music and Musical Instruments* (London: Kegan Paul, Trench, Trubner & Co., Ltd., 1923).

REYHER, PAUL: *Les Masques Anglais* (1512–1640) (Paris: Librairie Hachette et Cie., 1909).

RIMBAULT, EDWARD F. (ed.), *The Old Cheque-Book, or Book of Remembrance, of The Chapel Royal from 1561 to 1744* (London: Printed for the Camden Society and publ. by J. B. Nichols and Sons, 1872).

—— *The Rounds, Catches and Canons of England* (London, 1865).

ROBERTSON, DORA H.: *Sarum Close* (London: Jonathan Cape Ltd., 1938).

ROHR-SAUER, PHILIP VON: *English Metrical Psalms from 1600 to 1660* (Freiburg, 1938).

SCHOLES, PERCY A.: *The Puritans and Music* (London: Oxford University Press, 1937).

SIMPSON, CHRISTOPHER: *A Compendium of Practicall Musick* (London: Printed by William Godbid for Henry Brome, 2nd enlarged ed. in five parts, 1667).

—— *The Division-Violist*, lithographic facsimile of the second edition (1667) (London: J. Curwen, 1955).

SIMPSON, PERCY, and C. F. BELL: *Designs by Inigo Jones for Masques and Plays at Court*, printed for the Walpole and Malone Societies (London: Oxford University Press, 1924).

STEELE, MARY SUSAN: *Plays and Masques at Court During the Reigns of Elizabeth, James I, and Charles I, 1558–1642* (London: Oxford University Press, 1926).

TOVEY, SIR DONALD: 'Words and Music', in *Seventeenth-Century Studies Presented to Sir Herbert Grierson* (London: Oxford University Press, 1938).

VAN DEN BORREN, CHARLES: *The Sources of Keyboard Music in England* (London: Novello and Co., Ltd., 1913).

WALKER, ERNEST: *A History of Music in England* (Oxford: The Clarendon Press, 1952), 3rd. ed. revised and enlarged by J. A. Westrup.

WARLOCK, PETER (PHILIP HESELTINE): *The English Ayre* (London: Oxford University Press, 1926).

WELSFORD, ENID: *The Court Masque* (Cambridge University Press, 1927).

WESTRUP, J. A.: 'Domestic Music under the Stuarts', *Proceedings of the Musical Association*, Vol. LXVIII (1941–2).

—— 'Foreign Musicians in Stuart England', *The Musical Quarterly*, January 1941.

—— *Purcell* (3rd. ed., London: J. M. Dent and Sons Ltd., 1937).

WHITELOCKE, BULSTRODE: *Memorials of the English Affairs from the beginning of the Reign of Charles I* (London: 1682).

WOOD, ANTHONY: *The Life of Anthony á Wood from the year 1632 to 1672* (Oxford: Thomas Hearne, 1772).

—— Manuscript notes on the lives of the English musicians. Unpublished manuscript in the Bodleian Library (*Wood D. 19 (4)*, No. 106, folio 83).

WOODFILL, WALTER L.: *Musicians in English Society from Elizabeth to Charles I* (Princeton: Princeton University Press, 1953).

INDEX

INDEX

foreign influence, 5 f., 10, 13, 39, 51,
    62 ff., 77, 80, 83, 104, 106 f.,
    124f., 147, 151 f., 154, 161, 163,
    165 ff., 189, 206 ff., 210, 222,
    244, 259 f.
foreign musicians, 13, 62, 64, *124 f.*,
    189, 212
forms, instrumental, 10, *39 f.*, 43,
    47 ff., 63, 68 f., 80, 82, 82(2),
    88, 95, *100 f.*, 104, 106 ff.,
    111, 114, 122 f., 136, 139 f.,
    142, 146 f., 152, 208, 259
—— dances, 68 f., 81 ff., 86, 88, 95,
    100 f., 140, 146, 208
—— fantasias, 47 ff., 136
—— 'sonatas', 47, 106 ff., 122, 136
—— suites, 43
—— the *Consort Suites*, 39 ff., 43,
    47 ff.
—— the *'Harpe' Consorts*, 88, 100 f.,
    104
—— the *Lyra Viol and Bass Viol
    Suites*, 136, 140, 142 ff. (Ex.
    20)
—— the *Royall Consort*, 69, 80, 82,
    82(2)
—— the *Violin 'Sonatas'*, 106 ff., 111,
    114, 122 f., 136
See also dances, dance suites, and
    individual instrumental and
    dance forms, sectional structure
forms, poetic, 152 f.
forms, vocal, *150 ff.*, 158, 168 f., *182
    ff.* (incl. Ex. 29), 192, *201 f.*
    (Ex. 31), 207 f., 224, 230,
    242 ff. (Ex. 36), 249 f. (Ex.
    40), 256, 259
—— 'ballad', 165 ff. (incl. Exs. 22–
    23)
—— declamatory song, 150 ff. (incl.
    Ex. 21)
—— 'dialogue', 168 ff. (incl. Ex.
    24)
—— drinking songs, 180 ff. (incl.
    Ex. 28)
—— madrigals, 172 ff. (incl. Ex. 25–
    27)
—— masques, 206 ff., 224, 230

forms, vocal, religious, 235ff. (psalms,
    incl. Ex. 34–36), 249 ff. ('com-
    mon tune' psalms or verse
    anthems, incl. Ex. 40),
    256 f.
—— rounds, canons and catches,
    182 ff. (incl. Ex. 29), 247 f.
    (incl. Exs. 38–9)
See also anthems and other
    individual vocal forms
Fortune Theatre, 189
Foster, Captain Edmund, 23, 25 f.
Foundations of English Opera (Dent,
    1928), 209(1), 216(1), 224 (1, 2)
Fragmentea Aurea (Suckling, 1646),
    160
fragments, instrumental, 146 f.
fragments, vocal, 33, 172, *178 f.*,
    216 f., 219 f.
French influence, 107, 124, 151, 154,
    166ff., 189, *206 ff.*, 210, 222, 259
frets, 41, 127, *132*, 146
Froberger, Johann Jacob, 68
fugato technique, *40 ff.*, 49, 52, 58,
    97, 104, 111, 114, 119 f., 127,
    134, 136 f., 239
—— in the *Consort Suites*, 40 ff., 49,
    52, 58
—— in the fantasias, 40 f., 49, 52,
    58, 111, 134
—— in the *'Harpe' Consorts*, 97, 104
—— in keyboard parts, 119
—— in the *Lyra Viol and Bass Viol
    Suites*, 127, 134, 136 f.
—— in the psalms, 239
—— in the *Violin 'Sonatas'*, 111, 114,
    119 f.
See also fugue, imitation, 'points',
    'reports', *stretto*
'fuge', *see* fugue
fugue, 8, 48 f., 114, 120, 127, 134,
    136 f.; *see also fugato* technique
Fuller, Thomas, 5, 5–6(1), 6 f., 9 f.,
    20 f.
functional music in the theatre, 193;
    see also theatre music

Gabrieli, Giovanni, 63